GROWTH HACKIN

WRIT_
BETTER,
faster

HOW TO TRIPLE YOUR WRITING SPEED
AND WRITE MORE EVERY DAY

MONICA LEONELLE

Contents

ABOUT THE BOOK

About Write Better, Faster: How To Triple Your Writing Speed and Write More Every Day (Growth Hacking For Storytellers #1)

In 2012, fiction author Monica Leonelle made a life-changing decision to learn to write faster. Throughmonths of trial-and-error, hundreds of hours of experimentation, and dozens of manuscripts, she tweaked and honed until she could easily write 10,000 words in a day, at speeds over 3500+ words per hour!

She shares all her insights, secrets, hacks, and data in this tome dedicated to improving your writing speeds, skyrocketing your monthly word count, and publishing more books. You'll learn:

- The 4-step framework that Monica used to reach speeds of 3500+ new fiction words per hour
- The tracking systems you need to double or triple your writing speed in the next couple months
- The killer 4-step pre-production method Monica uses to combat writer's block, no matter what the project is!

- - The secrets to developing a daily writing habit that other authors don't talk about enough
- - How Monica went from publishing only one book per year from 2009-2013, to publishing 8 books in a single year in 2014

For serious authors, both beginner and advanced, who want to improve their output this year!

Write Better, Faster: How To Triple Your Writing Speed and Write More Every Day will help you kick your excuses and get more writing done. As part of the Growth Hacking For Storytellers series, it explores how to hack your writing routine to be more efficient, more productive, and have a ton of fun in the process!

For release dates on more books like this one by Monica Leonelle, plus free related content, go to:

ProseOnFire.com/Storytellers/

Chapter 1
INTRODUCTION

This book started as a simple, 2000 word blog post that a number of people asked me to write after I shared with them my astounding results in increasing my writing speed over a period of just a few months.

But before I even talk about the post, I'm going to talk about the roots of the post so that everything else in this book, from my initial starting point, to my eventual framework that I shared in the post, to now, this book, makes sense to someone who has never, ever read anything about me and is wondering who the heck I am.

Cool?

Cool.

Let's do this.

Who Am I?

My name is Monica Leonelle and I've been a fiction author for five years. I first started self-publishing in 2009 with the release of a non-fiction book about new media and was quickly bitten by the bug. Since then I've written and published twelve fiction books, with eight of them coming out in 2014 (nine, if you count a short story anthology I was a part of). These books total over half a million words across two separate pen names.

Before I started writing professionally, I specialized in business, digital marketing, copywriting, virality, and word-of-mouth. I went the traditional route with my education, earning an MBA with a focus in strategy and entrepreneurship, which I applied toward digital marketing at tech startups.

I've also been blogging consistently for nearly ten years and have been featured in Advertising Age, The Huffington Post, the AMEX OpenForum, GigaOm, Mashable, Social Media Today, and the Christian Science Monitor.

HOW MY JOURNEY STARTED

It all started back in 2012 when I was seriously stuck on my third book. I had two fiction series at that point, one an urban fantasy, the other cyberpunk sci-fi. I was struggling to write the follow-up to either of them.

I was also a newly minted freelance writer. I was going through a very difficult time in my personal life, trying to regain my freedom from certain people I had trusted, and I was over-correcting. I had quit my high-paying, plush job as the marketing director of a successful startup, I had quit my marriage, and I was spending time with a completely different crowd than I normally would—people who were driven by a different kind of success than the traditional kind that I had been pursuing and achieving for years.

Freelancing wasn't going well, period. Apparently you can't just start a new company to pay your bills, working only a few hours a week, so you can dedicate the rest of your time to what you really care about? Something like that. I had money, but had also been out of a steady job for a year and a half. I was still living like I made 6-figures, but wasn't making anything close to it. Savings were dwindling, and I needed to turn things around. Fast.

It was a tough and painful year, potentially one of the most difficult of my life. So obviously, I was reading a ton of advice from strangers on the internet. A lot of it, I didn't or couldn't use. But then, I came across two pieces that kicked off my journey to writing this book.

The first was that if you are stuck on a book, you should write something completely different and outside your comfort zone, then circle back.

The second was that successful freelance writers focused on writing speed above all else. The good ones were able to write 3000-4000 words per hour if under a tight deadline. My eyes widened when I read this. 3000 words?! I had been blogging for years and averaged around 900 words per hour, which many other writers had told me was fast. Now, I was in the remedial lane? What?!

THE DECISION TO WRITE FASTER

I decided then to focus on becoming a faster writer. The logic behind it made sense—as a freelancer, I was paid a flat rate per project or an hourly rate per service (if I consulted with the company on their marketing). In both cases, writing faster meant I could take on more projects and make more money. And at the least, even if I didn't have more clients, I could use the time I saved from having to freelance to work on my fiction books.

At the time, I didn't have a big freelance project that I could test my writing speed on. I also wasn't going to rush one of my "real" books or risk messing up a second-in-series. Instead, I decided on a brand new fiction project that was the opposite of my current work: light young adult fantasy and science fiction in third-person past tense. My new project was dark hardcore erotica in first-person, present tense (again, I over-corrected).

I had no idea how to write this type of story. This forced me to write a more detailed outline than I would have that included 3-5 paragraphs per chapter that explained what would happen in the chapter. (Later, I learned that these were "beats," which we'll discuss a few chapters from now.)

As I typed, I kept track of my starts and ends in a Google Spreadsheet. Although I could hit 900 words per hour fairly easily with non-fiction blog posts, I struggled to hit 600-700 words with fiction. The beats helped me with this, because I knew where the story was going and didn't have to pause to think about what to write next.

I had also stumbled on a technique that many writers swore by, called the Pomodoro Method. Like most newbie writers, I could sit down to write and not type a word for hours. I mean, I had to check Facebook, and then there was someone wrong on Twitter, and then—you know how that story ends. The Pomodoro Method was perfect for writers who couldn't focus.

I sat down to type this new story, making sure I had a simple timer app installed on my computer (you can also use e.ggtimer.com). 25 minutes writing, five minutes of break—simple enough! Suddenly, with the Pomodoro Method and the detailed beats I'd already written up, I was absolutely flying through my draft. I was well over a thousand words per hour, usually hitting closer to ~1500, and every once in awhile, breaking through to ~2000. I honestly couldn't believe it.

The end product, which was written primarily on Oct. 5th and 6th, then cleaned up a bit and finished off on Oct. 7th, totaled ~24,000 words. It was the fastest I'd ever written anything in my life. And it was good—better than either of my first two books. I knew I couldn't keep it to myself. So I set it aside, and in December that year, published it as the first book under a new pen name.

This was my first foray into what was really possible with writing speed. At the end of this, I thought, "Wow, if I could write a novella in two days, I should be able to publish one every week! 50 books in a year! I'm rich!" (Insert HUGE LOL here.)

IDENTIFYING PROBLEMS AND FINDING TWEAKS

I spent the next several months trying to replicate this success with other books, trying to improve my understanding of beats, of the Pomodoro method, but the experience never quite clicked for me in this way again.

Still, I was adamant that it was not a fluke. So I went back through the original event. Two of my most vivid memories from that period of flow were as follows:

My hands were killing me at the end from all that typing. When I tried to type my other books using pomodoros, I could feel the pain in my fingers. It is hard enough to write in the first place, but what do you think your lizard brain does when writing puts you in physical pain?

My fingers could not keep up with my thoughts. I recall writing the story in my head several sentences faster than

I could type it. Then, I would have to go back and get the words on the page. It slowed me down. I could type 70 words per minute, but was only clocking ~30 words per minute when I wrote for an extended period (something typing tests don't require).

So I went back and looked for a solution to these problems, determined to either figure out how to write a consistent 2000 words per hour, or find another thing like the Pomodoro Method that could give me big gains again.

I spent a lot of 2013 searching for a solution. The one I found was dictation, which felt like an absolute godsend to me and my poor, pained hands. I talk about dictation a lot in this book, particularly whether it will work for you and what you can do with it if it does. I did not think I would like it and felt very self-conscious talking out loud to myself the first few times—but then I got used to it and now I absolutely love how easy it is. This helped me increase my speeds again to ~3000 words per hour.

I kind of thought I was done at this point. I mean, I had hit the mythical 3000 words per hour that freelancers supposedly got. That was all I needed, right?

I wrote a few more books during this timeframe, though only one reached completion. I was definitely writing faster, ~2500 words per hour when you averaged out my writing speed over 30-50 pomodoros, but I still wasn't publishing much. I had a ton of drafts at 80%.

This bothered me to no end because my biggest roadblock to being a successful fiction author was how quickly I could produce content. Before embarking on improving my writing speed, I had the marketing chops from my previous career and the publishing chops from the four books now under my belt. I was editing other people's books as a freelancer and genuinely improving them. I thought I had everything I needed for success. I was fast now; why wasn't I successful?

WRITING CONSISTENTLY

The more I thought about it, the more I had to get honest with myself. Increasing my writing speed was invaluable, something I don't regret spending time on. But writing fast didn't necessarily mean I produced more content.

You see, my mindset toward writing fast was, "I'll do it to get it over with." I didn't love writing fiction, I loved having written fiction. And that was my problem.

Around August 2013, I had to accept the truth: I was not writing enough to change my circumstances. I had published a total of five books in 5 years (2009-2013). Four of them were fiction. The problem? Despite writing faster, I still wasn't writing more. I was writing just as many words as I usually did, I was just doing it in less time.

What I needed wasn't speed, it was consistency. Consistency would produce more words per day, which meant more words per month...

I decided to embark on my biggest experiment yet—full tracking in both a spreadsheet and a diary, with a new metric: instead of tracking words per hour, I was going to track total words per month. And I was going to figure out what was really holding me back with my writing.

My experiment lasted two months, each one in which I hit 50,000 total words for that month. This is basically doing National Novel Writing Month (#NaNoWriMo)—a November challenge to write a 50,000 word novel in one month—two months in a row.

In those two months, I learned more about myself and my writing process than I've learned from any book, from any curriculum, from any teacher or mentor. I highly recommend this sort of challenge to anyone and everyone. And you can, of course, read all about my experience—it's all in this book as well, with the full diary entries, word counts, and more in the appendix.

After that experiment, I was exhausted and still didn't have my perfect process, but I was getting a lot closer. I did have six brand new drafts, several of which I was able to publish last year, and the rest which will go out this year. I felt that even though I had not kept up with the tracking past the experiment, I had done something right, because in 2014, I published eight books total, completely wiping my previous record of one book a year. That is an 800% improvement. That is insane!

I also settled into the idea that I will never have the perfect process I'd been chasing for years. Even when you think your journey is over, it's not! I have not yet reached my destination on any of this. Eight books is amazing, but I'd love to double or triple that this year in 2015. What my experiments have taught me is that anything is possible and the smallest tweaks can produce wildly better results. I don't think any of us should ever stop striving for improvement. There is always so much more to learn and experience.

THE BIRTH OF THE 3500 WORDS ARTICLE

At the beginning of 2014, I told a friend of mine that I was freelancing with about my huge experiment that yielded me 100,000 brand new words of fiction in two months. In the process, we got to talking about writing speed. I mentioned during that talk that I had hit over 4,000 words per hour during a handful of my sessions.

He couldn't believe it. He told me, "I would love to see a blog post about how you did that."

It took me about nearly the entire year to write that blog post. There was so much detail and I was sure a blog post like that would take forever to do and would be well over 10,000 words. I didn't really have a reason to write it, either—it's not like readers cared! But when I started my writing blog at ProseOnFire.com, there was one week where I needed to post something quickly. This was a blessing in disguise, because all I could think of was this topic I had in my back pocket, about writing fast, and all I had time to do was provide the most basic information about what I did and what I learned.

That post was called How To Consistently Write 3500-4000 Words Per Hour, and it's still available for free online (just Google it).

I'll be the first to admit that the title is a bit gimmicky. What can I say—I'm a copywriter. I'm not going to call it, "How it took me two years, 100+ hours of experimentation, and 50,000 words of diary entries to figure out why I wrote 'all the time' and still sucked at getting published books—books that could actually earned me money—onto Amazon where people could actually buy them." That simply doesn't have quite the same ring to it—and it also doesn't sell the underlying premise of the article. The article, at its roots, is a smart framework that I believe anyone can use to drastically improve his or her writing speed, without having to do as much crap as I did.

The article was well-received and I started getting lots of emails and comments about it. I won't pretend I didn't know this would happen—I had seen articles about this topic go viral, and I knew from my own experiences that I loved articles where authors shared their processes.

The questions, concerns, criticisms, and suggestions flooded in, as I expected. A lot of people liked it. A lot of people had reasonable questions or wanted more detail on one part or another. Every time I answered a question via email, I had to decide: do I try to work this into the article as well, or do I leave the article in its simplest form to satisfy the masses?

It hurt, but I knew that most people didn't want to read my detailed account, complete with examples, about my outline, beats, sketches, and draft process.

I also knew that some people did. A lot of the information I left out of the original article was smart and well-thought-out—I just didn't have a place for in the article. I decided instead to write the "real" article, the one I had originally envisioned. That "real" article ballooned and ballooned until I acquiesced and made it into this book that you're reading right now. And that is the full story of how this book came to be.

WHAT THIS BOOK IS ABOUT

When I first started writing this, I thought it would be around 10,000 words of new content. I was wrong. The book is 90,000 words long, with 50,000 of that in the appendix with the diary.

The main point of writing it is to go into much more detail about each of the four steps in the framework and to address the feedback I received from the original article. That feedback from the article fell into three main areas:

- Questions that dug deeper into the details of one particular step in my 4-step framework
- Questions that muddled increasing writing speed with increasing writing hours (two *very* different things that must be addressed separately)
- Questions about how writing speed fits into a larger framework of producing a book

In writing this book I felt I could help authors do three things that would help them move drastically faster than other writers:

#1 - INCREASE YOUR WRITING SPEED

For me, this was the first step in increasing my productivity. To help, I've provided the original article, a section that digs deeper into each of the four steps, and a section that just answers frequently asked questions about my method and process.

I believe that what I provide in this book is all you need to know to drastically increase your writing speed—the rest is going to be in tracking your results, knowing yourself, and actually executing (a part that most people skip).

It took me several months to get this right, but it is easily one of the best things I ever did for my writing career.

#2 - INCREASE YOUR WRITING STAMINA

A lot of writers were confused about this concept, even without realizing it themselves. Increasing your writing speed isn't nearly enough to get your book done. It's just a tiny part. Several writers asked me about getting to 10,000 words a day, for example, but that has little to do with writing speed. You can get to 10,000 words a day writing at 1,000 words an hour—just write for 10 hours total. What they were really asking about was how to increase the number of hours they could write in a day, which takes a completely different mindset than the one used to increase writing speed.

I address a lot of what you need to know about this in the sections on focus, training, and energy (steps 2, 3, and 4). When you separate writing speed from number of hours spent writing, it makes it much easier to know which one to work on first and how to get started immediately.

#3 - IMPROVE YOUR BOOK PRODUCTION PROCESS

This book focuses primarily on writing a first draft. You can think of it as everything you need to go from idea to first draft.

However, writing doesn't alone make you a successful author. Later sections of this book delve deeper into the rest of the process—editing, publishing, and so on.

The rest of this book is dedicated to my actual data. A good chunk of the word count in this book (50,000 words—roughly 200 pages) is dedicated to a diary of two months in a row where I succeeded in hitting 50,000 fiction words per month (September and October of 2013). Because this is the same goal as National Novel Writing Month, I thought it could be useful for those trying to increase their writing speed.

I originally thought that including this diary might be self-aggrandizing, but when I started reading back over it a year later, it seemed like there was enough there to make it worth including. There is a breadth of insight in the narrative that helped me solidify my understanding of my own process, plus put together some of the larger frameworks in this book that I believe can help anyone do the same thing. This documentation of those two months is ugly and full of warts and embarrassing (for me), as it was written in real-time—but there is so much to learn from it and so much that I've learned, that is only obvious in hindsight.

If there is one takeaway from this section, I hope it's this—that beyond tracking just the quantitative data in spreadsheets, you should also track your qualitative data in the form of a diary. I did mine publicly, but you could just as easily do it privately. It will truly provide you with a wealth of information not only as you are writing and reflecting in the moment, but also a year later when you've forgotten several of the lessons you've already learned and need or want to re-implement them.

I hope you enjoy the book and everything I'm sharing with you, and I hope it inspires you to start experimenting with what works for you. Self-knowledge has always been the best productivity hack—something that is easy to see as you start your own journey to creating processes for all aspects of your writing business.

Chapter 2
THE FIRST STEP TO WRITING FASTER

Non-fiction is never objective. The amount of value you get out of a non-fiction book is directly related to how your beliefs and goals align with the author's.

That's why it's only fair to share a little more about myself, my beliefs, and my goals upfront.

MY BELIEFS

My name is Monica Leonelle. I'm a female, a thirty-year old (at the time of writing), a young adult author AND a romance author (long, long story) and a lover of all aspects of publishing.

I am...

Primarily a fiction author. The only non-fiction I do these days is to market my books (via a blog) and to share my knowledge and journey with other fiction authors (via books like this). Of course, you can apply all the techniques

I'm sharing to non-fiction, too, but this book is primarily aimed at fiction authors.

A former marketing and copywriting professional. I don't believe in excuses, I don't believe that the writing is going to happen on a mythical "someday," and I don't believe in "I'm not sure how." I look for actual results and metrics to track it as indicators of progress.

An achiever. I love goals and I love winning, even if it's only against my former self. I've tried to chill out over the years, and I've embraced pacing myself with my writing goals, but there will always be that aspect of my personality that will shine through in a lot of my content.

I BELIEVE...

That writing better comes from writing more. I've read a lot of first drafts of books, and the ones that have the most potential always come from the writers who have more words under their belts. You learn to write through experience, plain and simple. The writers I know who are satisfied with writing a few sentences a day are easily lapped by the ones who put fingers to keyboard regularly.

That speed and quality rarely have much to do with each other. A lot of writers believe that anything written quickly must be terrible. I believe that if your writing gets worse when you're going fast, it probably isn't great when you're going slow, either. Harsh, harsh truth, but one nonetheless. So yes, some writers may need to start by first improving their skill, then improving their speed... but don't buy into the inverse proportionality myth of speed and quality. If you are a good writer slow, you will probably be a better writer fast once you get used to it.

That efficiency is something to strive for. Time is a fixed quantity. To get more done, you must improve your efficiency. That gives you more time to contribute to the world however you want—with more writing, by taking care of your family, or anything else that is important to you.

I'M TRYING TO...

Make a living writing without sacrificing my creativity. I'm never going to chase money, but I am going to support potential paid sales as much as possible. I do this by prioritizing projects I want to do by how profitable I think they'll be—and if you read more of my books and posts, particularly the ones about virality, you'll see that I'm quite good at predicting this.

Write great stories. I'm not intrinsically motivated by money, but by the value I can share with others. This drives everything I do, including trying to write faster. It's simple—if I can produce my stories faster, I can write more stories, and I can add more value to others before I leave this earth. That's important to me.

Share what works for me so you can figure out what works for you. I don't think my exact process will be your exact process, but that's not the point. No one needs another guru to tell them how to do something; what they need instead is inspiration and frameworks for thinking about things and coming to their own conclusions. If you're looking for a formula, you won't find it here. What you'll find instead is a ton of insight and inspiration to get you started on YOUR process. You know best. Period.

If you don't share my background, beliefs, or goals, you may take issue with my work or approach to things. Just a friendly word of warning before we dive in.

WHY WRITE BETTER?

The title of this book is Write Better, Faster, but an obvious question is, why?

It may seem stupid to even question why we want to write better. Who wouldn't want to be a better writer?

Well, one thing to consider is how much time and energy it takes to become a better writer. For example, replace "writer" with "cellist." Why would you want to become a better cellist?

My personal answer to that question is, I wouldn't. That's why a better question might be, why is writing better an important goal to you?

After all, you can get by in this world (and even make a ton of money as you go) without being a great writer. Millions of people already do this. And in fact, writing is one of the worst-paid professions in the world:

- The average book sells fewer than 500 copies
- The average writer makes less than $10,000 per book advance.
- The average self-published author makes less $5000 in royalties per year.

This is not a profitable career path for many. So why try to get better at this skill?

Well, I don't advise doing it for the money or for the potential fame that could come with bestseller status. I also don't advise doing it for any other of the myriad of external validations—movie deals, red carpets, NYT bestseller list, and so on. In my experience, validation comes from external sources a lot less often than it needs to come from yourself.

The people who seem to succeed at increasing their writing speed do so out of a pure passion for storytelling and a bigger "why" than simply getting more writing done.

For example, as I shared earlier, I set down the path of increasing my writing speed because I wanted to get my stories into the world faster. I believe that telling stories that matter is what I was put on this earth to do. I believe that my job is to be as productive as possible during my lifetime. I also believe I will let down the world and myself by not sharing what I can while I'm here. All of these beliefs are powerful and push me to do more in less time.

What's your why, and how does writing better get you there? You should know the answer to that question, or else you won't be motivated enough to go through this transformation.

WHY WRITE FASTER?

Again, this seems like a benign question with an obvious answer, but there are plenty of reasons you don't want to write faster. For example, you don't want to write faster if the quality of your work is subpar to begin with. (This will only create more subpar work in less time.) You don't want to write faster if you're chasing a goal, like money, that is negatively affected by going faster (for example, if you're an hourly freelancer, it actually hurts your wage to get your work done faster).

These are all valid concerns to consider. My assumption in writing this book is that you, the reader, want to write faster because it will benefit your work. This is true for writers in most sectors of the industry, and specifically, it's true for novelists like me.

So let's consider how writing faster can help your career as an author:

You will write more in less time - this seems obvious, again, but it's important for a number of reasons. Most novelists are working on spec—they write something, then try to get paid for it (as opposed to work-for-hire, which is guaranteed payment when the assignment is complete). When you're writing on spec, you need more irons in the fire. If you're a novelist, you want as many (good) books out as possible. This will both increase your earnings and minimize your risk on any one title's sales.

You will increase your marketing efforts - much of the secret behind marketing content is content marketing. (How's that for a tongue twister?) Few people or companies will buy a piece of writing without first sampling that same author's writing. That means that you'll need free samples of your work available in order to sell anything. This could be on social media, in a blog post, on your website as a download, or even in the ebook marketplaces as a freebie. All of this means doing even more writing than you need to create your book.

You will get more practice writing - I'm always skeptical of anyone who considers himself a great writer when he hasn't put in the hours. Some industry leaders, like Dean Wesley Smith, say it takes about a million words of fiction before you sell through traditional channels. I've also found from personal experience that the best way to learn writing is to write every single day. Being able to write quickly means that you can get thousands of extra words in per day—and those words add up quickly.

You will get into a deeper flow, which produces better words - Furthermore, writing quickly gets you out of editing mode and into your left brain artist flow. Finding your flow puts you in this surreal state where you are working but not even aware of the words you're putting on the page. I've experienced this deeply spiritual writing many times, but the most vivid was when I wrote the 24,000 word novella under a brand new pen name. That book is published in the marketplace right now, almost verbatim, and was my most popular book when it first came out (since then, I've had another series hit larger, so now it is only my second most popular).

You will fall in love with writing - As humans, we love doing things we are good at. Writing faster doesn't necessarily make you good, but for the motivated and growth-oriented writer, it will definitely help. Writing faster often leads to writing better, which leads to feeling good about writing, which leads to writing more, which leads to writing even faster... it becomes the best kind of cycle, the kind your ego loves to feed on. A lot of writers love having written, but not writing itself. I used to be one of those writers. But when I started learning to write faster, I also fell in love with writing itself. I now find writing one of the most enjoyable aspects of my job and revel in the times that I get to do it in peace. Right now, I'm sitting in Hero Coffee Bar in Chicago, drinking the most delicious almond oolong tea, typing this book out for you... and I'm in absolute heaven. The information is flowing easily from my mind to my fingertips to your conscious. It's play, not work.

Those are only five reasons that you might want to go down this path of learning to write faster—I'm sure you can think of your own reasons too. The point is, again, to know why you're doing it and what you hope to gain. Learning to write faster and better is, by its transformative nature, going to make you uncomfortable. The end results are the part that will help you push through the challenges you face.

WHY GROWTH HACKING?

This series is called Growth Hacking for Storytellers, but what does that even mean?

For those of you unfamiliar with the term "growth hacking," growth hacking focuses exclusively on strategies and tactics (typically in digital marketing) that help grow a business or product.

The concept was first coined by Sean Ellis of Dropbox fame back in 2010 in a blog post. It has since changed the face of startup marketing, with Techcrunch guest writer Aaron Ginn explaining that a growth hacker has a "mindset of data, creativity, and curiosity."

We are going to apply these same mindsets—data, creativity, and curiosity—first to the concept of writing better and faster, then to other writer business topics throughout the series.

You see, as a storyteller, there are a number of tasks you could do, and plenty of people urging you to do them. Write a press release, go on a book signing tour, attend events, buy a course, tweet—all of these are potential ways to spend your time.

This series has no intention of spending your time, though. In the Growth Hacking for Storytellers series, I want to help you identify the small tweaks you can make to produce HUGE results and push your writing career forward faster, better, and smarter.

Learning to write faster is one of those tweaks and is going to significantly accelerate your progress as an author or writer. If you spend one month optimizing your productivity in this area, you will gain 20-40 years of extremely productive and optimized writing sessions. What an amazing way to invest your time, right?

I'm not here to tell you that you have to write fast. But I am able to share the life-changing impact that writing faster has made on my life and business. Optimizing my productivity has been one of the most important growth hacks I've stumbled upon in the last several years.

I think it can be just as life-changing a discovery for you. Are you ready?

Chapter 3
SET UP YOUR TRACKING SYSTEM

If you're serious about boosting your word count per hour (and I do believe it's a fun journey and a worthwhile skill to develop as a writer) there is one thing you must do.

YOU MUST TRACK YOUR PROGRESS.

You absolutely, 100% CANNOT skip this part. You will not succeed if you don't do this. I would not recommend even attempting this if you aren't going to bother with setting up and maintaining a tracking system.

HERE'S WHY:

To incite any real change, you must know what you're currently doing, what you want to do, and what the gap is - as Rachel Aaron pointed out in her brilliant book 2k to 10k (which I highly recommend as complimentary material to this book), few writers have any clue how they write books to begin with. Is it any surprise that they can't figure out how to write faster? Just like you would at any job, you need to give yourself a performance review. Benchmark your current metrics for at least a week or two—this will give you a starting point for improving your metrics.

You're self-sabatoging in ways you can't begin to see right now - as humans, we're quite bad at remembering what we actually do in any given day. That's why people wake up ten years later with 40 extra pounds, why employees are blindsided when they're fired, why people see a picture of themselves and are shocked by how much they've aged. Our brains are incredibly good at hiding the truth from us. It's a survival mechanism, plain and simple. And if you're struggling with writing faster, it's likely because this survival mechanism has kicked in. But your records will tell you the truth.

We don't spot patterns without hard data - you may have a vague gut feeling that you write better in the morning, but you won't actually know anything until you track your progress at different times. I have been completely wrong about my patterns in the past, thinking I couldn't write in the mornings—it's 10:37am right now and I've already typed about 1500 words, and I'm just at the beginning of my writing block. If you're so sure of your natural inclinations, prove it to yourself with actual performance metrics. You won't be sorry you confirmed what you already knew, and you might be surprised by how much you didn't know about yourself.

You have to approach this like a scientist would - You can try to implement just the content and tips in this book, but you won't achieve optimal results. That's because self-knowledge is the actual holy grail of productivity—not anything else I share in this book. A lot of this information is what I tried and what worked for me. But you need to figure out what you should try and test it to see what is going to work for you. You see, the whole entire project is an experiment you're going to do on yourself. My role in all of this is only to act as your mentor, to guide you in your thinking about what to try. You still have to do the work. And you will be completely lost if you don't set up your tracking system from the beginning.

THE HARSH TRUTHS OF TRACKING YOUR PROGRESS

If you've ever tried to track anything, from your calorie intake, to your workouts, to your steps per day, to your your weight, to your sales numbers or your traffic, you know that there's a lot holding you back from writing down and analyzing those numbers on a consistent basis.

HERE ARE THE HARSH TRUTHS OF TRACKING:

It's going to get old after awhile. If you love data, you will love seeing your numbers go up as you progress through this transformation... but eventually, you'll hit a point where keeping the numbers is a chore. I have already hit this point and don't bother keeping track of my numbers anymore. I have a good handle on what works for me and I've internalized a lot of it, so most of my writing time is spent in a moderate-to-optimal state.

It's going to take time to maintain your spreadsheets. You don't want to count this time as part of your writing time, because eventually you'll stop tracking it. I would plan to maintain this for 3-6 months, max (the higher end only if you're doing this extremely part-time).

You may be tempted to fudge the data. Resist this urge to lie to yourself. (Obvious, but worth stating explicitly.)

You'll need to mix things up during the experiment. If you write every morning for an hour, you're probably going to need to try writing at other times in the day. If you always type in the same spot, you might need to try a coffee shop or a dictation mic. If you use a jolt of coffee to get you going, you may need to switch to caffeine-free a few times. An experiment is just that, so don't be afraid to get out of your comfort zone. You will learn a lot less about yourself if you don't.

What gets measured gets managed. Peter Drucker, one of the forefathers and inventors of modern management, said that—and he was right! I don't talk much about key performance indicators (KPIs) in this book, but the bottom line is that if you focus heavily on fresh word count for awhile, that is what you're going to get in your results. Keep in mind that fresh word count is a key driver in books published, but it's not the only key driver. I ran into this personally, when I was writing 50,000 words per month but had no process in place to also edit and self-publish 50,000 words per month. Don't forget about this and set your expectations accordingly. I talk about this a lot more later in the book, but I want to point out from the outset that word count does not equal published books. That equation is a bit more complicated.

Tracking is going to make you work harder than you normally would. This is a known phenomenon called the Hawthorne Effect. What it means is that when you are being watched (even by yourself) you are more likely to follow through on your intentions. That means that your results are going to be better when you're tracking than they are when you're not tracking. Keep this is mind for when you go off of tracking. I would say that although I could write 4,000 words per hour and have on numerous occasions, I rarely do now that I'm not tracking. Could is still a valuable outcome. But it's not like I can crank out a 40,000 word novel in 10 hours on a daily basis.

You are a human, not a machine. Right now, I'm probably writing closer to 2,200-2,500 words per hour. It's 11:21am and I've added about 1,500 new words since I last told you my time (10:37am). I'm jumping around, as I usually do with non-fiction (I write more linearly with fiction, which accounts for the 4,000wph, but I can't recall ever achieving this with non-fiction). I'm sipping tea, listening in on conversations around me, and watching people walk by out the windows as I type. It's a relaxed environment. I'm not using my mic (which accounts for a huge boost in my word count). Right now, I'm trying to enjoy myself, not write as fast as I possibly can. So keep this in mind—even when you look at my diary in the appendix, you'll find that my true averages still only fall between 2,500-3,500 words per hour, when averaged out over an entire month. The point is that you're going to have bad days and you're going to eventually want to optimize for something else (like pleasure or enjoyability—where I'm at now). So don't take the numbers too literally. That last sentence will drive some of you absolutely insane, and give others of you a huge sense of relief.

Explore with an open mind. You really don't know what you're going to find. You may find that 4,000 words per hour is way, way out of your comfort zone. You may find that you need to write with music. You may find that you've been doing all the wrong things and your writing routine needs a complete overhaul. You may find that everything is already optimized! Approach this process with no expectations, and you'll be surprised; approach it with the goal of publishing 20 books next year, and you will only set yourself up for disappointment.

Don't compare yourself to others. This is the road to anger, bitterness, resentment, jealousy, disappointment, and self-loathing. Eyes on your own paper.

All progress is progress. If you get stuck (and you will), don't feel bad about stepping away for a moment. You'll see in my Life of a Writer diary in the appendix that I got really stuck during the second month. I took some time off from the experiment and got clear on what I needed and wanted. Forgiving myself and my shortcomings was key to that.

Transformations are wonderful, but they can also be all-consuming. As you're going through this transformation, try to ground it in realism and daily life. You can't drop everything and drive your word count up forever—that's just a recipe for burnout. Keep this experiment as close to real life as possible, and you'll get more realistic results you can live with in the process.

HOW TO TRACK YOUR PROGRESS

There are two most important metrics (MIMs) that you need to track:

- How many words per hour you're hitting (on average)
- How many hours per day you're writing (on average)

The goal for your entire journey will be to increase these numbers in a way that works for you.

You can adjust this goal to your preference, of course, but this is the basic driver of the experiment.

To track your MIMs, you need to record what you're doing throughout the experiment. You can do this in multiple ways and formats:

- By keeping spreadsheets of what you do (I recommend Microsoft Excel or Google Spreadsheets)
- By keeping a daily diary of what happened, at what times, and how you felt as you were trying to make it happen (I recommend Evernote, SimpleNote, or Google Docs)
- By allowing an automated program like RescueTime record your productivity for you
- By sharing your progress with others publicly through a blog or within a group (I recommend Google+ or Wordpress)

Put as much of this as you can in place, so you have more data. You'll be surprised by how much it helps you later.

If this seems daunting, remember that tracking is temporary. Eventually, you won't need to track what you're doing because you'll have enough data to draw conclusions about what you should do, and then you can just ingrain those conclusions in your habits and actions.

Here's my list of what I tracked quantitatively (numbers):

- Start time
- End time
- Date
- Total time spent
- First pomodoro, second pomodoro, etc.
- First set of pomodoros, second set of pomodoros, etc.
- Where I was at

- What inputs I used (mic, keyboard)
- Whether I was primarily writing or editing
- The title of the book
- The title of the series
- A notes column where I could write down mood

Here's my list of what I tracked qualitatively (rich textual data):

- Times
- How I felt
- What I was struggling with
- My original intentions
- What got in the way of those intentions
- Where I was, where I wanted to be
- New experiments I wanted to try
- Real-time evaluation of my progress
- Real-time adjustment of my goals and expectations

I did not use RescueTime, personally, but it may be helpful to corroborate your data at the end of the month, especially if you think you'll be tempted to lie to yourself. (Of course, you can lie to yourself just as easily via RescueTime—every system can be gamed.)

You may be wondering what you would ever do with all this data, or whether you need to collect it to begin with. My thought is collect all the data you can at first and adjust down as you go. If you find yourself not having any use for something, stop collecting it. But start at a place of abundance, just in case.

I evaluated myself from session to session, and then in detail on a monthly basis when I did this experiment. That's what I'd recommend to you as well. My monthly detailed analysis was fascinating for me and gave me even richer insight than I was getting from the day-to-day. You can see my evaluations in the appendix, named September Insights, October Resolutions (Life of a Writer: Day 38).

As you evaluate, here are some things you can do:

- See what you are doing now and do more of what's working
- Abandon what's not working
- Hypothesize some new theories about what would work for you and set up the experiment
- Compare your data from this month to last month and congratulate yourself on any improvement
- Add another goal and push yourself

At this point I've given you way more information than I intended to regarding tracking your progress, but I can't tell you how important it is to your success. I'll reiterate—if there's one takeaway you glean from this book, it should be to start tracking your data. The rest is all optional, but this is required.

If you have any questions, reach out to me on Twitter or Google+. My handle is @monicaleonelle on both. Please post publicly so I can respond publicly and help others as well.

Chapter 4
WRITING 3500-4000+ WORDS PER HOUR

This is the original article "How To Consistently Write 3500-4000 Words Per Hour" with no edits.

The steps roughly correspond to the eventual framework I've come up with, Knowledge, Flow, Training, and Energy, but not quite. That's why I'll go into each of those four steps in more detail in the coming chapters.

This article is also available for free online if you'd like to share with your friends. If you tweet it out or share it, don't forget to tag me too so I can thank you!

Twitter: @monicaleonelle
Facebook: http://facebook.com/monicaleonellegrace/

*****

It happens to every author, freelancer, or blogger at some point. We realize that our business model of creating valuable content is actually working—if only we had more content to give.

I fell down the productivity rabbit hole back at the 2012, when I was only writing 900–1200 words per hour. I knew that my goal and dream of becoming a full-time fiction author was possible, if only I could build my back catalog quickly. But novels were too long, especially mine. One of my novels was nearly 250,000 words done properly. Another had taken me months and months to write. And I was burnt out. There simply weren't enough hours in the day for writing.

So instead of giving up on my dream, I decided that I was simply going to learn to write faster. I studied suggestions from other people and made a list of nearly 30 different ways I could improve my writing pace. I ended up only needing four general principles, which I'm going to share with you today.

I applied the first principle and saw my word count jump to around 1600 words per hour. Not bad. I applied the next and I was suddenly in the 2000's. "2000 words!" I thought. Eventually, I had so optimized the crap out of my writing speed that I could write at a predictable 3500–4000 word pace.

HERE'S HOW I DID IT

STEP 1: KNOW WHAT YOU'RE WRITING

I've been writing nonfiction for long enough that I could do a simple bulleted outline and churn out tons of words quickly. Fiction was a little different, but I finally settled into a 4-step process:

Outline – I wrote roughly a paragraph per chapter about what would happen in the chapter.

Write Beats – I expanded the outline to roughly five paragraphs per chapter, this time indicating whether a section is dialogue, description, or internal monologue. Each of these three requires a different writing mindset, and most authors gravitate toward one a little more.

Sketch – I turned each beat from "tell" to "show," thinking of them as short instructions for what should be on the page. I didn't bother writing in connectors or transitions between the beats, just tried to hit between 300–500 words with each beat. Essentially, I sketched out the scene without drawing firm lines.

Draft – I cleaned the sketch to what I call "compile," which in software terms, means that the program actually runs (there are no syntax errors). For the fiction version of "compile," I consider it compilable when I could hand it to someone and they could read it with no missing parts. This didn't necessarily mean that the draft was perfect, but the draft communicated the story well enough that no one would say, "Hey, how did they jump from the bedroom to the restaurant?"

This process continues to work well for me today, especially because I've internalized a number of story structures and can easily apply them to my outline. In my opinion, get the outline right, you get the entire book right. I talk about this in my book, Nail Your Outline. This is true for non-fiction and articles, too, and you can easily adapt this structure to all sorts of non-fiction, including books, essays, articles, and blog posts.

Breaking the process out into extremely obvious steps that each only took a very small chunk of time to do was absolutely key to improving my writing speed.

Result: Jumped from ~800-900 words/hr to ~1600 words/hr.

STEP 2: FLOW (AND THE POMODORO METHOD)

When you have flow, the words are going to come out of you effortlessly. For me, the easiest way to get into flow was to use the Pomodoro Method.

The Pomodoro Method is a productivity tool in which you work for a concentrated, focused 25 minutes and then get a five minute break before starting again. People use it for all sorts of things, but I decided to use it just for writing, so as not to distract myself while writing.

This technique alone will help you see big gains in writing speed, especially if you've planned out your writing already.

It also helps you normalize your writing routine and tracking because the chunk of time is the same for every pomodoro (25 minutes long). My tracking spreadsheet suddenly became more useful in terms of what each number actually meant.

I recommend the Pomodoro Method to absolutely everybody, and every single person has said it helped them write faster. So try it. You will be surprised at how out of flow you are during a typical writing session without this.

Result: Jumped from ~1600 words/hr to ~2400 words/hr. Completed a novella that launched my second pen name in two days. You can nearly read my original draft word for word in that novella to this day, because I was in such a state of flow that I barely had any revisions for it.

STEP 3: TRAINING

The bad thing for me about using the Pomodoro Method was that my wrists and fingers were in serious pain by the end of each day. I couldn't physically keep up with the typing for reasons that were out of my control. No matter what I did ergonomically, I couldn't alleviate the issue.

Date	Avg. W/H	Time Start	Time Stop	WC	Location
6/29/2012	926	11:20:00	12:50:00	1389	Starbucks
6/29/2012	601	15:04:00	15:47:00	431	My Couch
7/8/2012	815	22:00:00	23:30:00	1223	Patrick's Couch
7/10/2012	799	17:32:00	18:13:00	546	Patrick's Couch
7/15/2012	847	10:12:00	10:23:00	155	My Couch
7/15/2012	916	10:47:00	11:14:00	412	My Couch
7/15/2012	890	12:27:00	13:30:00	934	My Couch
7/15/2012	934	14:13:00	15:18:00	1011	My Couch
7/16/2012	1,013	8:18:00	9:17:00	996	Starbucks
7/16/2012	753	9:30:00	10:03:00	414	Starbucks
7/17/2012	1,569	13:42:00	13:59:00	444	Patrick's Couch
7/17/2012	886	13:59:00	14:18:00	281	Patrick's Couch
7/17/2012	1,213	14:40:00	15:04:00	485	Patrick's Couch
7/17/2012	1,483	16:03:00	16:37:00	841	Patrick's Couch
7/19/2012	709	12:54:00	14:41:00	1265	My Couch
7/19/2012	1,050	14:45:00	16:48:00	2153	My Couch
7/19/2012	1,452	17:15:00	17:47:00	774	My Couch
8/18/2012	1,168	13:11:00	13:55:00	856	Chicago Public Library
8/18/2012	781	14:00:00	15:14:00	963	Chicago Public Library
8/18/2012	1,103	16:50:00	17:08:00	331	Patrick's Couch
8/18/2012	1,267	17:50:00	18:10:00	422	Patrick's Couch
8/21/2012	726	9:33:00	9:54:00	254	Chicago Public Library
8/21/2012	993	10:05:00	11:05:00	993	Chicago Public Library
8/21/2012	427	11:20:00	12:02:00	299	Chicago Public Library
8/24/2012	978	11:00:00	12:15:00	1223	Chicago Public Library
8/24/2012	842	14:09:00	15:00:00	716	Chicago Public Library
8/26/2012	733	13:25:00	13:47:00	269	Chicago Public Library
8/26/2012	669	14:15:00	15:54:00	1104	Chicago Public Library
8/26/2012	855	16:00:00	16:33:00	470	Chicago Public Library
8/26/2012	575	18:25:00	20:29:00	1189	Bedroom, Couch
8/26/2012	1,052	20:35:00	20:51:00	281	Patrick's Couch

Original Tracking – No Set Length of Session

Word Count/Hour is the second column.

Date	Set	Pomodoro #	Time Start	Time Stop	Words Start	Words Stop	Word Count	Words/Hour	Words/Minute	Writing/Editing	Location
10/5/2012	1	1	10:05:00	10:30:00	670	1247	577	1,384	23	Writing	My Couch
10/5/2012	1	2	10:35:00	11:00:00	1247	1878	631	1,513	25	Writing	My Couch
10/5/2012	1	3	11:05:00	11:30:00	1878	2602	724	1,736	29	Writing	My Couch
10/5/2012	1	4	11:35:00	12:00:00	2602	3520	918	2,201	37	Writing	My Couch
10/5/2012	2	1	14:30:00	14:55:00	0	807	807	1,935	32	Writing	My Couch
10/5/2012	2	2	15:00:00	15:25:00	807	1636	829	1,988	33	Writing	My Couch
10/5/2012	2	3	15:30:00	15:55:00	1636	2432	796	1,909	32	Writing	My Couch
10/5/2012	2	4	16:00:00	16:25:00	0	807	807	1,935	32	Writing	My Couch
10/5/2012	3	1	21:30:00	21:55:00	1279	1828	549	1,317	22	Writing	My Bed
10/5/2012	3	2	22:00:00	22:25:00	1828	2667	839	2,012	34	Writing	My Bed
10/5/2012	3	3	22:30:00	22:55:00	2667	3384	717	1,719	29	Writing	My Bed
10/5/2012	3	4	23:00:00	23:25:00	3384	3920	536	1,285	21	Writing	My Bed
10/6/2012	1	1	14:00:00	14:25:00	0	794	794	1,904	32	Writing	My Couch
10/6/2012	1	2	14:30:00	14:55:00	794	1338	544	1,305	22	Writing	My Couch
10/6/2012	1	3	15:00:00	15:25:00	1338	2025	687	1,647	27	Writing	My Couch
10/6/2012	1	4	15:30:00	15:55:00	2025	2820	795	1,906	32	Writing	My Couch
10/6/2012	2	1	21:45:00	22:10:00	0	818	818	1,957	33	Writing	My Bed
10/6/2012	2	2	22:15:00	22:40:00	818	1447	631	1,513	25	Writing	My Bed
10/6/2012	2	3	22:45:00	23:10:00	1447	2120	673	1,614	27	Writing	My Bed
10/6/2012	2	4	23:15:00	23:40:00	2120	2751	631	1,513	25	Writing	My Bed
10/7/2012	1	1	10:00:00	10:25:00	0	444	444	1,066	18	Writing	Patrick's Couch
10/7/2012	1	2	10:30:00	10:55:00	444	743	299	717	12	Writing	Patrick's Couch
10/7/2012	1	3	11:00:00	11:25:00	743	1254	511	1,225	20	Writing	Patrick's Couch
10/7/2012	1	4	11:30:00	11:55:00	1254	1537	283	679	11	Writing	Patrick's Couch
10/16/2012	1	1	11:30:00	11:55:00	0	592	592	1,420	24	Writing	B&N, back
10/16/2012	1	2	13:30:00	13:55:00	592	1145	553	1,326	22	Writing	Library
10/16/2012	1	3	14:00:00	14:25:00	1145	1746	601	1,441	24	Writing	Library
10/16/2012	1	4	14:30:00	14:55:00	0	524	524	1,257	21	Writing	Library
10/17/2012	1	1	11:00:00	11:25:00	524	1137	613	1,470	25	Writing	Library
10/17/2012	1	2	11:30:00	11:55:00	1137	1830	693	1,662	28	Writing	Library
10/17/2012	1	3	12:00:00	12:25:00	0	838	538	1,290	22	Writing	Library
10/17/2012	1	4	12:30:00	12:55:00			0	0	0	Writing	Library

Pomodoro Tracking – 25 Minute Sessions

Word Count/Hour is the 9th column.

I grew frustrated because I could think of my story faster than I could type it comfortably. So I did a little research and found the concept of dictation, which is likely where our entire culture is going in the next 10 years.

("Look kids, I remember back in my day when we had to press buttons on this slab of metal and wires just to communicate with each other. Imagine, typing in a word letter-by-letter. You kids are lucky!")

(Sidenote: my prediction is that spelling will go the way of handwriting in terms of life skills. The next generation simply won't need it.)

The concept of dictation is simple: the average person speaks at 150 words per minute, while the average person types at 35–40 words per minute. I typed at 70 words per minute, but couldn't do that for long periods of time with consistency due to my fingers and hands. So if my story was coming at me at a clip of ~30 words per minute or more, my hands couldn't keep up.

Dictation solved that. I took to it right away and saw huge gains again.

Now, not everyone will take to dictation like me. It makes sense for extroverts and incessant talkers like myself. Yes, there's some throat clearing to delete in the editing, but for the most part, my story unravelled at an unparalleled pace when I switched.

For introverts, the concept still applies. Make sure your physical input speed over long hours far outpaces your thinking speed, because that's the only way you'll be able to transfer your brain to (electronic) paper for extended periods of time.

Result: Jumped from ~2400 words/hr to ~3200 words/hr. I was killing it!

11/18/2012	1	1	13:03:00	13:15:00	0	571	571	2,855	48	Dragon Dictate	Dining Room
11/18/2012	1	2	13:20:00	13:45:00	0	1464	1464	3,511	59	Dragon Dictate	Dining Room
11/18/2012	1	3	14:00:00	14:25:00	0	1189	1189	2,851	48	Dragon Dictate	Dining Room
11/18/2012	1	4	14:35:00	15:00:00	0	1316	1316	3,156	53	Dragon Dictate	Dining Room
11/18/2012	2	1	20:20:00	20:44:00	0	1444	1444	3,610	60	Dragon Dictate	Bedroom
11/18/2012	2	2	20:50:00	21:15:00	0	1313	1313	3,149	52	Dragon Dictate	Bedroom
11/18/2012	2	3	21:20:00	21:35:00	1313	1890	577	2,308	38	Dragon Dictate	Bedroom
11/18/2012	2	4	21:50:00	22:15:00	0	1344	1344	3,223	54	Dragon Dictate	Bedroom
11/20/2012	1	1	0:10:00	0:37:00	0	1576	1576	3,502	58	Dragon Dictate	Dining Room
11/20/2012	1	2	0:40:00	1:09:00	0	1778	1778	3,681	61	Dragon Dictate	Dining Room
11/20/2012	1	3	1:15:00	1:40:00	0	1568	1588	3,760	63	Dragon Dictate	Dining Room
11/20/2012	1	4	1:50:00	2:15:00	0	1288	1288	3,089	51	Dragon Dictate	Dining Room
11/20/2012	1	1	18:00:00	18:25:00	0	1590	1590	3,813	64	Dragon Dictate	Dining Room
11/20/2012	1	2	18:30:00	18:49:00	0	914	914	2,883	48	Dragon Dictate	Dining Room

Pomodoro + Dragon Dictate Tracking

Word Count/Hour is the 9th column.

STEP 4: ENERGY

Energy will always, always improve your writing speed, but you've got to know yourself too. As an extrovert, a lot of my energy comes from external forces. This makes it difficult for me to be a writer because most of my time is spent by myself.

At the same time, when I write with other people, I don't want to write, I want to talk. So the most productive places for me are coffee shops where I don't know anyone... and not to make you introverts laugh, but "not knowing anyone" just honestly doesn't last that long for me, so I have to change coffee shops regularly just to get some peace.

This created a huge challenge for me because coffee shops provided me the most energy, but I couldn't dictate in coffee shops. I could dictate at home, but I felt like the atmosphere was chipping away at me more often than not, making my writing stagnate.

I found a really happy medium for myself when I started doing walk and talks. This unfortunately meant I had to wrangle with a ton of technology. (I used my iPad to record and carried a mini-recording studio with me in a backpack as I walked so that I could get good sound and use my expensive mic, which was the only one Dragon Dictate could translate correctly—yeesh.)

The upside was that I could walk to secluded areas of Chicago (a.k.a. the lakefront path below Soldier Field) and speak my novel out loud, in peace, with only a few strange looks from passerbys. The outdoors gave me tons of energy (the constant scenery changes and bustle of people were a plus) and I also got some movement in each day.

Again, your energy may come from other routines, like exercise, reading a good book, or sitting in a special chair and sipping tea, but knowing yourself is key. Figure out where your untapped energy source is and make sure you have a routine to draw from it every day.

Result: Jumped from ~3200 words/hr to ~3500–4000 words/hr!

WHEN DOES IT STOP?

After all of this effort (many, many months of experimenting, in my case), I lost interest in increasing my writing speed any further. One reason was because I sensed that any faster would start to degrade my quality of writing significantly. I was already starting to see deterioration at the ~4000 word/hr speed.

Another was because I hate doing things the same way all the time, and I started to get bored with the idea of going out for yet another walk and talk.

If you're a plodder, you will absolutely, 100% love optimizing your writing speed, because you love routine. I would love to love routine, but alas, I'm a natural burster who needs variety in her day-to-day.

So now, I don't write at 4000 words per hour every day, but I'm still happy I took the journey. I can write 4000 words per hour, if needed. That's always going to be a great skill to have. Additionally, I can write a lot more than 1200 words per hour even when I sit down to type at this point (around ~2800 wph—still an amazing speed). And I can dictate at my desk too, depending on what my mood is. Switching off between the different places and different ways I can "write" has increased the sheer number of hours I spend writing, which has helped me put out 6 books this year (with *hopefully* at least another five on the way before the end of the year—they are so close to being done!).

I hope this helps you figure out what works best for you to rapidly improve your writing speed. There are a lot of other tips out there, but most of the are too specific and work only for certain types of people (i.e. a plodder and not a burster, an introvert and not an extrovert, etc.) I've never seen any that genuinely matter besides these four above.

As always, my message in sharing this is going to be use the general framework and switch up the details for what works for YOU. That is how you'll achieve the best results. Know thyself. It's a freaking great productivity strategy!

Chapter 5
STEP #1 - KNOWLEDGE

The first step to writing faster is knowledge about what you're writing, which so many authors either scrimp on or skip completely.

Big mistake. I found that just this step basically doubled my word count per hour.

However, I actually understand the compulsion to skip pre-production and just sit down and write, because I used to do the exact same thing. I can tell you with confidence where that road led to for me—a bloated book that didn't make much sense or sell well.

It's only through years of refining that I've been able to come up with a solid process to create an amazing draft that works for me. Other writers have told me that my process is killer and leaves very little room for writer's block. Your mileage may vary, but I think this is a worthy framework to start from—you'll, of course, have to customize it to your own style and preferences.

Here's how it works:

STEP 1: OUTLINE

Pretty much everything I learned about outlining, I learned from reading only a few books (despite buying and reading over 50, so save yourself time and take my recommendations). I'll get to what those books are in a minute, but first, I want to explain the types of information you want to trace in your outlines.

PLOT ARC

You definitely want to know your plot, and it's easy enough to follow the 4-part story structure that is commonly taught for commercial work. *Story Engineering* by Larry Brooks is the BEST book on this topic—I can't recommend his book enough. He goes over inciting incidents, cliffhangers, plot points, pinch points, and more.

Most aspiring (and some actual) authors stop at the plot outline, when there are still a few other pieces of your book that you want to know more about before moving onto beats.

CHARACTER ARC(S)

You also want to outline major character arcs, which gets sticky if you have multiple characters or multiple viewpoints. A lot of fantasy authors have this problem, I've noticed. Still, there's no getting around doing character arc outlines for every major character, including the antagonist, because a character that people care about will change throughout the story and you've got to be able to show that. I also usually give myself three or four backstory/flashback/dream sequence sections per novel, though that's by no means a hard and fast rule—I just try not to overwhelm my readers with too much information about any one character. As it was explained to me, when you define your characters too sharply at their introduction, it sometimes leaves little room for them to grow. This works well for most tertiary characters, but not for protagonists, antagonists, and secondary characters, who need much more gray area in their personalities.

My favorite book(s) on this topic are by Victoria Lynn Schmidt, starting with *45 Master Characters*, and continuing with her other book *A Writer's Guide to Characterization* (though if you only read one, read 45 Master Characters).

I also subscribe to the television model of character arcs when I'm writing a series. The television model is something you'll probably recognize once you hear it; it's the idea that every secondary character gets an episode dedicated to them per season. One amazing show that follows this model exactly just came out in 2014, called *How To Get Away With Murder* (and yes, Shonda Rhimes is one of my storytelling idols—more on that in a different book).

Every storyteller should watch this show to get a better understanding of how to build character arcs. The show starts with a general pilot that sets up the concept of the entire series, focusing on the main character (the one who's on all the posters), Annalise Keating. She's a criminal defense attorney who puts together this crack team of first-year law students to work at her firm (hey, I never said the premise was plausible). In the second episode, we watch one of Annalise Keating's cases (like many new television shows, this one has a "freak-of-the-week" for the first 6-7 episodes so that new viewers can jump right in without a ton of context), but we also learn more about one of the first-years on this crack team while keeping the others in the background. The next episode focuses on another of the first-years, and then another... by the 6th or 7th episode, all the characters have had their moment in the sun, the larger arc has developed rapidly, AND the show has kept its pattern of one trial case solved per episode. It's really quite a feat to watch, and one that I haven't seen many other shows pull off so well.

Anyway, back to character arcs. Once you've done both your plot arc and your character arcs, you of course need to overlay them and start matching things up. This can be a bit challenging, or it can feel serendipitous (I've felt both for the same book). I'm not going to go into detail on this because it depends a lot on how you outline; what I will say is that this part is a bit like piecing together a puzzle. All of the little pieces you've gathered with eventually form the full picture, but you've got to figure out the connections to make it happen. Either way, if you can get this right, you'll be way ahead of at least 90% of writers who simply don't think about how much time they could save down the road by getting plot and character arcs right upfront.

WORLD-BUILDING ARCS

If you want to go a step further, it may also be helpful to do a world-building outline, especially if you write anything other than contemporary fiction. Few historical, fantasy, and science fiction authors think about this, which results in pockets of information dumps throughout their novel. I experienced this with an urban fantasy I was working on, where I threw like, everything anyone ever needed to know about the world into a single book. When I went back through and rewrote the book (it was my first one, so it needed to be rewritten for a plethora of reasons) I took entire plot lines and just moved them to later books in the series... they were merely open threads that slowed down the first book.

When it comes to creating a world-building outline, there aren't any real templates or books out there to recommend. What I do is limit myself to the least someone needs to know to understand the novel, and move pieces around accordingly. Less always seems to be more in these cases.

A great example of someone who can build a world slowly is J.K. Rowling.

(Spoiler Alert—not that anyone who hasn't made time to read the Harry Potter series yet deserves one—I'm now going to talk about the full plot of all seven books. Skip the next several pages or so if you haven't read the series and plan to.)

Imagine, for example, if she tried to cram in all the information about the horcruxes in book two, where the first one showed up? It would have been a confusing mess. Deciding where to reveal this information was an interesting choice on her part, and in a way revitalized the entire series in the sixth and seventh books, when we finally got the whole backstory on Voldemort.

Another amazing example of world-building is in this British television show called Black Mirror. It's a bit like The Twilight Zone and explores the way our digital lives impact us in dark ways. You can skip the first episode—it's gross and horrifying and not very good—but the second episode of the first season is called "Fifteen Million Merits" and is what I would consider a master class on world-building. The script itself is sparse of dialog, but the setting and the visuals give you all the information you need to immerse yourself. I love how every little piece, from the Wraith's Babes at the beginning, to the scenes with the apples, tell so much more about the world than words could.

I don't think outlining the world-building progression needs to be a big effort, especially not compared to the plot and character arcs. I tend to just make notes about when I'm going to dig in to each piece of information and try to keep those pieces spread out. If you are a color-coding type, you can easily visualize this by labeling the world-building sections of your outline in green.

One last thing I want to say about outlines, that they don't need to be this huge production. An outline is just a few sentences about each chapter + a list of things you want to touch on within the scene.

Throughout this section, I'm going to share a sample of this entire process from my own work. The book in question is a mashup of two popular Jane Austen works: Emma and Pride and Prejudice. I chose this particular project for the example because I wanted something that people roughly knew the story to, and I also wanted something that people could go to and read in full, free of charge. Emma + Elsie Meet Fitzwilliam Darcy is free either via my website (go to http://monicaleonelle.com/ee/ to download it) or for free on all eRetailers. So, if you'd like to really do your homework, you can grab it and see how the final book turned out, using this process.

Here's the original outline:

BOOK 1 - EMMA + ELSIE MEET FITZWILLIAM DARCY

Ch. 1 - Elsie

Intro to the two characters and how they became best friends. When Jane left for college and Miss Taylor started dating Mr. Weston, the two started hanging out. There are only 12 girls in their grade — the two of them, Catherine Linton, who is never allowed to leave her home or hang out, Lacey Bates, who started school several years late, and Charlotte Lucas, who is neighbors with Elsie, but who has... changed. Charlotte is not going to college... Shes happy working a simple job in the town. Emma is obsessed with Miss Taylor's wedding since it's the first time she'll be a bridesmaid. Elsie is excited that her sister, Jane is coming home for the wedding.

Ch. 2 - Emma

She has checklist after checklist of what needs to be done for the wedding. She wants everything to be perfect. While working on the checklists Jace Knightley comes over to tell her about some new people that moved to town that she should invite. She freaks out, but Jace says it's fine because they have an open wedding.

Ch. 3 - Elsie

She sees Jane for the first time in months. Jane is with a girl she doesn't recognize, who introduces herself as Caroline Bingley. Jane met Caroline through her studies in social work and Caroline's brother just so happens to be renting one of the mansions in town for the summer. Jane is kind, as always, but Elsie is skeptical of this new girl.

Ch. 4 - Jane

Caroline exhibits mean girl tendencies that Jane doesn't have a clue about. She's sugary sweet even though she doesn't like Jane at all. Jane takes her to see everything around town and doesn't notice that Caroline is disdainful of the area. Finally, Caroline and Jane meet Jane's mother and she commits a faux pas in front of Caroline. Then, Jane's mom insists that Jane spend some time at their manor, because she's always loved it since she was a little girl.

Ch. 5 - Emma

Emma bursts into her father's study, where Jace is talking to him about something important. She needs someone to take pictures of her getting dressed. She needs Jace's help to get dressed... her dress doesn't work with her tan. She calls him, claiming it's an emergency. Allude to his past girlfriends. He comes to the rescue as usual.

Ch. 6 - Jane

Jane meets Bingley. Something magical passes between them, which Caroline isn't okay with. Caroline has so many plans for her brother, and Jane is totally not the girl she pictures him with. But Jane can't see that at all. He's interested in her social work, she's interested in his foundations, etc.

Ch. 7 - Elsie

Elsie sits with her family and we meet them. What does her mom care about? She wants to make sure her daughters get out and experience the world, rather than stay in Rosebelle and settle down with farmers. Elsie sees William Darcy and realizes he's incredibly attractive, but not as attractive as Bingley, who is sitting next to Jane at the wedding. William is a bad boy, seemingly. His edge is harder, and she wonders about him.

Ch. 8 - Emma

She walks down the aisle with Jace who is the best man. The whole time, she misses his subtle hints that he's in love with her. She's clueless! He asks her to save a dance for him at the reception, and she agrees out of surprise.

Ch. 9 - Jane

Jane and Charles dance for the second time that night. There is something magnetic and electric between them. He is the kindest, most gentle man she has ever met. She feels entirely swept off her feet.

Ch. 10 - Elsie

At the reception, she watches Jane get swept off her feet by Bingley. she secretly hopes that William will ask her, but she overhears him saying horrible things about her hometown to Caroline Bingley. Also, horrible things about her.

Ch. 11 - Emma

Emma finds Elsie in the bathroom crying, and goes into friend mode. She breezes past Jace who was patiently waiting for her, and the girls find a place to sit. Emma vows to take down William Darcy while he's here for hurting her friend.

Ch. 12 - Jane

They go off by themselves and something intense happens between them. Jane is caught up in the moment and can't help but act on her connection with Bingley. Sexy time! (It is a New Adult series, after all.)

STEP 2: BEATS

After the outline is done, I then continue to build out the story, writing down the highlights for each chapter/scene (mine are basically the same, though sometimes a chapter is a couple scenes strung together with transitions).

A number of people who read the original article asked me what exactly "beats" were. My short definition is, you can do beats however you want. Similar to an outline, beats are very personal. The way I do mine is I attempt to "tell" a mythical someone what my story is about. Later, I'll convert "tell" to "show" (the preferred method of reading a story), but for now, I just want to get down what exactly the story is.

This part immediately makes the gaps in my story painfully obvious. Have you ever thought you had a great story, and then when you tried to tell someone, you realized it's actually terrible? This happened to me a lot in my youth—I had an amazing night out with my friends, and I'd be talking about it at lunch the next day, and then I'd realize that the story basically amounted to "we got drunk and partied."

Your beats will tell you if you actually have a story that someone else cares about and will also help you nail down the details in a way that outlining doesn't force you to.

For example, if you're outlining, you can write stuff like, "Harry Potter goes up against Professor Quirrell and wins." Unfortunately, that sentence is almost useless when you get to the actual writing part. There are way too many details that you still need to figure out—and if you go straight to the draft, you will spin your wheels and waste your potential for flow trying to decide on the most basic of plot points. In the book Willpower, the author points out that decision-making is one of the largest taxes on your willpower throughout the day. That's why people like President Obama don't spend time on pointless decisions, like what to wear in the morning (his entire wardrobe is coordinated to gray and blue suits). If you buy into the research, you can probably see why it's so hard to keep writing when you have no clue what your story is about. Writing, at the end of the day, is a series of decisions, and you'll make thousands of them throughout your novel without even realizing it. You're eating up all your willpower, making these decisions—which makes it hard to then apply that same willpower to the act of putting fingers to keyboard.

Beating is a way to make a ton of decisions about your novel without the added pressure of making it "sound good." Going back to the original sentence, "Harry Potter goes up against Professor Quirrell and wins."—let's dig into those decisions now. If you were telling someone this story, you wouldn't be able to get away with that single sentence. You would need to expand. The first thing the other person would ask is, "Well, how? Where do they battle? What is the weapon? What happens to Professor Quirrell afterward? Does Harry actually kill him, or just stun him? How does a child take down an adult wizard inhabited by the darkest lord of all time?"

Your beats are where you can work out all the answers to these questions. Just start by asking yourself one question you have about a sentence in your outline. With every question, you'll find an answer and another few questions... keep on prodding yourself until you've developed a nice narrative that you could share with someone else to explain your scene. You'll end up beating out several chapters worth of content and answer all the basic questions someone might have about your story.

Following this simple process alone is going to be insanely more helpful than your outline. It also takes a lot less time than you think—I can usually beat out my entire book in a day or two, and this saves me hundreds of hours during both the writing AND editing processes, because I don't waste time going down paths that don't lead to a successful story.

Let me expand on that. As Larry Brooks says in Story Engineering (my absolute favorite book on plotting), too many writers waste words on trying to find their plot, and end up having to cut huge sections and entire chapters from their final draft. This is not only painful and time consuming, but also 100% avoidable. He subscribes to the idea that finding your story in pre-production, before you do all that drafting, is vastly more efficient—and I have to agree, based on my personal experience. I rarely need to cut sections from my drafts anymore, because the story is clean and whole from the beats. I'm able to spot and address issues before I even start drafting, because they become apparent when reading through the beats. This results in significantly less writing, significantly less rewriting, and significantly less editing. It sets me up for success all the way through the rest of my process.

In my beats, I also like to add in other little notes to myself. For example, I like to add in a beat that reminds me to describe the setting, especially if it hasn't been done before in the book. Same goes for characters—you usually need to give them at least a sentence, especially if they are tertiary and fairly one-note. (Like the Dursleys in Harry Potter.)

You'll also want to experiment with your length of outline to length of beats ratio and length of beats to length of draft ratio.

For me, one sentence in my outline usually equates to 1-3 paragraphs in my beats. And one paragraph in my beats usually equates to 300-500 words of draft.

Why is this useful? Because once you figure out what those amounts are for you, you'll be able to predict how much time you need to complete a draft. A big part of drafting is knowing when something is done.

Another way this has helped me is I can push myself a little more. I can say stuff to myself like, "Oh, I'll just do one more beat, it will only take 10 minutes." A great productivity tip that so many gurus will tell you is when you are overwhelmed with a task, it's often because you need to break it up into manageable chunks. That's what knowing these ratios helps you do—and most writers can manage 300-500 words per day, no matter how busy they are.

Finally, knowing this information takes a lot of the mystery out of how to go from outline to draft. Mystery = Fear. Fear = Resistance. Resistance = Procrastination. Remove your procrastination at the source, and you won't have to push yourself to write ever again.

I've included the outline and the beats below so you can see them side by side. A lot changes from one to the other!

BOOK 1 - EMMA + ELSIE MEET FITZWILLIAM DARCY

Ch. 1 - Elsie

Intro to the two characters and how they became best friends. When Jane left for college and Miss Taylor started dating Mr. Weston, the two started hanging out. There are only 12 girls in their grade — the two of them, Catherine Linton, who is never allowed to leave her home or hang out, Lacey Bates, who started school several years late, and Charlotte Lucas, who is neighbors with Elsie, but who has... changed. Charlotte is not going to college... Shes happy working a simple job in the town. Emma is obsessed with Miss Taylor's wedding since it's the first time she'll be a bridesmaid. Elsie is excited that her sister, Jane is coming home for the wedding.

Beats:

It's Friday. Emma is going crazy with her to-do list of last minute items that will make her bff Miss Taylor's wedding to die for.

Elsie is over at her house, looking through a scrapbook of their high school years, which Emma has just completed in the last week. It goes all the way up until graduation and includes every little thing that Emma has achieved over the entirety of her four years. There's a section where

Emma refers to herself "smart AND beautiful" which she can hardly keep from laughing at.

She finally gets Emma to put down the to-do list with the promise of gossip.

The Gossip: Remember the hot older guy that they looked up when they were putting together the seating chart? Charles Bingley, totally rich, totally perfect for Emma—if she were looking for a boyfriend, which she isn't. He's bringing a friend who is totally hotter, totally older, totally richer.

And no, they're not gay.

She reminds Emma that she invited her over for a reason—she wanted to show her "the wall." The wall is a full-display board with images of their high school times scattered about. There are neon pens so people can add fun comments to the pictures.

She sees pictures of everyone from their school—

She comments that all the images on the wall include Emma, which she has no problem with.

Then, Emma realizes that if the Bingleys are bringing friends, they have to add more seating at the wedding. They need to rearrange the tables! She calls to her daddy and says she needs to get Jace on the phone to handle his best man duties.

Explain why they're friends in this opening: Emma's sister moved out early, having gotten married very young. Elsie and Emma were in the same grade, and their friendship developed as a result of proximity. It was solidified when they were forced to play tennis in pairs—and turned out to be pretty good together. Emma hated the sport and eventually quit, while Elsie went on to play singles. When her older sister Jane left, and when Miss Taylor started dating Mr. Weston, they started spending a lot more time together.

Ch. 2 - Emma

She has checklist after checklist of what needs to be done for the wedding. She wants everything to be perfect. While working on the checklists Jace Knightley comes over to tell her about some new people that moved to town that she should invite. She freaks out, but Jace says it's fine because they have an open wedding.

Beats:

Emma drags Elsie into the dining room, where Jace Knightly is speaking to her father.

What are they talking about?

She interrupts them, taking over the conversation.

Jace knows the guy who's coming—Fitzwilliam Darcy, who they look up online. Elsie seems attracted to him, Jace is a bit jealous at the thought that Emma might be, but Emma is completely oblivious and focused on the seating charts.

Emma's father is complaining about Miss Taylor leaving them. Show that Emma is dispensing sage advice for him, well beyond her years—he is more the child and she is the parent.

Her father can't handle the stress of something like Miss Taylor's wedding, and Emma protects him from it. She wonders vaguely how she's going to deal when Miss Taylor moves out, especially since her father can't spar with her. And also, who will her father live with?

She asks him about his medicine, making sure he takes it, making sure he's comfortable, making sure he has everything he needs. She's the clear mistress of the house and in charge of everything. She forces him to get some rest before dinner.

She tells him about the party she is having, and while Jace doesn't think it's a particularly smart idea, the father allows it.

Elsie tells Emma and Jace to stop flirting, which causes them to break apart. She gets a text from Jane, and runs off, leaving the two of them alone, flirting at the seating chart.

Ch. 3 - Elsie

She sees Jane for the first time in months. Jane is with a girl she doesn't recognize, who introduces herself as Caroline Bingley. Jane met Caroline through her studies in social work and Caroline's brother just so happens to be renting one of the mansions in town for the summer. Jane is kind, as always, but Elsie is skeptical of this new girl.

Beats:

Elsie is so excited to meet up with Jane at their local coffee shop, she leaves Emma's house directly and goes straight. She wants to get Jane alone, without the company of their pesky sisters, so she can catch her up on everything that's been happening since she's been away at college.

Jane is not alone, though. She's with a girl named Caroline Bingley, who seems nice at first, though Elsie is immediately suspicious of her motives. Jane is a really sweet girl, and Caroline seems like a vulture, preying on her good graces.

What is the underlying conversation here? Just that Elsie wants to tell Jane everything, while Caroline is a bit gossipy-er than everyone else.

Caroline talks about Fitzwilliam Darcy as if he's spoken for, already. She went on one date with him, once, and she's essentially bringing him as her date to the wedding.

As they talk about the wedding, Caroline seems to look down a bit on Miss Taylor and Mr. Weston, citing that Mr. Weston is way too old for her.

Elsie concludes that Caroline is a bit of a snob, though Jane seems not to notice her two-faced nature. Do they have a discussion about it?

Ch. 4 - Jane

Caroline exhibits mean girl tendencies that Jane doesn't have a clue about. She's sugary sweet even though she doesn't like Jane at all. Jane takes her to see everything around town and doesn't notice that Caroline is disdainful of the area. Finally, Caroline and Jane meet Jane's mother and she commits a faux pas in front of Caroline. Then, Jane's mom insists that Jane spend some time at their manor, because she's always loved it since she was a little girl.

Beats:

Jane takes Caroline on a tour of their town, discussing her social work as they go. Caroline has a way of saying nice things when she's really being passive aggressive, and Jane doesn't really notice.

She does, however, notice that her sister Elsie has a bit of tension with Caroline. She wishes that they'd get along, because it would make the entire tour much more pleasant.

The town is a bit of a creature of its own. The things Jane talks about include:

- the history - Rosebelle and Ravensbelle
- how she loves that everyone knows each other
- how devastating the New Orleans disaster was and how grateful she was that Caroline's brother was part of the relief efforts.
- how sweet the little school was that she went to— all the grades were awesome and she had so many wonderful townsfolk
- the wedding, which a number of people in the town are helping to set up

Jane and Caroline and Elsie stumble across Mrs. Bennet, who has her youngest three daughters with her. The four of them are a bit of a train wreck, and Caroline doesn't hide her distaste, though Jane doesn't totally notice.

Mrs. Bennet asks when they will get to meet Charles Bingley, and insists that Jane stay at Netherfield at some point, since she always loved that area. And since she's so interested in what Charles is doing! Mrs. Bennet is transparent about what she wants and Caroline is disdainful of her and the younger girls, Lydia and Kitty. "Catherine is such a lovely name."

Ch. 5 - Emma

Emma bursts into her father's study, where Jace is talking to him about something important. She needs someone to take pictures of her getting dressed. She needs Jace's help to get dressed... her dress doesn't work with her tan. She calls him, claiming it's an emergency. Allude to his past girlfriends. He comes to the rescue as usual.

Beats:

Emma is running a personal errand for Miss Taylor, for the wedding. She goes to Mrs. Goddards and meets one of the girls that works there, Harriet Smith.

What is the personal errand? Miss Taylor made a special gift for Mr. Weston that she promised she'd pick up. Mrs. Goddards does something—what does it do? Harriet Smith is the girl at the counter, who is totally obsessed with Emma, having heard of her already.

On her way home, she gets caught in the middle of the swampland with no gas, having not filled her tank when Jace told her to.

She texts Elsie, but she can't come get her because their mom is using her car. Elsie's family is having financial trouble, which means that the five Bennet sisters have to share EVERYTHING. Emma can't imagine it.

Then she texts Charlotte, who can't help her either. She has to work.

She doesn't want to text Jace, but she's running so late, she finally does. He gives her a *really* hard time, and she's irritated by his condescension.

Just as she's about to beg him, Chuck Bingley stops and offers her a ride back into town. Darcy is with him and is... a little cold.

Jace freaks out a bit that she's taking a ride from strangers and confronts her when she gets back, only to find out that she was safe the whole time.

Ch. 6 - Jane

Jane meets Bingley. Something magical passes between them, which Caroline isn't okay with. Caroline has so many plans for her brother, and Jane is totally not the girl she pictures him with. But Jane can't see that at all. He's interested in her social work, she's interested in his foundations, etc.

Beats:

Jane meets Chuck the next day when she is getting ready at Caroline's house. Something magical passes between them, which Caroline isn't okay with.

Caroline has so many plans for her brother, and mentions that there are a number of women in his life.

Jane and Chuck keep chatting over lunch. He's interested in her social work, she's interested in his foundations, etc.

Jane doesn't really notice the edge in Caroline's voice, and neither does Chuck.

But Darcy does and comes to his bro's rescue by dragging Caroline away from them, finally. Jane interprets it as a bit cold, but Fitz is actually helping her get more time with Chuck, rather than shunning the two of them altogether.

This gives Chuck the chance to take her on a tour. Netherfield is incredible—he gives her a tour, even though she's seen it before. She admits that she's snuck in in the past, before she knew that his family owned it. She tells a fun anecdote about her family, then talks about her sister, Elsie.

He says he wants to meet this fabulous Elsie she speaks of, and she says she'll be at the wedding.

When they get back, Chuck tells everyone that they are going to be sitting next to the Bennets. Caroline wrinkles her nose at the thought, while none of the rest care. Jane notices Caroline speaking to Fitz specifically, whispering with him, but doesn't think much of it.

Ch. 7 - Elsie

Elsie sits with her family and we meet them. What does her mom care about? She wants to make sure her daughters get out and experience the world, rather than stay in Rosebelle and settle down with farmers. Elsie sees William Darcy and realizes he's incredibly attractive, but not as attractive as Bingley, who is sitting next to Jane at the wedding. William is a bad boy, seemingly. His edge is harder, and she wonders about him.

Beats:

Describe the wedding from Elsie's POV.

Elsie sits with her family at the wedding and we meet them again. What does her mom care about?

She wants to make sure her daughters get out and experience the world, rather than stay in Rosebelle and settle down with farmers. She makes this extremely apparent with all the questions she asks Bingley about his work, his family, etc.

Caroline seems to be a bit annoyed, as is her older sister, Mrs. Hurst. They are whispering a bit in that way that Elsie knows only too well, considering that she has five sisters.

Lydia and Catherine are extremely gossipy about something that's happening at their high school, a football camp of some sort. Lydia just turned fourteen and she's really difficult, getting a little too boy crazy, etc. Catherine does whatever she does, like a puppy who follows her everywhere, even though Lydia is the younger one. They keep gossiping and Elsie notices Fitz eyeing them...

She also can't believe that Mary actually brought a BOOK to the wedding. A BOOK. She's reading it before the ceremony starts.

Elsie sees Fitz and realizes he's incredibly attractive, but not as attractive as Bingley, who is sitting next to Jane. Aside from her mother asking questions, Chuck is really into Jane—he's the one who insisted that his whole group sit next to her family at the ceremony.

Elsie is sitting next to Fitz. Fitz catches her eye—he's a bit mysterious, a bit too quiet. He's also looking at her oddly.

She attempts to talk to him, but gets a brush off. Caroline is sitting on the other side of him and keeps drawing his attention back to her.

She's telling him all about the Churchill family—recount the entire story here. This is from Emma Chapter 2.

Elsie already knows the story and fills in the details for the reader, anything that Caroline doesn't say.

Finally, the ceremony starts.

Ch. 8 - Emma

She walks down the aisle with Jace who is the best man. The whole time, she misses his subtle hints that he's in love with her. She's clueless! He asks her to save a dance for him at the reception, and she agrees out of surprise.

Beats:

The Wedding!

She's never been in a wedding before because she was too young when her sister got married. Now she is the maid-of-honor and she's so happy for Miss Taylor that she wants the moment to be perfect.

She fidgets with Miss Taylor's dress and tells her that everything is about to change and she doesn't know what she'll do without her.

She walks down the aisle, looking for Elsie in the crowd. Elsie smiles and makes a little motion with her head; the Bingleys and their party are sitting right next to her family. Emma gives her the slightest nod to express her excitement.

She looks up at the altar and finds Jace staring at her, watching her. She can't help but notice how great he looks in his tux. But it's weird—he's older than her, and last she checked, he was dating some college girl. Plus, it would be weird, and her dad would never accept it, and Bella and John would never be on board. She pushes it out of her mind.

They walk out of the church together and while their in the procession line, she asks if he's still mad at her. He's not, and asks if she's still mad at him. He's not.

They take a ton of pictures together, where he has to help her into weird positions. She nearly falls and he catches her, laughing easily again at her silliness.

He holds her hand slightly longer than usual and tells her that he'll see her again when they dance.

Ch. 9 - Jane

Jane and Charles dance for the second time that night. There is something magnetic and electric between them. He is the kindest, most gentle man she has ever met. She feels entirely swept off her feet.

Beats:

Jane and Charles dance for the second time that night. There is something magnetic and electric between them. He is the kindest, most gentle man she has ever met. She feels entirely swept off her feet.

What do they talk about? Jane could ask him about his family, his friends. He's known Fitz since they were kids, and he tells some sort of cute story here about why they are best friends.

Elsie is her best friend, but they aren't as close since she moved away. She spends a little more time with Emma Woodhouse than Jane thinks is best, but she continues to say kind things about Emma and tries not to upset the balance.

Chuck is the same; he mentions that Jace is a college buddy and speaks very highly of Emma, who is his brother's sister-in-law. He describes Emma as a force of nature. She describes Elsie as one of the wittiest people she knows. She'll always make you laugh. She loves that he is not concerned with gossiping about people, but rather talking about larger issues in the world.

He dips her, telling her he shouldn't be paying so much attention to her when there are so many other girls at the party. But he only wants to spend time with her. He can tell she's something special.

She feels the same way about him. She asks him if he wants to get out of there at some point that night, and he agrees to, as soon as it's not rude to do so.

Ch. 10 - Elsie

At the reception, she watches Jane get swept off her feet by Bingley. she secretly hopes that William will ask her, but she overhears him saying horrible things about her hometown to Caroline Bingley. Also, horrible things about her.

Beats:

At the reception, she watches Jane get swept off her feet by Bingley. He's so charming, so funny, so cordial. He is the sweetest guy to her sweetest girl, and though he asks everyone to dance, she's the one he dances with most.

Chuck asks her to dance as well, and he twirls her around, but it's obvious that he's only interested in Jane. They move to a group and Chuck tries to get Fitz to dance with them.

He says he doesn't dance. He refuses to join their party, even when Chuck tries to introduce him to Elsie. He rejects the offer.

A few minutes later, she sees him dancing with Caroline. That's odd.

Elsie, having nothing better to do, runs to grab a drink and look for Emma. Where is that girl?

Later on, she overhears Jace and Darcy talking. He asks if Fitz is seeing any pretty girls he likes, and Fitz says the only pretty one there is Jane. Jace points out Elsie, and Darcy says she's "not hot enough for the effort."

She goes to the bathroom. Caroline and Mrs. Hurst walk in, and Caroline is telling Mrs. Hurst all the terrible things that Fitz has said about the town, the Bennets, and Elsie. Mrs. Hurst sort of agrees, especially about little Lydia and Mrs. Bennet. They aren't sure what to think of Jane, but Caroline calls Elsie "standoffish."

The women leave and Elsie bursts out of the bathroom, trying to keep her cool. She can hold it together. Emma walks in with her own emergency and Elsie realizes that she's *not* okay with what just happened. She is sad—she doesn't need a boyfriend, but she kind of wants one, and she's going off to college never having one, and Fitz was the first guy she'd been attracted to in forever...

Ch. 11 - Emma

Emma finds Elsie in the bathroom crying, and goes into friend mode. She breezes past Jace who was patiently waiting for her, and the girls find a place to sit. Emma vows to take down William Darcy while he's here for hurting her friend.

Beats:

Emma and Mrs. Weston find Elsie in the bathroom, upset from what happened earlier with Fitz. She goes into full-on friend mode.

Mrs. Weston tells Emma it's okay to take off, since the wedding is almost over and she's leaving soon. Emma is worried about the gifts, the arrangements, etc. but Mrs. Weston waves her off, saying she's done more than her duties.

They leave, breezing through the crowd without thinking of much. They head to their favorite spot, Sweet Kisses, which is this over-the-top southern dessert diner where they always go to have girl time. It's not open, but the guy who owns it has given Emma the key—she helped him design the place for free.

She makes her friend some dessert and they sit down in the back, talking. Elsie recounts everything that happened with Darcy, and Emma agrees he is standoffish.

But, he wasn't outright rude to Emma, like he was to Elsie. She talks Elsie up and vows to take down Darcy. Elsie says she doesn't want that, she just wants to forget about him.

Emma drives her home, then goes home herself to find Jace sitting on her porch. She totally forgot that she was supposed to dance with him.

He's brought her some cake, but she refuses because she's just eaten dessert. He's about to tell her something, but then notices she's shivering. He tells her to go inside and get some sleep.

Ch. 12 - Jane

They go off by themselves and something intense happens between them. Jane is caught up in the moment and can't help but act on her connection with Bingley. Sexy time! (It is a New Adult series, after all.)

Beats:

Jane takes Chuck to this place she's known since she was a kid. It's secluded and perfect for hanging out under the stars and talking all night.

He points out something about the constellations, something romantic, and she totally eats it up.

They kiss—it's electrifying. She doesn't want things to end; neither does he.

...

...

Jane sneaks into her house at 6 in the morning, where Elsie is waiting for her. Her smile is a little lopsided and she assumes that Elsie is hiding something from her.

Now that you've seen my beats, know that lots of people do beats differently. You can tweak this, add to it, or subtract from it—your choice. (You know best, always—don't ever forget it!)

For example, my friends over at Sterling and Stone go several steps beyond beats, creating an entire pre-production package that includes characters, locations, world-building, and the beats that I described above. (You can see their work firsthand in a project called Fiction Unboxed, which has an affordable book accompaniment if you're curious, but aren't ready to plunk down for the entire shebang.) This is great for them because they need to collaborate and are able to add visuals (they "cast" their characters and "scout" their locations—really cool) to help each other see the same visions as they work.

I've never been one to do this type of thing, though I think it becomes more and more helpful as a series goes on (and usually, it's too intensive to do once you're on book 5). Point being, you need to do enough in pre-production to hit your personal goals, while not spending too much time in pre-production to the point that you never start writing. As important as I believe pre-production is, I've also seen writers who stay in pre-production for years. It is painful and piteous to watch a writer stay stuck in this mode.

You must weigh the value and knowledge you'll get from pre-production (a lot) against the value and knowledge you'll get from drafting (a lot more). Your goal at the outline and beats level should be to learn enough about your characters, setting, world, and plot to get started with actually writing. You will always, always learn a lot more about each of these areas as you write—eventually, you must just start!

STEP 3: SKETCH OR SKELETON

(Note: I use sketch and skeleton interchangeably throughout this book.)

What exactly is the sketch? A lot of readers have asked. Well, I think of it the same way an artist might think of it—it's a "rough draft" of what you are eventually going to draw.

Isn't that just the draft? Maybe... but for some writers, it's better if it's an entirely separate step. You may or may not need this step, based on whether or not you are an under-writer or an over-writer. Over-writers will definitely not need it, and it will probably drive them crazy. For me, as an under-writer, I like it because my mind works out some parts of my story in more detail than others, and I

69

can get stuck on those "others" and not make nearly as much progress as I want.

I basically use the sketch step to turn the beats (the "tell") into a draft (the "show"), and then to make notes about anything that's not yet fully formed in my mind, but that I know will eventually need to be in the draft (i.e. transitions).

As inspiration hits, I start detailing the sketch—drawing in the lines of the sketch, if you will. This allows me to skip around and work on whatever I feel like while still making progress overall. It ensures that if I'm doing writing blocks, I'm spending them productively, because I'm gravitating toward whatever inspires me at that moment. This helps keeps me motivated and in flow.

I find myself skipping around when I'm feeling excited about one section but not another, or when I feel like writing dialogue and not description. If I'm sketching, I almost always skip transitions between beats, because they bore me to tears!

Even as I write this book, I keep skipping between the steps in this section, leaving a few unfinished sentences and a few sections blank to fill in later. This helps me stay inspired about what I'm writing. Whatever works for you. I tend to have author A.D.D. and hop around a lot. If you don't have this problem, then you probably don't need a sketch step.

The last thing I'll say about the sketch is that it can bring a sense of playfulness to your work, allowing you a somewhat carefree way of drafting without all the pressure of Writing (the one with the capital 'W'). If you struggle with the prospect of Writing, but you have no trouble jotting down some parts of your draft in full while making notes on the rest to come back to later, then you may appreciate sketching for the freedom it provides.

All of that said, I frequently don't use the sketch, and instead skip straight to a full draft. This is true especially when I do a walk and talk to get a draft going quickly. But if I'm in a moseying mood, or if I'm short on time, or if I'm phoning it in (yes, I still do that—it's going to happen if you write thousands of words every day), or if I don't have my mic with me, then I'll just open my laptop and write a little section of a scene this way.

This is a sketch of my first chapter mixed with parts of draft:

Chapter 1 - Elsie

"Emma."

Her best friend paced back and forth in front of her dresser, mumbling to herself.

"Flowers, shoes, necklace..."

"Emma," Elsie repeated.

"Gift!" Emma exclaimed, marking something on the small notepad she was holding. She set the pad on her dresser, scribbling furiously.

Elsie heaved a huge, exasperated sigh. "Emma!"

Emma spun around. "Elsie! You're here." She tilted her head, letting her blonde, bouncy curls fall to one side. "When did you get here?"

"Set it down."

"What?"

"The pen, the book, your body in a chair. Step away from the to-do list before your head explodes."

"I am the maid of honor," Emma declared solemnly. "I will not rest until my list is complete and I've ensured that Annabeth's wedding is absolutely, 100% perfect."

"But Emma," she said, a light grin dancing on her lips. She plopped down onto her best friend's 4-post princess bed, sprawling out across the crisp, fresh, and pristinely lightweight comforter. She was bursting to tell her what she had just learned, but Emma was wrapped up in her own world, as usual.

"No buts," Emma said, digging through her purse. She pulled out tubes of lipstick, notepads with scratchings all over them, dozens of tiny barrettes, hair clips, and bobby pins, before finding what she was looking for—her keys.

Elsie knew what that meant—Emma had once again invited her over before having to run out the door. "Let me guess—you're leaving."

Emma gave her a pouty face. "I'm really sorry... It's an emergency, I swear. A real one this time! Talk later?"

"You're going to want to hear this before you go," Elsie said in a singsong voice. She sat up, slightly annoyed by Emma's dismissal. "Where are you going anyway?"

"Oh, what time is it?" Emma made a point of looking at her watch, an heirloom of her mother's. Her mother had passed away when she was a child, and Elsie had never once seen her without it on.

"Time for you to listen to the exciting news I have," Elsie rang out.

"Oh my gosh, okay. I have a solid thirty minutes before I absolutely have to leave, or Annabeth's wedding will be ruined. Do you want that on your conscience, Elsie? Ruined." Emma's eyes bulged open to demonstrate her point. "Go ahead, then. What's your gossip?"

"Charles Bingley," Elsie said, as if it explained everything. When Emma raised an eyebrow at her, she heaved another sigh. "Remember when we looked up all the wedding guests to do the seating charts?" Elsie could still picture almost every detail of the LSU junior's Facebook profile, but Emma's eyes were completely blank as she tapped her pen against her notebook, fidgeting.

"Remember? Charles Bingley—tall, handsome, older, totally rich—totally perfect for you and your ridiculously high standards?"

"My standards aren't ridiculous!" Emma exclaimed, bringing back an argument they had on a regular basis. "Why does everyone think I need a boyfriend, all of a sudden? It's the summer before we whisk off to Louisiana State University, where I may or may not want to focus on my future instead of searching for a husband with all the rest of the M.R.S. majors." She smirked. "Besides, most women still get married for money. I already have money."

Elsie grinned at her friend's relentless determination to stay happily single. "Anyway... Charles—or Chuck, according to Lydia—"

"Oh my gosh," Emma interrupted. "Please don't tell me your baby sister knows a college student. She does realize she's like, fifteen, right?"

Elsie shook her head—her sister Lydia was a wild child, untamable and out of control—way past Elsie's guidance, and her parents didn't exactly lay down the law. "Two more years," she said, looking up at the ceiling. "In two more years she officially can't be a star on Sixteen and Pregnant."

"Good luck with that," Emma said. "That little firecracker is one sexually charged—"

"Not the point," Elsie said, cutting her off. "Chuck is bringing friends to the wedding," she rushed out, before they could go off-topic again.

Emma set her to-do list aside, finally intrigued by the conversation. Elsie smiled, glad to have her friend's full attention.

"Chuck and his two sisters were supposed to come to the wedding by themselves, remember? Old friends of the Churchills, Mr. Weston's deceased wife was a Churchill—"

"I know, I know," Emma said, gesturing with her hands. The whole town of Rosebelle knew the sad story of Mr. Weston losing his wife after only three years of marriage, then losing his baby son shortly after, sending him off to his wife's sister's house to be raised.

"Skip to the good part."

"So, Chuck is bringing a friend..." Elsie said, delighting in the fact that Emma had sat down, purse and keys discarded, and was practically on the edge of her seat.

"Who?!" Emma asked impatiently.

Elsie smiled. "We don't know yet."

"Oh," Emma said, draping her body over the arm of the chair.

"But."

Emma picked up a stuffed animal she was sharing the chair with and chucked it across the room, nearly creaming her in the face. "Elsie, you're killing me! Spit it out right now, or so help me—"

"We do know that he's tall, handsome, older, totally rich—even richer than the Bingleys."

"His boyfriend?!" Emma exclaimed. "Oh my gosh—of course, Charles Bingley is allowed a plus one, but I just wasn't expecting it." She stood up, throwing open her closet. "I have to get them something special for the reception—a gay couple in Rosebelle! This should get interesting—"

"They're not gay." Elsie hunched over, her stomach in pain from how much she was laughing. "Not that there's anything wrong if they were. I just meant that now there are two guys who will be fighting over the fabulous Emma

Woodhouse, first-time maid-ofhonor, newly minted adult, soon-to-be college girl, reigning prom queen of Rosebelle—"

"Oh my gosh," Emma said letting a giggle escape. "I doubt college guys care about all that high school silliness." Elsie smirked—Emma had spent months quietly campaigning for that particular tiara, even once saying that it was 'by far the most important moment of her high school career.'

Emma sat down next to her on the bed. "Besides, what about you?" She grinned mischievously. "Oh, please let me set you up with one of them, pretty please?"

Elsie shook her head. "No way."

"Come on! Look at how well I did for Annabeth."

Elsie held one finger up. "Annabeth is one person you set up, and even that one almost ended in disaster. If it weren't for your scheming and a very lucky guess—"

Emma waved a hand in the air. "Successful women make their own luck, Elsie. Everyone knows that."

Elsie widened her eyes with exasperation, and a warning. "Not the point! The answer is hell no."

"Well, then you're not allowed to set me up either!" Emma said. "It's decided, then. Neither of us will get swept away by tall, dark, handsome men at Annabeth's wedding."

"Fine," Elsie said.

"Fine," Emma repeated.

[Elsie is over at her house, looking through a scrapbook of their high school years, which Emma has just completed in the last week. It goes all the way up until graduation and includes every little thing that Emma has achieved over the entirety of her four years. There's a section where

Emma refers to herself "smart AND beautiful" which she can hardly keep from laughing at.]

[She reminds Emma that she invited her over for a reason—she wanted to show her "the wall." The wall is a full-display board with images of their high school times scattered about. There are neon pens so people can add fun comments to the pictures. She sees pictures of everyone from their school—She comments that all the images on the wall include Emma, which she has no problem with.]

[Then, Emma realizes that if the Bingleys are bringing friends, they have to add more seating at the wedding. They need to rearrange the tables! She calls to her daddy and says she needs to get Jace on the phone to handle his best man duties.]

From the sketch, it probably looks like I'm not actually that far along—but trust me, I am. Filling in the sections is the fun part. Making all the decisions is the hard part—a lot of writers try to do it all at once while also trying to get the character and setting right—and the writing itself goes very, very slowly as a result.

Also, you can't tell from just this example, but I work on the scenes out of order. It's often easier (for me) to stay in one character's head for an extended period of time, so that the chapters sound different based on the character.

Finally, this really is a sketch, not a draft... really. I'll spend real time on moving these from sketches to drafts, which I talk about in the next section. After that, I move them through my entire editing process, which I share in later parts of this book. The end result of each of these chapters will likely be very different, especially because the characters are evolving as I learn more about them.

STEP 4: DRAFT

It's finally time for that dreaded draft! Only, you've done so much work already, with the beats and the sketching, that it likely doesn't seem that hard anymore. In fact, you can see the framework of your scene coming together already, in bits and pieces, and all you need to do is start stringing those pieces together.

I learned most of what I understand about drafting novels from my background in computer science and software programming. The way I write is to go from the high level, big picture view of my novel and then work my way down to the details. If you can get all the "chunks" into their correct places, then you can fiddle with the inner workings of the "chunks" and tweak as much as you want.

During the drafting stage, I first rearrange my chunks how I want them (they are usually already in the correct order, because I already arranged them in order in the beats). Next, I add any transitions necessary, which are usually in the form of narrative summary. For example, your characters are having a conversation in the dining room with the wrench. Then, they are having a conversation in the garage with the scissors. You need to narrate (in just a few sentences, usually) the physical distance between those two chunks so your reader follows the characters along as they move.

Finally, I clean up the chunks themselves, which for the first draft usually just means that I finish them off so I don't have any missing sentences or sections. I also tend to add "color" here—descriptions, funny looks, jokes—but you can also do this during editing.

My goal of the draft round is to get my scene or chapter into a "compile." In software programming, "compile" means that your code can at least run. It doesn't mean your code is good, elegant, or even does what it's intended to do; it just means that it runs.

For both fiction and non-fiction, "compile" means that you complete your sentences and thoughts without completely losing the reader. It doesn't mean that your draft is good, elegant, or even does what it's intended to do; it just means that the reader can comprehend it.

That's all I have to share about drafting; if you've followed these steps, you've done so much of the work by this point, which should make the draft smooth sailing.

Here's the first scene:

Chapter 1 - Elsie

"Emma."

Her best friend paced back and forth in front of her dresser, mumbling to herself. "Garter, shoes, necklace…"

"Emma," Elsie repeated.

"Surprise… oh my gosh, the surprise!" Emma made a fist at the air, like she was cursing it, before marking something on the small notepad she was holding. She set the pad on her dresser, scribbling furiously. "I can't believe I almost forgot to—"

Elsie heaved a huge, exasperated sigh. "Emma!"

Emma spun around. "Elsie, you're here." She tilted her head, letting her blonde, bouncy curls fall to one side. "Wait. When did you get here?"

"Set it down."

"What?"

"The pen, the book, your body in a chair. Step away from the to-do list before your head explodes."

"I am the maid of honor," Emma declared solemnly. "I will not rest until my list is complete and I've ensured that Annabeth's wedding is absolutely, one-hundred percent perfect."

Elsie watched her friend, a light grin dancing on her lips. She flipped her iron-straight chestnut hair over her shoulder and plopped down onto her best friend's four-post princess bed, sprawling out across the crisp, lightweight comforter. She was bursting to tell Emma what she had just learned, but Emma was wrapped up in her own world, as usual. "But—" she said.

"No buts," Emma said, digging through her purse. She pulled out tubes of lipstick, notepads with scratchings all over them, and dozens of tiny barrettes, hair clips, and bobby pins, before finding what she was looking for—her keys.

Elsie groaned. Emma had once again invited her over just before having to run out the door. "Let me guess— you're leaving."

Emma's lips formed an exaggerated pout. "I'm sorry... It's an emergency, I swear. A real one this time! Talk later?"

"You're going to want to hear this before you go," Elsie said in a singsong voice. She sat up, slightly annoyed by Emma's dismissal. "Where are you going anyway?"

"What time is it?" Emma made a point of looking at her watch, an heirloom of her mother's. Her mother had passed away when she was a child, and Elsie had rarely seen her without it on.

"Time for you to listen to the exciting news I have," Elsie rang out.

"Okay, okay. I have a solid thirty minutes before I absolutely have to leave, or Annabeth's wedding will be ruined. Do you want that on your conscience, Elsie?

Ruined." Emma's eyes bulged open to demonstrate her point. "Go ahead, then. What's your gossip?"

"Charles Bingley," Elsie said, not being able to contain her excitement any longer. When Emma raised an eyebrow at her, she heaved another sigh. "Remember when we looked up all the wedding guests to do the seating charts?" Elsie could still picture almost every detail of the Louisiana State University junior's Facebook profile, but Emma's eyes were completely blank as she tapped her pen against her notebook, fidgeting.

"Remember? Charles Bingley—tall, handsome, older, extremely wealthy—totally perfect for you and your ridiculously high standards?"

"My standards aren't ridiculous!" Emma exclaimed, bringing back an argument they had on a regular basis. "Why does everyone think I need a boyfriend? It's the summer before we whisk off to LSU, where I want to focus on a future that doesn't necessarily include studying for an M.R.S. degree." She smirked as she annunciated each letter in 'Mrs.' "Besides, I already have money. I don't need to marry into it."

Elsie grinned at her friend's relentless determination to stay happily single—and her horrible habit of reminding everyone that her father was the richest man in Rosebelle, aside from their neighbors, the Knightleys. "Anyway... Charles—or Chuck, according to Lydia—"

"Lydia?" Emma interrupted. "Please don't tell me your baby sister knows a college student. She does realize she's, like, fifteen, right?"

Elsie shook her head. Her sister Lydia was a wild child, untamable and out of control—way past Elsie's influence. Their parents didn't exactly lay down the law either

"One more year," she said, looking up at the ceiling. "In one more year, she will be driving. Driving, Ems."

"As in, able to physically transport herself to parties she shouldn't be at where she will attach herself to age-inappropriate boyfriends," Emma said. She shrugged. "That little firecracker is one sexually charged—"

"Not the point," Elsie said, cutting her off. She hated that her sister had such a reputation already, after only one year in high school. "Lydia said that Chuck is bringing friends to the wedding," she rushed out, before they could go off-topic again.

Emma set her to-do list aside, finally intrigued by the conversation. Elsie smiled, glad to have her friend's full attention.

"Chuck and his two sisters were supposed to come to the wedding by themselves, remember?" Elsie ticked off the facts on her fingers. "Old friends of Mr. Weston's first wife's family, the Churchills—"

"I know, I know," Emma said, gesturing with her hands. "Skip to the good part."

Elsie grinned at her impatience. The whole town of Rosebelle knew that Mr. Weston sent his baby son off to his brother-in-law to be raised after his wife died.

"So, Chuck is bringing a friend..." Elsie said, delighting in the fact that Emma had sat down, purse and keys discarded, and was practically on the edge of her seat.

"Who?!" Emma asked impatiently.

Elsie smiled. "We don't know yet."

"I see," Emma said, draping her body over the arm of the chair.

"But..."

Emma picked up a stuffed animal she was sharing the chair with and chucked it across the room, nearly creaming her in the face. "Elsie, you're killing me! Spit it out right now, or so help me—"

"We do know that he's tall, handsome, older, and extremely, extremely wealthy—even richer than the Bingleys." Elsie beamed.

"His boyfriend?!" Emma exclaimed. "Wow. Of course, Charles Bingley is allowed a plus one, but I wasn't expecting this." She stood up, grabbing her to-do list. "A gay couple in Rosebelle! This should get interesting."

Elsie hunched over, her stomach in pain from how much she was laughing. "I can assure you they are both straight—Lydia does her homework. My point is that now there are two guys who will be fighting over the fabulous Emma Woodhouse, first-time maid-of-honor, newly minted adult a.k.a. legal, soon-to-be college girl, reigning prom queen of Rosebelle—"

"Prom queen?" Emma repeated, clearly trying to hold back her smile. "I doubt college guys care about all that high school silliness."

Elsie smirked—Emma had spent months quietly campaigning for that particular tiara, even once saying that it was 'by far the most important moment of her high school career.'

Emma sat down next to her on the bed. "Besides, what about you?" She grinned mischievously. "Please, please, please let me set you up with one of them?"

Elsie shook her head. "No way."

"Come on! Look at how well I did for Annabeth."

Elsie held one finger up. "Annabeth is one person you set up, and even that one almost ended in disaster. If it weren't for your scheming and a very lucky guess—"

Emma waved a hand dismissively. "Successful women make their own luck, Els. Everyone knows that."

Elsie widened her eyes with exasperation. "Not the point! The answer is hell no."

"Then you're not allowed to set me up either!" Emma said. "It's decided, then. Neither of us will get swept away by tall, dark, handsome college men at Annabeth's wedding."

"Fine," Elsie said.

"Fine," Emma repeated.

"So..." Elsie said, filling the lull in the conversation. "Do you have time to show me the wall?"

"Yes—right!" Emma pressed a finger to her forehead. "That's why you're here in the first place. I swear, this wedding is making me lose my mind."

"Come on," Elsie said, grabbing her friend's arm and dragging her out of the chair. "The wedding will be over tomorrow, but apparently the wall will be forever, immortalizing Emma Woodhouse's brilliant high school career."

Emma laughed as they walked down the stairs, passing the first floor of the house and going straight down to the basement. "You make me sound so self-absorbed."

"Hello—you basically put a shrine to yourself in your father's basement. I know the two of you are close, but really?"

"You know my father can't live without me," Emma said. "I honestly don't know how he's going to take it when I leave for school."

"Baton Rouge is only what—a two or three hour drive?"

"We're talking about my father. A two or three minute drive is an ordeal for him."

She was right, to some extent. Elsie had known Mr. Woodhouse almost her entire life, and he was by far one of the fussiest men she'd ever met. It wasn't that he was unkind, or incompetent. He was just... Specific. Particular. And, at times, implacable.

He also rarely left their house, which had often left her wondering how he built an entire franchise of car dealerships during his youth. Emma said that things changed a lot when her mother died, and her older sister Bella was always saying that their dad wasn't the same afterward, but still—the Mr. Woodhouse that Elsie knew was definitely not a business mogul.

Luckily, John Knightley had married Mr. Woodhouse's eldest daughter, Bella, and thus handled most of the day-to-day business decisions at the company in addition to whatever role he played in his own family's company.

His brother, Jace, also helped out Mr. Woodhouse. He lived just down the street from Emma, so he was around all the time. At least, whenever he wasn't working on his Masters in Business Administration at Louisiana State University.

The Woodhouses were filthy rich as a result of their chain of dealerships and whatever other investments they had acquired. Emma took full advantage of her family's money and connections to make the most of her high school experience. Many of the girls in their grade couldn't stand Emma because of it, but Elsie had never felt jealous.

"Ready?" Emma asked when they reached the basement landing.

"Do I have to cover my eyes or something?" Elsie asked.

"Well, you're really only going to get a peek, because the actual unveiling is happening at my graduation party. Remember?"

"Emma Jane Woodhouse, are you telling me that I walked all the way over here from the other side of town to get a lame peek at the Shrine to Emma?"

"Psh. The other side of town is like, two miles away."

"Two miles is far without a car!"

"I told you," Emma said in the more serious voice. "If you want to borrow a car from one of my father's dealerships, we're more than happy to loan you one."

Elsie stopped laughing. "You know my dad will kill me if he finds out I told you about our... situation." Her family used to be one of the more prominent ones in Rosebelle, with a popular and successful tourism business. They had nowhere near the level of wealth of the Woodhouses, but it had certainly had been a growing fortune. All of that was washed away with Hurricane Katrina, when tourists abandoned the area in droves. With her mother's determined marketing, things were finally starting to turn around, but the family had nearly depleted their savings and were still barely staying afloat, even with the recent growth.

Now that they were about to have two daughters in college, the Bennet family was really strapped for cash. They had already sold much of their land and were even contemplating selling the house. Mrs. Bennet had already put out seeds of their cover story. According to her, they were tired of the high maintenance of their estate and were considering downsizing now that her daughters were leaving the nest. Elsie's younger sister Mary was going to be a junior in high school next year, and Jane was going to be a sophomore in college, so the storm of having three daughters in school all at once was coming—and they couldn't be certain that the tourism business would pick up quickly enough to cover all the expenses.

Emma fidgeted with the curtains that really did cover an entire, large wall of her basement, pinning a small subsection of the curtains to itself to isolate the peek she intended to give Elsie.

Elsie didn't even feel surprised by how massive the Shrine to Emma truly was. Emma always went all-out. Always.

"Ta-dah," Emma said, holding up her hands in presentation as she stepped away from the wall and revealed her masterpiece.

"Smart, beautiful, strong?" Elsie read the words blown up in huge letters underneath Emma's picture.

"It's the quote from the yearbook, remember?" Emma grinned at her, completely clueless.

Elsie bit her lip to keep from laughing. "It's... Lovely."

Emma narrowed her eyes at her. "Shut up."

A giggle escaped from Elsie's mouth.

Emma frowned, glancing up at the wall as if for the first time. "Is it stupid?" She tilted her head, staring hard at her portrait and the words underneath it. "On second thought, I didn't realize how vain it sounded until you just read it out loud."

Elsie couldn't take it anymore—she started laughing uncontrollably.

To her surprise, Emma joined in. "It's a little much, isn't it?" she asked. "I think I'm just going to take this whole thing down. It's just—it's not the classy, elegant decor I want for my high school graduation party."

Elsie picked up one of the neon pens that was resting in the tray lining the bottom of the wall. "Does that mean I get to sign the Shrine to Emma with a penis beforehand?"

Emma snatched the pink pen out of Elsie's hand. "Don't be vulgar, Elizabeth Bennet." She put the pen back in the tray and walked to the other side of the room, staring up at the wall. "I'm imagining a completely redone design that emphasizes adulthood—and, truly, planning this wedding really gave me tons of ideas for how to redo the entire basement."

Elsie knew she should have expected this—Emma basically ran her father's household, with her mother gone and her sister moved out. That meant that Emma spent an inordinate amount of time on Pinterest picking out new fabrics, drapes, furniture, accessories, light fixtures, and more, always identifying new rooms that needed 'a little something'. The only difference between Emma and a regular teenager was that Emma actually had the resources to redecorate her entire home every year, so their rooms were always in flux—that is, most rooms, since Mr. Woodhouse didn't appreciate change unless it happened gradually. The few rooms that he stuck to stayed relatively the same, aside from the little objects that Emma might sneak in here and there. The rest of the house, vast compared to most homes, was like a revolving door of Martha Stewart magazine layouts.

"Oh, no," Emma said, her eyes wide. "I just realized—how many friends are the Bingleys bringing now?"

"Lydia only mentioned the one—"

"Ugh—this is a disaster!" Emma grabbed Elsie's hand and dragged her toward the steps. "One friend in rich people language is like an entire bus full of people. We have to rearrange it all again!"

Emma ran up the steps, and Elsie knew that they could only be going to one place—to the seating charts!

I've found that this entire process for going from idea to draft works very, very well for big picture types who subscribe to a top-down approach to problem solving.

If you are a detail-oriented person and tend to work your way up to the big picture, however, there's a chance this won't help you. To be honest, I have no idea what would help you. I've watched detail-to-big-picture writers write, and they usually spend a lot of time tossing out huge sections of their work. They are more likely to be pantsers (writers who write by the seat of their pants rather than from an outline) and they are prone to spending hours and hours working on the details of a chapter that they later hit the delete button on.

I won't pretend to comprehend the inner workings of detail-oriented writers' minds, but I do know someone who has a lot of empathy for this writing style, because she uses it herself. My friend Susan Pogorzelski is one of the most interesting writers I've ever known, and she consults detail-oriented writers on writing and self-publishing. So if you're struggling with this process of outline to draft, and you've tried the process I described and it's not working at all for you, perhaps reach out to her at susan@ brownbeaglebooks.com.

I believe I've given you more than enough about my process to help you formulate your own process for gaining more knowledge about what you're writing and for getting the draft done quickly and efficiently. The main takeaways I hope you gain from this section are:

Going from outline straight to draft is a great way to get stuck - I can't say enough about the Beats step—it will easily help you double your word count per hour and also make writing much more fun for you.

Breaking down your work into small, doable, 15 minute tasks is a winning strategy - Our minds simply can't process huge projects. Beats help you compartmentalize sections of your work. The best combatant for procrastination is to always know exactly what you need to do next. This is even more important for parents of little ones and full-time employees, who will need to write in the "in-betweens" of the day.

Having a solid outline is going to save you lots of mistakes, rewrites, and wasted energy throughout your entire writing process - I didn't get to say enough about this, but I write a lot more about outlines in my book, *Nail Your Outline*. I also recommend *Story Engineering* by Larry Brooks if you're looking for a template or framework.

Before I move on to the next section, I wanted to give you just a few more ways you can spot a need for adjustment and refinement of your process.

A LOW WORD COUNT PER HOUR MEANS YOU NEED MORE PLANNING

Whenever I drop below about 1500 words per hour, I know that I need to step back and do some more planning on the scene. (Note: your metric will be different, depending on how fast you write, but a good benchmark is a number at about 50-60% of your average writing speed.)

Some writers mistake slow writing for a need to push themselves harder or focus more (if they see that their writing is poking along at all—again, most writers have no clue). What it actually means is that you have no clue where your story is going. You either haven't visualized your scene well enough, haven't made enough decisions about your scene, or (for non-fiction) haven't collected enough data or done enough research.

This is where your tracking spreadsheets are essential. A lot of writers don't think of their word count speed as a monitoring metric, but it makes so much sense. If you were running significantly slower than you could, wouldn't you wonder if you were sick or had an injury? If you were at work and were only producing at half your usual pace, wouldn't your boss sit you down and start asking about your home life, your health, your mental state?

You don't have a boss, so you need to spot this pattern on your own. If you're going slow on a scene, you have a lot of options:

- Set it aside and come back to it later. Your subconscious hasn't done enough of the work yet... but it will.
- Go back to your outline to see if you made a wrong turn.
- Ask yourself more questions about your story. What is the first thing someone would ask if you tried to describe this story to them? Now, answer that question.
- Go back through your diary and look for patterns. There might be some insight there that is only obvious in hindsight, but that would make a huge difference in your process.
- Ask a friend or critique partner for feedback. Others can see your mistakes more easily than you can.

All of this is relative, of course, so your "low" word count may be a completely different number. What's important is to know your numbers and see warning bells when your numbers are off (likewise, to feel giddiness when your numbers skyrocket, as I expect them to once you implement even just a few sections in this book).

AN URGE TO PROCRASTINATE MEANS YOU'VE TAKEN A WRONG TURN IN THE STORY ITSELF

If you are reading this book, you are not a lazy person. That means you are motivated, smart, and proactive, and you can figure out anything life throws at you.

Furthermore, this 4-step process actively combats a lot of the fears writers face when they start. It's already working for you to break through the barriers that are holding you back from hitting your writing goals.

So if you have done all these steps, and you love writing, and you want to write your story, and you're still procrastinating, it's probably because something about your story is wrong and you aren't facing it.

You see, your gut knows you've taken a wrong turn in your story long before your mind does. There are many times when I'm procrastinating and have no idea where I've gone wrong. In those situations, I can't identify any one part of the story that's wrong; the only thing I know is that something is wrong.

Again, you have a lot of options:

- Take a break from the book. You probably have other projects you can work on in the meantime, and pushing back a release date is understandable and commonplace, as long as it's communicated well.

- Toss a compiled version of what you have so far on your Kindle and experience it like a reader would. How does it make you feel? Try to block out all your urges to rewrite and instead get lost in the characters and story. This has helped me more than once get out of my own head and into my readers' heads.

Use one of the tactics under the "Low Word Count" section. They will all work in this case, too.

DIFFICULTY WITH ANY OF THESE STEPS MEANS YOU

NEED A DIFFERENT STEP

For some writers, this entire 4-step process will be complete overkill. For others, it won't be nearly enough. I touched on this earlier, but you truly need to use self-knowledge to adapt this process to what you're trying to do.

How do you do this? There are several options:

- Find more writers' processes to emulate. Many, many writers write about how they get things done and post it online for free. There are also a ton of comprehensive paid resources that dive crazy deep into the authors' processes. My two favorite ones that are so relevant to writing faster are 2k to 10k by Rachel Aaron and Fiction Unboxed by Sean Platt and Johnny B. Truant. I mentioned both of these already in this book. I also loved Speed Writing for Nonfiction Writers: How to Double or Triple Your Daily Word Count by Ryan Healy.

- Study your own past successes. You don't have to steal from others, you can steal from other areas of your life where you've already succeeded. Chances are, something in that area will help you in this area. Great examples of areas with corollary goals and tactics to writing faster and more are weight loss, training for any sport (marathons especially are superbly metaphorical), hacking any sort of system (like a corporation, a college or university, or a particular industry), or learning a language. Trace back over your steps in any of these areas, and you'll probably spot some strategies and tactics that worked for you then, that will also work for your writing goals.

- Launch a new experiment on yourself. Just try

something different. Don't worry about whether it's better—just do something else. Record your results and adjust from there.

The goal of the Knowledge step is to get it in whatever way you need it, and then tweak from there. Find ways to get through the Knowledge step faster, more efficiently, with more overall savings on your entire process.

To reiterate: this section alone basically doubled my word count per hour. If it does the same for you, please tweet me and let me know! I'd love to collect more data on this. I'm at @monicaleonelle.

And if you enjoyed this section, you'll love one of my other books, *Nail Your Outline: Add Tension, Build Emotion, and Keep Your Readers Addicted*. I talk in even more detail about why becoming a good outliner can save you tons of time and help you build your stories (and your business!) much faster.

Chapter 6
STEP #2 - FLOW

We've all experienced it at least once—complete and total immersion in a project, book, or goal. When we were in that place of total immersion, we were making inhuman progress, losing track of time, coming up with way-better-than-our-usual ideas, and soaring free mentally and emotionally.

We were in flow, and damn did it feel effortless!

Flow is the state of complete immersion in the activity at hand, no matter what that activity is. When you're in flow, your body moves without your mind's conscious intervention—you don't have to think, you just do. This hyper focused state allows you to move incredibly quickly though your tasks, your project, or whatever else you're working on.

Every writer longs for the state of flow while he or she is writing. It helps you write better, faster, and more. It appeases both writers who love to write and writers who love to have written. And it means that our stories are being told and spreading value to others.

But how do you achieve a state of flow? It's a question I asked myself several times before, that took me many years to come up with answers to. What helped me most was falling into a state of flow accidentally and then observing the steps I took leading up to it. Through trial and error, I've come up with a list of writing-specific techniques that I believe can get any writer closer to a state of flow.

We've already talked about a number of tips that will help you achieve a state of flow. For example, we talked about having a larger "why" for what you're doing in the introduction section, and we talked about how knowledge of what you're about to write can eliminate mystery about what to do next as you're writing. A few other traits of flow:

- Losing track of time
- Concentration and focus
- Engaging and re-engaging in the task at hand
- Eliminating distractions
- Eliminating negative thoughts
- Taking ownership of your results
- Knowing the next small step to take

Achieving the state of flow seems like a very personal process to me, in all the years I've studied it. As such, I'm going to share some of the rituals that have helped me achieve flow with writing, with the caveat that you may want to brainstorm on the traits I've shared above to figure out what works for you.

Even if some of the following tips are not for you, I hope they will inspire you to come up with your own techniques and tricks for getting into flow.

Word of warning: many of these tips would work for the workplace as well, but I encourage you to use them just for writing when possible, especially since you are chasing the specific goal of writing better and faster. Mixing the two might put you in a state of mind for your day job when you're supposed to be writing, or vice-versa.

Have a System For Emptying Thoughts

Have you ever noticed that a lot of productivity hacks basically amount to deleting? Well, if the Flow step had a theme it would be "Delete!" Here are ways we delete to be more productive and efficient:

- Eat less or cut out specific foods to lose weight, gain focus, develop muscle
- Get rid of stuff in your closet to organize it
- Clear meetings on your calendar to do more creative work
- Archive, filter, and delete most of your emails to clean your inbox
- Unsubscribe from, log out of, and quit social media to get a life again

Since deletion is a key step in any productivity improvement, my first rule of achieving flow is to empty your mind—the place where all your creative work comes from—in any way that you can.

You can do this in a hundred different ways. Many, many uber-productive people turn to meditation, yoga, or both.

As an ENTP and an idea person, I tend to get sidetracked by my own ideas. For me, journaling has been the best source of release and easiest way to empty my mind. I have stacks of black 5.5" x 8.5" Moleskines that are full of ideas and insights I'll likely never get to in my lifetime. But having them down on paper somehow allows my mind to release them and close the open loop.

Journaling has been one of the most important writing practices I've ever encountered. Writing truly takes all of your energy, attention, and being while you're doing it, so you can't have other threads spinning in the background. Journaling helped me hit "delete" on those threads.

During my original challenge to change my writing habits (covered in the diary in the appendix), I didn't do enough journaling and it derailed me every time, leaving me with days where I didn't write nearly enough. Now, I journal the way most people exercise—daily, first thing, plus whenever my mind feels mushy or I find myself not making writing progress on my projects.

CROSS UNNECESSARY DECISIONS AND TASKS OFF YOUR LIST

A big part of writing is making space for writing. My fiancé, Patrick, has been hugely influential in my thinking on this.

I asked him one day, "Do you think I need to work somewhere with no access to the internet?"

He said, "You don't need more motivation to write. You love writing. You just need to set aside blocks of time to do it."

I realized immediately the truth in this. A writing career doesn't require a ton of productivity aerobatics to make things work. It actually requires a lot of space—in your mind, in your surroundings, and yes, even in your schedule.

There is literally only one way to make space for more writing, and that is to start crossing off your to-dos rather than checking them off. For a long time, I thought I could do it all, but nope! The first thing to go in a busy schedule is your creative work. It's just too taxing, too ambivalent, too difficult to check off—creative projects are endless in how much they require from you.

Right now, if you are not writing as much, it's largely because you're busy during the day. While logically, you probably have a few hours to spare, mentally, you're spent. The harsh truth about writing more is that you need to figure out what you're going to give up and let go of in order to get more time to get it done.

So, you have to turn off the internet for a few hours, give up your B and C-list television shows (you know, the generic stuff you watch when nothing else is on, like House Hunters and Sleepy Hollow), and stop playing video games (except for Shadow of Mordor, because that is one seriously beautiful game). None of this will kill you, and a lot of it will probably make you happier. You may be tempted to cling to these little comforts, but here are some easy ways to make that space:

Log out of Facebook - because God, do you have any idea how many times you check that thing? Just logging out will make you realize how addicted you are. And hitting the login page of Facebook is a nice slap on the wrist, without making you feel like you are never going to speak to your 843 friends again.

Unplug the internet or go to a coffee shop - I love coffee shops. Tea is a fun pairing with writing and always gets me in the mood. And crappy shared internet is close enough to no internet, because when a site takes nearly a minute to load, you will get bored and give up.

Delete shows from your DVR - This is easily one of my favorite productivity strategies, ever. If I need more time, I just start deleting things, leaving groups, unsubscribing from newsletters, turning off notifications, quitting habits. If I feel bummed after a few days of quitting, I simply add it back—but that doesn't happen 90% of the time. Typically, without the constant reminder that something is there, I pretty much forget it completely. We live in an On Demand world, so you can always come back to it later. New Girl, for example, is funny, but I can watch it on Netflix someday. In the meantime, my books are getting done!

Set times for eating - I eat between 1pm and 8pm every day, unless there are extenuating circumstances. Usually, I eat a salad or leftovers for lunch, and then whatever Patrick wants for dinner. Very few snacks in between, since we don't keep a lot of them around the house. Is all of this weird? Well, I like to call it quirky. But basically, it prevents a ton of thinking regarding food.

Wear a "uniform" to work - I live in Chicago, so my uniform is basically thick tights, sweater boots, and a comfortable sweater. This cuts down on the time I spend to get ready and is also "public"-ready, which means I can actually wear it outside without looking like I just rolled out of bed.

Save alcohol and smoking for the weekends, or cut them out completely - They just makes you miserable, anyway, and when your body is off its addictions for even a short amount of time, it's easier to not go back to them. Maybe it's because I recently hit my thirties, but as of late, I've been limiting myself to two drinks max in one sitting. Anything more ruins my next day of writing.

Mostly, you need to identify your soft addictions and give them up, at least during this process. Easier said than done, of course.

CREATE SYSTEMS THAT COMBAT DISTRACTIONS

Concentration is key to achieving flow, and you can't concentrate if you are distracted. Again, there are hundreds of ways to distract yourself, and more pop up every day.

It's really, really not your fault. As one of my favorite bloggers, Rebecca Healy, writes, "companies are now spending millions and billions of dollars perfecting the addictive crunch of a chip until the whole bag is gone, the auto-play of the next episode until you've watched the entire season, the notification alert until all of your time is spent." The world is working against you, trying to push their own agendas; productivity has become synonymous with navigating this veritable field of land mines so that your own agenda doesn't blow up in your face every single day.

A lot of your daily grind is going to be one large game of Distraction Whack-a-Mole. Here are some of the obvious and easy things you can do:

Turn off the damn internet. I've never met a writer who can get into flow while simultaneously having easy internet access. Put all your devices on airplane mode and let yourself spend a few hours notification-free. It's not going to kill you, and in fact, it will probably be the huge relief you need to finally relax and get some writing done.

Put up passive barriers everywhere. A passive barrier is something that is small but annoying to remove in order to do something that you might do. For example, a passive barrier to going to the gym might be having to de-ice your car. While I was doing my daily writing habit challenge, I maintained a separate account on my computer that was essentially on lockdown, so I couldn't get on the internet. It was so annoying to close out all my programs and switch over that I could do many distraction-free hours of writing in the mornings. This unfortunately worked the other way as well; if I was on my internet account, it was that much more difficult to get back to writing. My prerogative quickly became to put up as many passive barriers as possible for things I didn't want to do, and to remove those passive barriers for things I did want to do. This meant doing stuff like not switching over to the internet account until the evening, and then switching back before I went to bed. I don't need this barrier anymore because I've gotten used to spending long periods of time writing, but when I first started I was like a crack addict with the internet.

Close the door. You will not understand the power of a door against your loved ones until you don't have one. In my one bedroom + den apartment that I share with Patrick and my little west highland terrier, Mia, I basically work in a walk-in closet that's been gutted and repurposed as an "office." There is no door. Which means that if I want any peace or interruption-free time, I have to leave or work in our bedroom or bathroom (the only two rooms in our entire apartment that have doors—yay, open floor plan). If you are lucky enough to have a door, establish the rules with your family. You need your loved ones on your team, rooting for you, honoring your boundaries. They must respect your work time and treat it as sacred as you treat it, or you won't see much success with this.

There is a lot of detail to these three items that I'm leaving out, but that's basically the premise. Don't get overwhelmed; remember, this is a game of whack-a-mole. You don't try to hit them all at once; you wait for the moles to poke their ugly heads above ground, then BAM!

USE THE POMODORO METHOD

One of the best ways to win at Distraction Whack-a-Mole (if "winning" is even possible—ugh) is to time box your distractions and essentially limit your exposure. Time boxing is a technique where you spend a small, concentrated amount of time on something, then quit when the time is up. If you've ever used a calendar, then you have some experience with time boxing.

My time boxing method of choice is the Pomodoro Method because it is 25 minutes on with five minute breaks. I used the Pomodoro Method only for writing, which feels important to me. I feel like if I tried to use it for something else, like clearing my inbox, I would be in the headspace of my email during my set writing times. (I never tested it though, so see for yourself.)

The five minute breaks were essential to my progress, especially at first. They allowed me to record my numbers on the spreadsheet, get up and walk around for a minute, go to the bathroom or get a quick snack or look at my phone without feeling crazy.

I also loved the Pomodoro Method because it normalized all my writing sessions. I originally tracked my writing sessions by just starting when I felt like it and ending when I felt like it. This meant that sometimes my sessions were seven minutes long, while others were 77 minutes long. It was really hard to see patterns at a glance this way. The 25 minute sessions helped me compare and contrast sessions easily.

One of the questions I had about Pomodoro (and something that a ton of people have asked when I told them about my progress with it) is, "Are the time boxes set, or can you adjust them?" I searched online and never found a good answer as to whether 25 minutes was an optimal length of focus, so I tried it myself. I found that, for me, somewhere closer to 40 minutes was more optimal, only because when I got started with a scene or section, I would be roaring along and the buzzer would go off, pulling me out of flow. I liked 40 minutes because I could usually finish a draft 2,500 word scene (my average scene length) and I could still do a five minute break for a round 45 minutes of time total. In three hours, I could do four pomodoros, which is equal to one set.

Your mileage may vary; for example, if you only have an hour to write every day, doing two pomodoros at 25 minutes each is probably more effective.

If you're not sure, I recommend starting with 25 on, five off, and adjusting from there. I will say that when I first started, 25 minutes was painfully long for me. This was because I was addicted to distractions. Practice cured my addictions.

You can slowly increase your pomodoros in five minute increments as well, which will improve your "writing stamina," or the total amount of time you spend writing per day.

A few more notes on what to do on your five minute breaks: One thing I don't do is check email or Facebook. Those apps are designed to suck you in, so they aren't ideal for 5 minute breaks. I've also heard of people who do 50 pushups or whatever. Awesome idea if 50 pushups is easy or refreshing for you, but if not, don't pick this up. Don't do anything that's going to drain your energy on your break. That's a recipe to burnout.

LET MOTIVATION TAKE OVER

Confession time: I don't use the Pomodoro Method as often anymore unless I'm on a deadline or trying to tackle a section that I'm particularly frustrated and/or bored by. I also don't always turn off my internet (I think it's on right now, actually, in case I need to look up a quote).

What I've found is that you don't need a lot of these tips to get into flow once you have the motivation. When you feel motivated, it's much easier to slide into flow. These tips are great when you're starting out or if you don't have a lot of practice with writing tons of words every day. But, like tracking your progress, like self-editing, like plotting and story structure—really, like a lot of aspects of writing—once you practice enough, you begin to internalize what you've learned.

This has happened to me in two other areas of my life. First, when I was studying jujitsu, and I began reacting from muscle memory during my sparring matches, rather than from any thoughtful or logical process on my part. I had been over the moves so many times, perfected the positioning of my hands, arms, legs, and posture, and calculated the right amount of force to use so many times that the instinctual part of me finally took over. This took several years, lots of training, and constant vigilance—but even today, over 10 years after my last jujitsu class, I still have a lot of the self-defense skills I learned there (which was, of course, the point—when someone is attacking, you don't want to hesitate over what to do next).

The second time it happened to me was with singing. I sang for most of my school age years, always participating in the choir until I got to college. When I knew a song, I didn't have to think about the words, the notes, anything—I could just go up there and add my energy and perform.

Writing is a bit like this too, though so many writers, even professional ones, never get to the point where they can perform at a high level even without the proper routines and preparation. Learning to write faster and putting in more hours has gotten me to this level. I've been working on this book for the last ~6 hours (with lots of breaks, including a lunch one) and added ~11,000 brand new words, nearly all of which will make it into the final draft. I don't feel fatigued, I've taken natural breaks for food and more tea (I'm working at a coffee shop as I type this), and I'm still people-watching through the windows outside. It's only in the last hour that I've felt a little more distracted with checking my phone for messages, which means I've only got another section or two in me—but thus far, everything has flowed naturally, with no need for passive barriers, pomodoros, word count tracking, or any of the other tips I'm sharing in this section.

Motivation + preparation and training has given me the ability to hit my flow easily and efficiently. It's real, tangible, and available to you, too.

I tell you this because it can be challenging to implement all these changes to your routine, but the light at the end of the tunnel is that you probably won't need them forever. Once you go through the transformation, it's quite easy to maintain your progress simply by writing on a regular basis.

This is not just true of writing, but of many, many habits we are able to install in our lives. For example, when you first start a cooking routine, it's painful and almost all-consuming. But once you've been doing it for several months, you can whip up dinner in 30 minutes fairly easily. You've internalized a number of recipes, you know just what to buy on your weekly grocery run, and you have a great system for processing dirty dishes after your meal is finished.

The same is true for people who are able to maintain their weight after losing one hundred pounds, or people who learn their way around a new city, or people who become new parents overnight—you just get used to doing something and you adapt. We humans are so moldable, if only we harness our abilities and put that energy toward something good that makes our lives better.

Now, don't get me wrong—I still have to put in the hours to see the results.

Increasing your writing speed is like riding a bike, though. You don't forget how to do it.

Achieving flow was another huge, huge boost in word count for me, allowing me to break through the 2000 words per hour barrier, which is a dream for most writers. I obviously didn't stop there, but I'm quite happy with that result on most days. Any day where I can hit over 5,000 new words, despite everything life throws at me, is a productive day in my book.

If you're struggling with this step, see if anything below helps get you unstuck:

FORCING YOURSELF MEANS YOU NEED TO STEP BACK

Writers are a crazy group of people in general, but one of the craziest things I see them do is push themselves in any way.

Here's the thing: writing is damn enjoyable. It's fun. You are creating something, using your talents, putting your thoughts on a screen. If you aren't having fun doing this—if you have to push yourself in any way—then something is wrong.

Some writers will disagree with me, and my guess is that those writers should not really be writers. The best writers I know are the ones who do it compulsively, even if it's just for themselves, even if they have to write it all out by hand, even if they don't have the right tools, even when they don't have the time, even when they should be working on other things. None of this sounds like forcing or pushing to me.

There are a few occasions when I've felt like I had to push myself:

- When the scene or the content was all wrong (and as a result, not very good)
- When I hadn't done the legwork needed - like beating out my content or getting my research done
- When I didn't want to create the specific content (I wasn't interested in the topic or the upside)
- When I was exhausted and not respecting my physical, mental, and emotional restraints, usually due to not taking care of myself

Another thing you can see in my diary entries is that I try (for months, really) to get excited about writing freelance articles. Even though I talk about it for weeks on end, I make very little progress. Why? Because I didn't want to do it!

It's hard enough to do things you do want to do. Setting goals for things you don't want to do is just going to waste a lot of time and energy stressing out about things that just aren't going to happen, no matter how hard you push yourself.

NOT FOLLOWING WHIMS MEANS YOU NEED MORE SPACE IN YOUR SCHEDULE

The creative life is by its nature, inconsistent. When you're struck with a new idea that has you giddy inside, sometimes you need to drop everything and explore it. If you leave enough space in your schedule, this can be quite a productive use of your time. I try to put at least five hours of brainstorming per week on my calendar, because it gives me the freedom to do just this.

Whenever an idea strikes, I can explore it right away—I just move whatever I had planned to the brainstorming section on my calendar.

Anyone who has been a creator long enough knows that inspiration is fleeting. Capture it when it strikes!

MISSING YOUR RHYTHMS MEANS YOU'RE TAKING THE WRONG ADVICE

I used to read a lot of advice. I would read, "write in the morning before anyone gets up," or "write in the middle of the night because it's quiet." The truth is that you should write according to your natural rhythms and ignore most other advice about it.

Through a lot of experimentation, I learned that my natural rhythm for writing is to start around 10 AM and continue until about 3 PM, taking breaks for food, water, and so on. 3 PM is basically my nap time... I'm so sleepy and since I work from home, I'm often cuddling with my dog at this point. Once I wake up, I start doing chores and cooking for the family, and don't circle back around to writing again until later in the evening, when I seem to catch my second wind for several hours before bedtime.

For awhile, I was trying to write in the middle of the day, and it just did not work for me, no matter what the research showed. When I started coordinating my writing schedule around this natural ebb and flow of my energy, I got much better results.

The point of all this is too many writers both give and take advice to do something very specific... but I've found that the instructions are way too detailed to be universal. You've got to figure out what your natural flow is and just work within that framework. Yes, this probably means you have to accept your nature... but once you do that, you can almost always make your natural strengths and preferences work in your favor.

For me, I had to accept that my body likes a nap around 3 PM. It's likely biological—my mom has, since before I can remember, been a 3 PM napper as well. During the holidays, you can usually find us napping on matching couches in their living room with the dog curled up next to one of us.

The goal of the Flow step is to move you away from the distractions of your life and toward a creative lifestyle. For most of us, this means developing better boundaries that create space for us to actually do the work we want and need to do on our writing careers. Once you get into your flow, your writing will come out much easier and faster.

As I said in the original article, my word count increased another 50% from Step 1—which was nearly 3x my natural writing speed that I was hitting only a few months earlier. Not bad!

Chapter 7
STEP #3 - TRAINING

You have the formula and the four steps that will drastically increase your writing speed—but is that all you need?

Probably not. You see, even armed with this information, you aren't suddenly going to start having 20,000 word days, working 6-8 hours on writing.

Why?

Because speed is only one component of the equation. While I genuinely believe that improving word count per hour is one of the best things you can do for your writing career, I also know from experience that it's not enough.

Think of it like training for a marathon. In that situation, it is definitely valuable to work on your speed, because you can finish the marathon significantly faster if you trim, say, two minutes off each mile.

Still, you won't finish the marathon unless you build your stamina over long distances and lengths of time. This requires habits, discipline, and plain old lacing up the shoes every day.

In fact, you're probably better off in the short term just running every day at your usual slow pace. Someone who runs 5-10 miles every day, even at a slow pace, is always going to do better than someone who can sprint 5 miles after not practicing for a month. Slow and steady wins the race nine times out of ten.

I've found that the same is true with books. You'll get a lot more done writing slowly every day, than doing a few sprint sessions a month. Writing fast is a superpower— but it only makes a real difference if you already have the good habit of writing every day in place. It's only when you combine speed with solid habit that you start to break records.

So how do you develop that habit? I am no expert on building habits, not even close, but I have realized that building a habit takes attacking it from all sides—the physical, the emotional, and the mental. You need a game plan for all aspects of your life. Here are a few tips that helped me:

KNOW YOUR HABIT-FORMING STYLE

Are you a questioner, obliger, rebel, upholder?

Writing consistently is entirely about how you form habits. Are you a good habit-former? If so, you probably put together a writing routine with ease. If not, you may be struggling to get started, not just with writing but with a number of other routines in your life!

The 4 Rubin Tendencies (developed by Gretchen Rubin) will help you determine what kind of habit-former you are and what will motivate you to make writing a part of your daily routine.

USE THE TRIGGER, BEHAVIOR, REWARD FRAMEWORK

A number of researchers have also come up with a simple framework of trigger, behavior, reward, which are the three elements of effective habit formation.

For example:

Trigger: my alarm goes off.

Behavior: I sit at my desk and start typing.

Reward: I get to check off a box on my list of to-do's for the day. (I know—my reward is lame, but I love checking things off. You can pick anything that motivates you.)

Lastly, you may want to look into BJ Fogg's simple process for habit formation called Tiny Habits, which will help you get started with habits in general. They really matter, so don't skimp on the process if you need to study habit formation first!

STACK HABITS

People do this with exercise all the time. For example, someone might want to improve themselves by listening to podcasts, and start a running habit. Instead of doing these two things separately they do them at once! Easy peasy.

You can do the same thing with writing, and in fact, I did for nearly a month. I still frequently do writing (via dictation) or even editing and proofreading (via Kindle) while I do a little movement (either walking or climbing stairs).

This may not work for others, but I love moving while writing. Sitting still is a challenge for me. I get very slouchy and bored and usually feel like a nap around 3pm or so.

If you can't stack a habit with writing, perhaps you can stack habits in other areas of your life to make more room for writing?

ADD IN A BUFFER AROUND TRAVEL DAYS

Falling off the horse—it happens to the best of us. And when it does, it is surprisingly hard to get back on, even if we've been on for months and months previously.

There's a common myth about habits that if you do something regularly for a long period of time, it becomes ingrained, and you'll just keep doing it.

But it's not true in the slightest, in my experience. And it makes sense when you think about how many things you've started and quit over the years.

Television is always a great example, in my opinion. For example, you spend all year from fall to spring watching your favorite shows every week. Then, over the summer, you get out of the habit. And when you come back to the new fall season, you have a lot of shows that you simply don't care about anymore. So you don't pick them up. But suddenly, you're obsessed with Gotham, or How To Get Away With Murder, and you block off your whole Thursday night for it.

Another one that I see a lot in my own life is a snack or drink habit. For example, I'll be on a tea kick and drink it every day for months. But then, the weather will change, or I'll change jobs, or I'll move, and suddenly, I don't drink tea at all.

We greatly underestimate how much our environments and external circumstances dictate our habits. Both good and bad habits can be surprisingly hard to start and surprisingly easy to quit, and vice-versa.

The same is true with writing. Never think that because you've been writing every day for months, you can take a few days off and hop right back on. I know plenty of people who struggle with this, including myself!

It's better to start from a place of knowing it will be hard to get back on the horse, and making a plan for it whenever you have travel, vacation, or a holiday to contend with. Budget a few days buffer on both sides, and know that you are going to be in a bit of pain when you get back. But remember how great it feels to be writing every day, because the pain is worth in when you come out on the other side.

WRITING IS A PHYSICAL GAME, NOT JUST A MENTAL ONE

Ergonomics are much more important than you would think.

First of all, sitting is the new smoking. It is really freaking unhealthy to sit for long periods of time without regular breaks.

Second, typing causes a lot of issues in your wrists. You need a comfortable keyboard, alternating writing positions, chairs, and places, and potentially even multiple inputs (I use both a keyboard and a microphone + Dragon Dictate setup).

Third, eye strain can really mess you up. I experienced eye strain during my challenge, and it made it extremely hard to work. I literally had to close my eyes for a lot of the time (luckily, I'm not a pecker—I can type with closed eyes just fine thanks to 5th grade computer classes on those awful hunk-of-metal Apple monitors). I was eventually able to cure my eye strain with better blinking habits, a humidifier in my office area, and cutting back on drinking alcohol or anything else that caused dehydration, like coffee and soda (I still drink caffeine free tea because it's the least offensive of the non-water liquids.), but this minor injury negatively affected my results for at least a week.

WRITE AND WALK AROUND AND WRITE

Both Dean Wesley Smith and Kris Rusch are career writers who know lots of other career writers. They say that pretty much every career writer follows the pattern of write, break, write, break, with the breaks happening on the hour, roughly. So they might write for an hour, break for fifteen minutes, write for an hour, wash the dishes, write for an hour, watch a show, and so on.

I found that this was true for me as well. I would write for less than 3 hours total during the day, but somehow that was spread out throughout the entire day. Say what you will about switching costs, but for some reason, writing fiction does require breaks for a lot of people.

To me, this is okay—sitting for long periods of time is terrible for you anyway. But it also means that writing needs to happen in-between your regular life of friends, family, chores, and work.

I tend to write in the mornings and evenings, but I'm more likely to write in the afternoon, too, when I have already written in the morning.

CREATE A PLAN FOR RESISTANCE

For whatever reason, writing a novel is intimidating, even though it's the same amount of work as writing ~10,000 twitter updates (which a surprising number of people have done). A big project is not fun to stare at, especially when you're starting with a blank page.

I'm going to copy and paste a section of my very first entry from when I started my Daily Fiction Writing Habit Challenge back in August of 2013. You can read it again in the first entry of my Life of a Writer diary in the appendix, but it's so relevant that I wanted to post it here as well:

8:30 am -

Sat down at the computer after getting up and showered. I usually wake up around 7:00 am and spend a few hours moseying around in bed, reading on my Kindle or checking various things like email and blogs on my iPad. I typically don't get up until after P leaves for work, but today is Sunday and I was extra excited for a book I wrote beats for yesterday.

The book is under a pen name, it's the third in a series, and I haven't finished edits on #2 yet, so the only one published is #1. Weird, I know. I'm the type of person who loves to work in bursts of energy but can lose interest quickly, so I've found that the best way to keep working is to have tons of projects going at once. That way, I can work on the one that's most interesting to me at the moment and go until I'm tired or bored, then switch to another one, which suddenly looks fresh and fun again.

Anyway, I honestly haven't written a first draft in awhile. I probably haven't put new words on screen in a few weeks, and I haven't drafted something new in months. (Unacceptable, hence, why I'm starting this challenge.) I could tell that I was out of practice because I felt tons of anxiety as I sat down at my computer.

Luckily, I had already prepared for that fear I was feeling. My laptop was already set to my writing account, with all the files up and ready to go.

BUT... I still felt a ton of resistance. I decided to go make tea before I wrote. I left a red cup full of tea on P's nightstand and made two mugs for myself. I sat back down at the computer.

Then, I realized that because I don't have internet under my new account, I couldn't update my spreadsheet where I track my word count. That uses Google Spreadsheet, and I couldn't access Drive. So I opened up Excel and created a new spreadsheet, which took another 20 minutes or so.

Finally, around 9:25 am, I was all set up and ready to write. You know how people say the hardest thing about getting something done is starting? I have a trick for getting started on anything I'm nervous about doing: I tell myself I'm going to do one Pomodoro of it, and then if I hate it, I can quit.

So I set my timer for 25 minutes and took off, dictating my first scene via Dragon Dictate, using beats that I wrote yesterday. After 25 minutes, I was feeling okay but still wanted a break. Got 897 words done, for an average of 2150 words/hour.

Not terrible, but certainly not my best. I'm hoping that in the weeks to come, my times improve. But, I can't really beat myself up about it because 897 words is more fiction than I've written in the last two weeks.

Also, it probably seems a little crazy that it took me nearly an hour to prepare for a 25 minute writing session. That's due to lack of practice. Think of it as if you were training for a marathon, but you hadn't gone jogging in 6 months. You're not going to go balls-to-the-wall on your first run, are you? You're going to take a nice and slow jog and try to hit 2 miles without keeling over.

That's how this challenge feels to me. Fear, anxiety, and the lizard brain are real. I've budgeted time to contend with them every day because I know they are my biggest enemies. I also know from experience that they get easier to contend with over time, though they never truly go away.

The moral of the story is that you are going to face resistance. *The War of Art* is an amazing book by Steven Pressfield that will help you understand how deeply penetrating this resistance is in your daily life—and how it will likely never, ever go away for you.

Accept that you will meet resistance to your goals and make a plan to combat them. Some of the best plans include:

- A way to easily remind yourself of the next step - To me, this is where knowledge comes in at full force.
- A small enough task to start with even when you don't want to - Most runners will tell you to just lace up your shoes and step out the door if you want to start a running habit. Writing is similar; it feels great while you're doing it in flow, but it's hard to overcome your initial resistance to it.
- A silly routine that puts you in the mindset (for example, drinking tea or going to a coffee shop)
- Some fancy if-then-else prioritizing - If it's before 10am, I'll do a pomodoro, else if it's after 12pm, I'll grab lunch, else I'll take out the dog, then do a pomodoro.

HAVE A PLAN TO DEAL WITH PERSONAL CRAP

My personal life has derailed my writing plans more often than I care to admit. This happens to every writer I know, whether it be health issues, emergencies, their relationships with others in their life (a spouse, children, or other family members) or the typical emotional ups and downs of life.

Again, the solution here is twofold:

- Budget time and space for unforeseen setbacks
- Have a plan for how you'll get back on track quickly

I believe (especially after reading back through my diary) that as long as you are not a dramatic person (we all know those people who constantly have "emergencies"... ugh) that personal crap is completely fine and doesn't have to derail your life.

Coming up with your training plan for writing more needs to be personal and custom. You have to find your own rhythm for working so that you can get work done consistently. These are a few of the pieces that tripped me up, and you can probably find corollaries in your own life!

Chapter 8

STEP #4 - ENERGY

[Note: in this section, i'm going to talk about energy in very, very loose terms. I'm not talking about physical energy, like calories in, calories out, and i'm not talking about physics itself, like forces acting upon one another. I'm talking about creative energy in a looser sense, in a way that cannot be measured, but rather felt and experienced. I apologize if this causes confusion for those detail-oriented, logic-based writers out there—I just don't have any other good words to describe the phenomenon I experienced as I tried to up my word count. Sorry about this!]

Over the course of my years as a creative, I've come to the conclusion that energy is a huge factor in how much I can accomplish each day.

I hit 50,000 words per month for two months straight, working only about 50 hours total and detailed it in diary entries that you'll find in the appendix.

But by the end of my two months, I was incredibly burnt out and didn't write another word of fiction for months afterward.

Now, some of this can be attributed to end-of-the-year slowdown and holidays, which always trip me up, but most of it should probably be attributed to the fact that I did not have an ounce of creative energy left to do the work!

I will never let that happen again. What I realized after that experience is that we all have a well of creative energy that we draw from. At the end of those two months, my well was completely dry. I didn't write again because it took me months and months to refill that well.

If you can buy into this premise/analogy I'm using to describe my experience, then you may be wondering what the hell this well of creative energy is, exactly. Here's how I would explain the equation. You use energy and deplete your creative well by creating art. You gain energy and replenish your creative well by getting inspired.

Weird, I know. But if you can stick with me, you may find that this rings true and logical to you, even if the details and math and science are a lot more loosey goosey than tracking your word count.

What this means to me is that in order to stay consistent with your writing, you MUST replenish your creative energy well on a regular basis. This isn't a suggestion; it's a work task that you must make time for on a consistent basis, the same way writing is a work task that you must make time for on a consistent basis.

After my crazy two months and subsequent lack-of-crazy two months, I've settled into routines and systems that both replenish and deplete my energy on a consistent basis. This equation is pretty easy to understand; basically, you never want to be creatively bankrupt. You can maybe charge your purchases on a credit card for a few months, but the piper will come after you for payment, eventually.

How do you replenish this energy and get inspired? (And what does it even mean to be "inspired," anyway?) Well, it's going to be different for each person. Some very common elements of inspiration are:

Nature - Going outside is one of the healthiest things you can do in a society like ours, where we spend so much time at desks and in front of screens. Even a 30 minute walk can make a huge difference.

Exercise - As my grandpa (who has had three heart surgeries) has told me, "The number one piece of advice I'd give young people is to get your heart rate up at least once every day." The benefits of exercise extend beyond the physical and exercise has more recently been shown to improve mental and emotional health. Exercise can serve as inspiration time too, especially if you combine it with one of the others on this list.

Ending Your Work Day - One of the most common shared traits of the uber successful is that they have specified work hours and specified play hours. I love working at night, but I don't do it much anymore because it doesn't give me a break from work. Nowadays, my evening routine does not include working on fiction; instead, it includes cooking for my fiancé, writing in my journal, and cuddling with my fiancé and my dog. If I do work on fiction, it's because I want to, not because I still have leftover tasks.

Spending Time With Loved Ones - Even if you're an introvert, you'll be surprised by how much certain people in your life can renew your energy. Spending time with your family is crucial to having strong, healthy, and meaningful relationships, but don't forget to schedule time with extended family and friends as well:

- Date nights for just the two of you
- Couples nights for double dates
- Family nights when you have kids
- Girls nights or Bro nights for friends
- Several yearly extended visits with family and friends out of town
- Weekend getaways
- Several yearly vacations and staycations for just the family
- Unplugged weekends

Careful Media Consumption - Consuming media doesn't make us happy, research shows, but consuming specific media can probably inspire us. Many writers read non-fiction business books, while others read books in their genre, while others still watch scripted television or head to a museum. As long as you consume purposefully and have specific reasons for what you consume, you can draw a lot of energy from other's art. (And how cool is it that part of your "job" is to enjoy what others create?)

A Related Hobby - Cross-training is important for both athletes and artists, so don't be afraid to spend some of your time practicing an instrument, painting, kickboxing, or learning survival tactics. It all contributes to your writing!

Down Time - Waiting in lines, standing in the shower, sitting on a train or in a car, trying to quiet your mind before bed—all are times that you can designate for brainstorming, thinking, chatting with others, sussing out good ideas, or consuming others' ideas.

Inspiration is literally all around us, and especially for fiction writers, everything "counts." When I focused too much on word count, I did so at the expense of all the things I enjoyed, which eventually did me in. If you are the type of person who already has a regular workout routine, or who already finds ways to unplug on a regular basis, you probably won't encounter this issue.

DEVELOPING SYSTEMS TO REFILL YOUR CREATIVE ENERGY WELL USING INSPIRATION

If you are like the average person, you may need to get serious about developing a system for staying inspired, the same way you develop a system for getting more writing done. There are a few distinctions that will help you pull your system together:

ARE YOU AN EXTROVERT OR AN INTROVERT, OR SOMEWHERE IN-BETWEEN?

This to me is one of the most important distinctions when understanding creative energy. Many people have the misconception that extroverts are outgoing and introverts are homebodies, which is not quite true. If we are going by the Myers-Briggs definition, extroverts are people who gain energy externally, which means that they get energy from their environments. Introverts are people who gain energy internally, which means they get energy from spending time alone. This corresponds roughly to the misconception, but doesn't completely explain discrepancies.

What does this mean? Depending on your answer, you'll be able to decide:

- Whether you're going to book lots of time with new people or people you don't see often (better for extroverts) or with close friends and family (introverts)
- Whether you're going to work in an busy spot (extroverts) or in an office alone (introverts)
- Whether you're going to exercise outside (extroverts) or inside (introverts)
- Whether you're going to listen to music or background noise (extroverts) or have complete silence (introverts)
- Are you a routine person or a stimulation person, or somewhere in-between?

Most people gravitate toward one of two types of work—doing something different every day or hour (prevalent in management or any other job where you're reactionary to problems) vs. having a routine of what you're expected to accomplish each day (prevalent to sales, speaking, etc.). If you picture the extremes of these two types of work at the ends of a spectrum, where would you fall on it?

Depending on your answer, you'll be able to decide:

- Whether you're going to work on multiple projects at a time (better for writers who need stimulation) or stick to one and focus (better for writers who like routine)
- Whether you're going to vary locations (coffee shop one day, living room the next, bookstore the day after) or whether you need to have a dedicated space on your home
- Whether you can stick to a time block at the same time each day (from 2-4pm each day) or whether you want an overall goal of time spent (2 hours a day, whenever you can fit them in)

- Whether you need to write sequentially or whether you can hop around within your manuscript

Knowing the answers to these questions will help you decide what kind of writing routine you'll have and what's going to work for you to actually sit down and produce words.

ARE YOU A "BURST-OF-ENERGY" PERSON OR A "SLOW-AND-STEADY" PERSON, OR SOMEWHERE IN-BETWEEN?

When it comes to writing, your manuscript progress will be almost entirely driven by how much energy you have to devote to the project. Energy levels vary not only by person but also by external factors, like how well you're sleeping, eating, exercising, what your natural circadian rhythm is set at, and what hours of the day you feel most productive.

In addition to those things, some people are the hardcore, I'm-going-to-kick-out-this-draft-in-two-weeks types and others would rather write 500 words a day on the draft.

Depending on your answer, you'll be able to decide:

- Whether you're going to set a small daily word count goal and try to hit it every day (slow-and-steady) or clear your weekend, hole up in a hotel room, and crank out your story all at once (burst-of-energy)
- Whether you'll write, then edit, then write, then edit or whether you'll do a block of both each day.
- Whether you'll have strict deadlines or follow your whims

Most people will fall somewhere in the middle on almost all of these scales, but once you know this you can plan and block off times for your drafting, based on how you like to work.

DON'T IGNORE THIS STEP

I understand that the way I've presented creative energy in this book comes across as wishy-washy pseudoscience at times—but I still believe in it because I've seen the results in both myself and others.

Take this step seriously. I've observed dozens of professional writers and have concluded that the successful-yet-manic-depressive-and-alcoholic writer is the exception rather than the norm. (And hey—Stephen King backs me up in his memoir, *On Writing*.)

Most of the successful writers I know have better-than-average personal habits that include regular workout and diet routines, regular contact with friends and family, and limited "soft addictions"—internet, porn, mobile gaming, and so on. Most writers have also escaped workaholicism, social media addiction, and impulsive or perseverating email checking, because it simply depletes this creative energy well.

Ignoring the creative energy well is like ignoring the gas tank on your car—you can get away with it for short periods, but eventually the car stops moving. Don't let this happen to you, because it is not easy to get back on the road again.

Energy is all about knowing yourself and listening when your body, mind, or soul needs to take a break. Ideally, you'll schedule them on your calendar!

And if you've ever needed an excuse to improve another area of your life—food, exercise, smoking, socializing, and so on, let your writing goals drive you forward! It all contributes to your ability to perform at peak level when you are at work. Better writing, better stories, successful author career.

Chapter 9
QUESTIONS

How Do You Maintain Quality?

The first response I get to sharing my framework typically falls into one of three categories:

A) This is AWESOME—can't wait to try it!

B) This is AWESOME—but I could never do it because...

C) You must write shitty novels!

For anyone who is in the last category, I'm going to speak some serious straight talk with you:

Writing faster does not equal writing worse, as long as you aren't rushing, which is a completely different thing.

In fact, for many, writing faster actually helps them write better, for a number of reasons.

1. WHEN YOU WRITE FASTER, YOU WRITE MORE.

Practice improves your skill, and hitting higher word counts can (though doesn't necessarily) help you improve your storytelling (or structuring) skills. The more work you have, the more work you can publish (in any form, not just in books) which means that you'll receive more feedback, which helps you improve. Writing more also gives you the opportunity to take on more projects, which means you can vary your work, try different styles in parallel, and in turn, improve your skill set further.

2. WHEN YOU WRITE FASTER, YOU DISCONNECT FROM YOUR EDITING SIDE.

Writing with Dragon Dictate helped me separate the writing from the editing so I could produce drafts from the heart, rather than from the mind. These drafts were full of passion, voice, and energy—everything needed to produce a great story and everything that's hard (if not impossible) to attain through an editing lens.

3. WHEN YOU WRITE FASTER, YOU'RE FORCED TO PLAN YOUR STORY BEFOREHAND.

Writing slow allowed me to make up the story as I went, to ignore plot, ignore character, ignore structure, and more. Writing faster forces me to write outlines and beats (I can't write fast without a map), which are very, very important planning processes for creating a better book altogether. Getting the planning right for each book means that I do less writing, editing, and revising down the line, which means I can spend more time writing, which is more words and more practice and more feedback...

Overall, writing faster has helped me vastly improve my craft, my processes, and my efficiency at publishing books. I've gotten on a schedule that allows me to publish at least a book (usually more) each month, which means that I'm happy, productive, and in flow. I'm making swift progress now, and I'm also earning money and readers for my efforts. Contrast this with a 18 months ago, when I had three books total from 3-4 years of effort... the difference is astounding!

You may be tempted to think, "Let me see that work of hers... where's the proof that she's producing anything of quality?" Really, you don't need to see my work or investigate me to know that my claims are true, that you can write 2-3 times faster with these simple tips and either maintain or improve quality.

1. QUALITY IS SUBJECTIVE.

You may think my work is great or terrible, but it doesn't actually matter. It could be that you simply don't like my style of writing. It could be that you don't like the subjects I write about. It could also be that you aren't as skilled as you think at judging writing skill. It could be that your immediate reaction to someone else's success is defensiveness. It could be that you can't see yourself achieving the same results, thus you don't want to consider that someone else is. There are many ways the brain tries to protect its human, so it's hard to trust your own instincts about the quality of someone else's work.

2. THE QUESTION ISN'T WHETHER I WRITE HIGH-QUALITY; IT'S WHETHER MY QUALITY IS MAINTAINED WHEN SWITCHING FROM A SLOW WRITING PACE TO A FASTER WRITING PACE.

That question is much easier to answer without throwing judgement, shade, or insults at my work. You can do this by looking at my work and trying to distinguish which books I wrote quickly and which I wrote slowly. I can promise you won't figure it out, and you'll probably get it wrong!

Now, you may say, "Well, what if she edited a poor first draft into something acceptable, and that's why her work maintains its quality level?" But... does it matter, even if that's the case? If I spend the same amount of time (or even a little more) editing my drafts, but write one draft significantly faster than the other, isn't the faster overall process better, or at the least, more efficient, if the end result is the same?

When you look at creating a first draft faster, think about it in terms of the entire process of publishing a book from front to end. Within that process, you may have four steps. If you do one step two times faster, but it causes your other three steps to go two times slower, then you have a less efficient process. If you do one step two times faster and the rest stay the same, however, you have a more efficient process. When you're looking at quality of the draft, you must think about how it affects all the processes and steps afterward.

3. THE QUESTION ISN'T REALLY EVEN WHETHER MY QUALITY IS MAINTAINED WHEN SWITCHING FROM A SLOW WRITING PACE TO A FASTER WRITING PACE. THE QUESTION IS WHETHER YOUR QUALITY IS MAINTAINED WHEN SWITCHING... RIGHT?

I'm assuming you are reading this, not because you particularly care about my life, but because you'd like to improve your own.

So, in fact, any evaluation of the quality of my writing is rendered completely useless. The best way to test my claims is to literally test my claims... on yourself!

Only then, you can judge for yourself whether or not the tips work for you and whether you want to continue to incorporate them into your work schedule.

If you're asking about the quality of my work in any way, you're probably asking the wrong question. Because the real question is, can this work for you? And you are the only person who can answer it.

4. DOES WORD COUNT INCLUDE PRE-PRODUCTION? WHAT ABOUT EDITING AND REVISIONS?

The short answer is, no, it doesn't include any pre-production, post-production, or publishing.

The long answer is to explain how my pre-production, post-production, and publishing processes have changed since I started writing faster.

BEFORE USING MY FRAMEWORK

Outline - I plotted lightly and used basic storytelling structure with four sections (sometimes condensed to three).

First Draft - I wrote down as much as I could think of for the scene, usually starting with dialog. I was very much an underwriter and would often come up with chapters that were 1000 words or so. I wasn't good at filling in details or adding transitions.

Second Draft - I went back and simply wrote more. I tried to add at least 50% more words to each section. I also rewrote a lot of what I already had, changing lines of dialog, rearranging sections, and more.

Third Draft - I went back through each section and ticked off items on a list: descriptions of people, descriptions of setting, transitions, etc. When the list was checked, I considered the draft "revised."

Editing - Once all the chapters/scenes were in the state of "revised," I then started looking at them on a higher level—how they all worked together. I started at the beginning of the book and just chugged through it, changing whatever I wanted as I went. I also rearranged chapters and cut chapters and made notes about chapters that I might want to add. It was quite chaotic!

2nd Editing - After the first editing I tried to put all the chapters in the correct order and wrote the extra chapters I thought I needed. I threw away chapters I didn't need, often amounting to tens of thousands of words. And then I started over, basically doing the same thing as the first editing.

3rd Editing - This process of editing could repeat several times until I was sick of it. Then I would hand it to an editor to see what he thought. But he would hand it back with tons of comments and questions and my approach would basically be to go through the editing process again with my editor's suggested changes.

Proofing & Publishing - Once I had spent a sufficient number of months on editing, I would proof the book to get it ready for publishing.

There were several issues that made this process incredibly inefficient:

#1 - I wrote way more content than I ended up using, which amounted to hours and hours of wasted time. I realized that if I could avoid writing that content to begin with, I could drastically reduce the book's time spent in draft.

#2 - I couldn't predict how long my draft was going to be. This was terrible, because it made it impossible to predict when it would be done (a release date), which is an impossible way to run a business.

#3 - I couldn't predict how long it would take me to edit something, because I didn't know what I needed to add, cut, or rewrite beforehand. I also didn't really have an end point to editing, and stopped when I couldn't stand to do it anymore. This didn't produce any specific result in the end, and I relied too much on editors to safeguard me from publishing something that was "bad."

It occurred to me (especially after reading Story Engineering) that I was searching for my outline through the process of drafting, rather than through the process of outlining. To Larry Brook's point, this makes zero sense and is a huge time suck.

The solution (which he provided) was simple: find problems in your plot in the pre-production phase, before you draft pages and pages of content that doesn't make it into the book. Getting a solid grasp on your story at this phase saves hours and hours down the line.

AFTER USING MY FRAMEWORK

My process now looks very different from how it was when I started:

Outline - I still do an outline, but I'm quite a bit better at predicting word count from an outline. All of my chapters are one scene and every scene runs about 2500 words. I also have chapter structures that I can plug in my stories to. I have these models in place because it cuts out a lot of decision making with the outlining process and also it ties my word count prediction directly to the amount of money I can earn from each project. This lets me sort projects by value to my business as well. Here's my list:

6 scenes - Used for serials that I put in subscription programs like KDP Select. I sell these for $2.99 and bundle in packs of 4 for $6.99 - $9.99.

8 scenes - Used for novellas under my romance pen name. I sell these for $3.99 and bundle in packs of 3 for $6.99 - $9.99.

12 scenes - Used for novellas under my Monica Leonelle pen name. I go a little longer on these compared to the romance books because Monica Leonelle houses fantasy, sci-fi, and more, which tend to have more viewpoint characters and world-building. I sell these for $3.99 and bundle in packs of 3 for $6.99 - $9.99.

24 scenes - Used for short novels under my Monica Leonelle pen name. I sell these for $5.99 - $6.99 each.

36 scenes - Used for full-length novels (usually standalone). I sell these for at least $6.99 or more.

Beats - I always do beats these days, which you've already read about. At this point, I usually try to get feedback from someone on my idea and I also poke at my idea for challenges with structure. This saves dozens of hours and rewrites down the line.

Sketches - I'm still an under-writer, so while my sketches have gotten better (I don't usually need to double word count afterward) I still tend to skip over transitions and description and add them in at a later date. This is the part I do with Dragon Dictate—it's really fast!

Draft - The draft is done when it's ready to "compile," as I said before. I now produce fairly clean drafts, in part because I do so much pre-production, and in part because I've written a lot more words and gotten better at my work in general.

Edit/Revisions - I don't do these for all my projects anymore. After reading Story Engineering and doing my own tests in the marketplace, it became obvious to me that readers care much, much, much more about reading an amazing story than they care about reading perfectly stylized sentences. My area of genius is much more in the former area, which meant that I could outsource the latter to others who were stronger at it.

Additional Eyes - I currently work with two editors + a company that "produces" some of my work. To combat consistency issues, I work with one editors on each series and handle some of my series myself. Since every series has a slightly different style anyway, I don't have to worry too much about consistency, and since each editor is working on specific series, they are able to maintain characterization, style, and more fairly easily. I do have some series that I produce entirely by myself still, and for those, I follow a simple editing process that focuses on my weaknesses at the scene-by-scene level. I don't do the larger adjustments with moving chapters around or cutting whole sections, because I've worked out a lot of those issues during my pre-production process.

Proofing - I proof my books without professional help, for better or for worse. I read through them several times on various devices, Sometimes my fiancé also reads through them, and usually, because I've worked with a ghostwriter on it, that person has also caught a lot of the problems. A lot of people will disagree with that approach, but those people have probably never paid someone over $1000 and still found copywriting and proofing errors in their final drafts. I believe 100% in putting great work out there, but disagree that hiring an editor to do the proof makes a significant difference in quality or sales, any more than a single typo in a blog post means no one will want to share it.

That's my entire process before I publish, from beginning to end, and why I can fairly easily predict not only how long a project will take me, but how much I can potentially earn from it. Even if you don't care about writing faster, I still encourage you to find your word count per hour, because being able to tie production time to revenue has been a game changer for me in the past year.

5. WHY ISN'T THIS WORKING FOR ME? WHY CAN'T I GET TO CONSISTENT 10K DAYS?

If you need some troubleshooting advice, I encourage you to understand a few things about my process that aren't 100% explicit in the article:

#1 - THIS IS WHAT WORKED FOR ME AND MY PRODUCTIVITY CHALLENGES; YOU MUST FIGURE OUT WHAT WORKS FOR YOU AND YOUR PRODUCTIVITY CHALLENGES

We are not the same person. You will have different fears and triggers to tackle and different motivators and rewards to spur you on. That's why I recommend a more qualitative form of tracking besides just your word counts, like diary entries, as qualitative forms will guide you in understanding your behavior in terms of the trigger, action, reward framework that BJ Fogg puts forward for understanding habits.

With any system, you must do a "translation" to make it work for you. No one else's system is going to work for you out-of-the-box, so make sure you put in the work to do that translation. And if you're stuck on how to translate, start trying to use the system out of the box and take notes about which aspects aren't working for you. Then, brainstorm how you can adjust the system accordingly.

#2 - YOU NEED TO GIVE YOURSELF TIME TO EXPERIMENT, GAIN FEEDBACK, AND ADJUST.

I spent two months of just studying word count to reach many of my conclusions about it. To refine my full publishing process, I spent years working with others— editors, ghostwriters, beta readers, critiquers—and with putting my work out into the marketplace and studying the feedback I gained from book reviews. Your opinion on and understanding of all these matters will form slowly, over time, and your intuition will improve the fastest with personal experience.

As such, don't expect to turn your word count around overnight. It could take you 1-3 months of focus on just this metric to see results. And once you've gotten those results, you then need to figure out how this small piece— word count—fits into your larger process.

Writing as a career is a long game, so focus on improving your word count over the next 3-6 months, not over the next week, and you will be significantly happier with your results.

#3 - WORD COUNT IS NOT A PERFECT METRIC TO TRACK

One thing I want to stress that I didn't stress enough in the article is the idea that racking up word count is a small part of the full publishing process. You'll see in my diary in the appendix how I misunderstand this at the beginning of my journey to write more, which leads to a backlog/ bottleneck of edits in my larger publishing process. As I started receiving feedback on the article, I realized that a lot of readers (other authors) were making the same faulty jump in logic—that more words equals the results they want—money, fame, published books, and so on.

Word count is an interesting metric, because as much as we judge ourselves and other writers by the number of words we can produce in an hour or a day, that metric doesn't give us a good picture of the overall health of our progress. Remember that for every word you type, you need editing, revision, and proofing processes to reevaluate those words before the book "goes to print." Increasing your word count will do nothing if you can't handle that word count in terms of editing and publishing the content. I ran into a situation during my challenge where I was the bottleneck.

A great way to look at and keep track of workflow is using Trello, which is essentially like a matrix of notecards that you might keep on the wall.

When you focus on word count, your full production process starts to look like Figure 3:

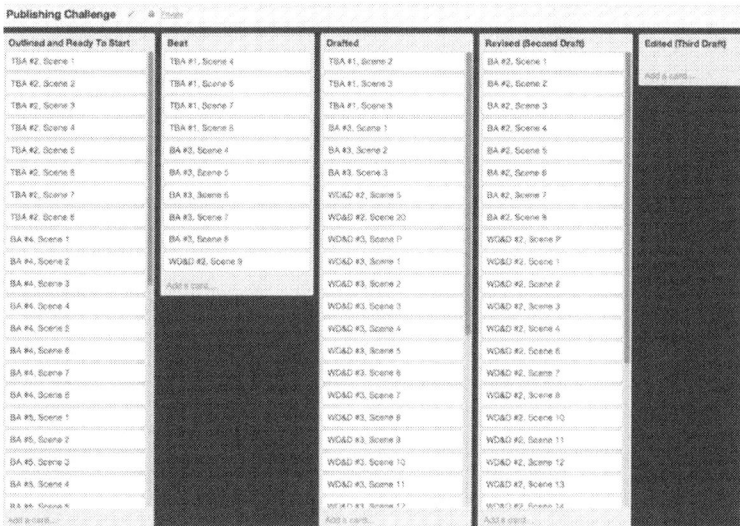

You won't want to edit, because it doesn't improve your metrics (you aren't tracking it).

Ideally, you want your full production process to look more like Figure 4:

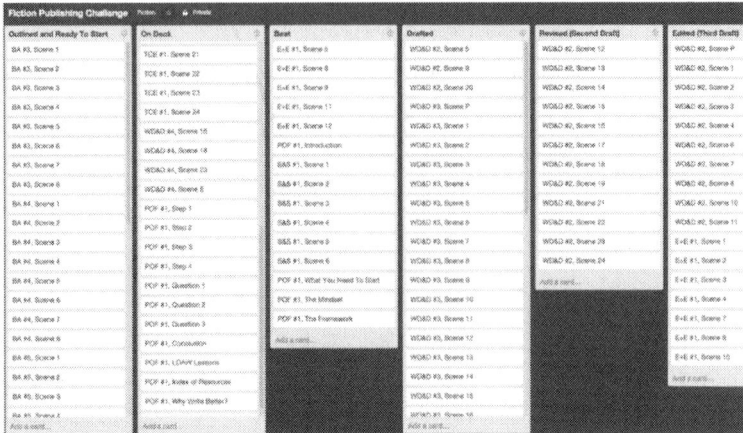

You want your whole process to be lean, where you are not producing too much in any of the columns. You want to have just-in-time production.

#4 - IMPROVING YOUR WRITING SPEED IS A SKILL THAT WORKS BEST WHEN YOU'VE ALREADY GOT THE "ASS IN CHAIR" SKILL DOWN PAT

Writing fast is a valuable skill, but only if you sit yourself down and actually do it.

For the longest time, I focused heavily on optimizing word count and trying to get as many words as possible in as little time as possible. My attitude was, "I can work on this for two hours a day, get the same results as someone working eight hours a day, and then spend the other six hours doing something else." (Which is classic Tim Ferriss, 4-Hour Workweek mentality.)

Now, I barely track word count because I spend plenty of time each day sitting down writing. It took me awhile to shift to this perspective, but I finally realized, "What else do I want to be doing with my time besides writing my stories?" Sure, I could watch a few extra hours of television, but did that make me happy, fulfilled, or inspired?

Instead of trying to optimize my hours, I then decided to focus on making writing more fun for myself—which has actually led to several 15k days, more so than my original pushes used to. Some days I write slower than 3,500 words per hour, but I write for many more hours, and that gives better results. Other days I need to churn out articles or get through rough draft scenes to hit a deadline, so I fall back on my skill set, do my focused pomodoros, and get it done.

I want to stress that no matter what writing speed you end up hitting, this skill works best when paired with the "ass in chair" skill. If you aren't getting results, the latter could be a good place to start making adjustments. I learned this as I was going through my "write fast" phase, which I think you'll see as you read my diary in the appendix.

All of this is to say that when efficiency fails, put in the hours. You will still be way ahead of most other writers!

As an analogy, consider diet and exercise. Most professionals say that diet will get you 80% of the weight loss results and exercise will get you the other 20%. Writing fast is in the 20%; "ass in chair" is the 80%. Just like exercise can get you ripped and take you to a whole different level of athleticism that diet can't help you with, writing fast can help you go pro... but it's not going to work if you're simultaneously stuffing your face (not making time to write).

#5 - YOUR WRITING PROGRESS DEPENDS ON YOUR LIFESTYLE

No career happens in a vacuum, and writing is no exception. If anything, writing as a career requires more changes to your personal schedule, your routines, and your habits than the average career, because you're working so independently.

As a result, your lifestyle is going to greatly dictate how easily you can apply these concepts.

Unfortunately, this means that if you don't have your shit together, you don't have a strong chance of succeeding at applying these concepts.

If your writing speed isn't improving, it may be beneficial to look at the larger picture of your life and identify key habits that are affecting your ability to produce. Maybe you're used to spending most of your workday at the day job on Facebook, and now that you're trying to write, you're seeing the same habit creep through. Maybe your home or your schedule is disorganized and as a result you can't find an hour to sit down and write. Maybe your relationships are in shambles and you don't have a support system in place to make this dream a reality. Maybe your health is terrible and you can't focus due to exhaustion, pain, or physical inability. All of these other factors matter so much; don't neglect these aspects of your life. Make improvements in these areas first and then come back to your writing speed. The results will come much easier!

If you're still stuck after reflecting on some of these troubleshooting points, feel free to reach out to me at monicaleonelle@gmail.com. Sometimes it's hard to see what the issue is when you're in the thick of it, but usually another writer can spot the issue easily. I will be kind, but honest about what I see.

WHAT NEXT?

Thank you so much for reading through the framework! I hope I've given you tons of ideas on how to improve your writing process.

What else? What's next?

STEP 1: YOU CAN ACCESS MORE RESOURCES

You can grab one of my other Growth Hacking books. Go to ProseOnFire.com/Storytellers/. Aren't the covers fun?

You can also get a free presentation (no email sign-up required) about building your email list in three steps. It's really good! The resources page here:

ProseOnFire.com/ListBuilding/

What it contains:

- Links to the presentation called The 3-Step Framework For Building Your Email List as an Author
- A list of my favorite list building tools (many of them free to use)
- The 10 Stages of Audience for Fiction Authors sampler,

which goes through the Sales Funnel Gap Analysis I developed—totally free! If you're struggling with your sales funnel, you will love these worksheets.

STEP 2: YOU CAN JOIN MY EMAIL LIST AND FOLLOW ME ON G+

I write a new blog post about what I'm learning right now every Thursday. Go to

http://proseonfire.com/contact-me/

I write new lessons I'm implementing frequently on G+. Go to

https://plus.google.com/u/0/+MonicaLeonelle/posts

STEP 3: YOU CAN IMPLEMENT, IMPLEMENT, IMPLEMENT

Hopefully you've taken a ton of notes throughout the book (and the appendix is definitely worth a look as well for hidden gems). Now it's time to set up your own experiment and start kicking ass on this writing stuff. You can do it! Feel free to keep me updated by chatting me on Twitter or Facebook. Here's my info:

Facebook: Facebook.com/MonicaLeonelleGrace/
Twitter: @monicaleonelle

Good luck with everything, and check the next page for the Index of Resources and Appendix.

ORIGINAL ARTICLES

You can find my weekly articles at

ProseOnFire.com/blog/

You can read my 2-month experiment in the Life of a Writer Diary (See Appendix to read in full).

Don't forget to sign up for more information on future books in this series:

ProseOnFire.com/Storytellers/

So many good books coming up!

STORYTELLING

For the best book on plotting and story structure, try *Story Engineering* by Larry Brooks.

For the best book on character arcs, try *45 Master Characters* by Victoria Lynn Schmidt.

For fiction examples that help you with Step 1: Knowledge, try:

- The complete *Harry Potter* series by J.K. Rowling
- *How To Get Away With Murder* television series, (specifically, the first 6-7 episodes of Season 1)
- *Black Mirror* television series (specifically, Season 1, Episode 2 "Fifteen Million Merits")
- *Emma + Elsie Meet Fitzwilliam Darcy (Emma + Elsie #1)* by Monica Leonelle and Maddy Raven

For an in-depth look at another group of authors' writing processes, try *Fiction Unboxed* by Sean Platt and Johnny B. Truant. They wrote a novel in 30 days!

For detail-oriented writers who need serious help with their writing process, reach out to Susan Pogorzelski at susanpogorzelski.com.

Still struggling with outlining? Try *Take Off Your Pants!* by Libbie Hawker. It works for both pantsers and plotters!

Keep a lookout for *Nail Your Story: Add Tension, Build Emotion, and Keep Your Readers Addicted (Growth Hacking For Storytellers #2)* by Monica Leonelle, which is available now:

ProseOnFire.com/nailyourstory/

And if you want to work one-on-one with me on your outline, grab one of the Nail Your Outline Sessions with myself and Amy Teegan. Go here to learn more:

ProseOnFire.com/nail-your-outline-sessions/

WRITING BUSINESS

Learn how to run your writing business with *Write. Publish. Repeat.* by Sean Platt, Johnny B. Truant, and David W. Wright.

To learn a lot more about writing fast, try *2k to 10k* by Rachel Aaron. It is a lot like this book!

For an excellent list of different tweaks you can make to your writing process to speed up, try *Writing Fast For Non-Fiction Writers* by Ryan Healy.

For the most interesting memoir on writing (and probably one of the most recommended by other authors), try *On Writing* by Stephen King.

Learn about publishing from a veteran writer who has seen all sides from Kristine Kathryn Rusch's blog, kriswrites.com.

BUILDING HABITS

Need to build a habit, like now? Try the Tiny Habits program by BJ Fogg. He's a PhD, and it's free!

Tinyhabits.com

Want to learn some new strategies to build habits based on your personality and inclinations? Try Better Than Before by Gretchen Rubin. You can also learn all about your habit-building style at:

https://www.surveygizmo.com/s3/1950137/Four-Tendencies-January-2015

Curious about willpower, habit, and how they work together? Try *Willpower* by Roy F. Baumeister and John Tierney.

Combat resistance with *The War of Art* by Steven Pressfield.

Build a writing habit ASAP with inspiration from Dean Wesley Smith's blog at deanwesleysmith.com.

PRODUCTIVITY

No one knows more about insanely weird productivity hacks than Tim. Try *The 4-Hour Workweek* by Tim Ferriss.

Get my full Walk 'n Talk setup, my most optimal writing configuration that has produced 4000+ words per hour speeds, at:

proseonfire.com/dictation/.

TRACKING

Get my tracking spreadsheet completely free!

ProseOnFire.com/tracking

Use Trello to create a list view of your publishing progress. (It's free!)

Use Asana to keep track of all your to-dos. (It's free!)

Use MenuCountdown on Mac or e.ggtimer.com/ to keep track of your pomodoros.

MORE FROM MONICA

Looking to build an email list? Check out the easy-to-implement 3-step Email List-Building Framework (webinar replay):

ProseOnFire.com/3step

Trying to write a fiction book or books? You will probably love my First 5 Pages Scorecard, which helps you rate how effective your novel opening chapter is in hooking your readers. Perfect if you are trying to optimize your ebook sample! ProseOnFire.com/first1000

Want to get a list of EVERY tool I use for my business (including my full dictation setup, all the software I use, and more?) Get my Author Equipment List so you never need to search for the perfect tool again.

ProseOnFire.com/equipment

IF YOU ENJOYED THIS BOOK

If you enjoyed this book, there are two things you can do that will really help spread the word about it:

#1: YOU CAN WRITE A REVIEW

As an independent author, reviews are one of the most important ways I have to get the word out. Your review will encourage others to grab the book. You can share anything, but here are a few ideas:

- What you liked about the book
- What you didn't like about the book
- Your favorite chapter/part in the book
- Three things you are going to implement from the book
- The results you hope to get or have already gotten from the book

Go to ProseOnFire.com/pof1 if you want to leave a review and help others discover a new way to write!

Also, make sure you send it to me at monicaleonelle@ gmail.com (my personal email address) so I can thank you properly for your support.

When you do, also tell me a little about yourself (optional, of course). Perhaps name ONE thing you want to change about your writing process. I'd love to hear from you—my email pals often inspire blog posts, which I love to dedicate to them!

#2: YOU CAN TELL THREE AUTHORS YOU KNOW ABOUT THIS BOOK

There are probably a few author friends who could benefit from this information, right? Why not send them an email or text with the title of the book right now? Takes just a few seconds, and you can do it from your phone!

Email or Text: Check out Write Better, Faster, by Monica Leonelle on all retailers! I enjoyed it and thought you would too.

I greatly appreciate all your support! Please let me know if I'm able to help you with anything in the future: monicaleonelle@gmail.com.

Sign Up For More
Be the first to know about upcoming books.

ProseOnFire.com/Storytellers/

APPENDIX: LIFE OF A WRITER DIARY

The following is a diary i wrote from the last week in august 2013 to the end of october 2013. It's pulled straight from blog posts, so there are missing links, odd references, and every once in awhile, some wonky formatting. Still, i included it because i thought it might help others as either an example of what they could write about while tracking their progress, or as a place to glean insight from someone who has tried this before. Most of the lessons are tied up in a neat bow in the first half of this book, but many of them are demonstrated in the narrative in this diary.

If you want all the data from the experiment, it's right there in the diary, listed at the bottom of each entry.

The diary ends abruptly, so there's also a neat summary of what's happened with my writing since the experiment.

I hope the diary helps! Enjoy.

THE BEGINNING OF A MUCH NEEDED DAILY FICTION-WRITING HABIT (LIFE OF A WRITER: DAY 1)

This is a new series about the daily life of a writer from my perspective, inspired by Dean Wesley Smith's Writing in

Public series. I watched him do it all of August and realized that not only was the series incredibly motivating, but also that reading it had become a daily habit for me.

I admire both DWS and his wife, Kristine Kathryn Rusch. They've taught me a lot about the publishing industry from the perspective of mid-list, career writers. I'm both inspired by them and wanting to be more like them. Writers write. That's the lesson I've learned. But putting it into practice is not so easy.

This is my attempt to create a daily writing habit.

I was going to do a weekly post on what I'm working on, but I like the idea of the daily post a little more, even though it might seem repetitive and/or narcissistic for some people. I get that most people don't want a "What I ate today" version of my work schedule.

But whatever — just skip it if you're annoyed. Right now, I need the accountability. As Gretchen Rubin said, "What you do every day matters more than what you do once in a while." If I want to develop a habit of writing fiction every day, then I should be accountable every day too.

That's my primary reason for doing this series. But I also have other reasons.

Here's the second one: I currently have 3 "pilots" (first books in a series) out, and I'm getting more and more requests for the second one in each series every day. For one of my books, under a different pen name, I'm getting a near-daily request by email, review, or through comments on the blog. The pressure is on for getting it out, but actually, that's not my biggest concern.

My biggest concern is that I will always be playing catch up with fans. They will always be able to read faster than I can produce. So these requests will get more frequent and more urgent as my series grow. And I'd like a way for fans to know that, yes, I hear them, and yes, I'm working as hard as I can to get the next book out.

My third reason has to do with other writers. I have learned so much from hearing how other writers at all different skill levels work and have been able to adapt their work habits into my own process. Still, I'm doing things that no one else talks about, or at least not in the same way. So I'm putting this out there because it may help another writer with what they are struggling with, or with motivation, or with just getting the work done.

And finally, my fourth reason is to prove a point — that you can make money as a writer. I've shared in posts before that I mix freelance writing with fiction writing to make up the majority of my income. And while I'm not rich by any means, I am making actual money as a writer.

And that is an important message for people to hear.

THE CHALLENGE

The main challenge is to develop a daily writing habit; however, each month I'm going to set a monthly word count goal as well. For September, I want to hit at least 50,000 words of fiction, which is the same goal that NaNoWriMo sets for its participants. I feel that if a newbie writer can achieve that word count in a month, I should be able to as well.

50,000 words averages out to 1,667 words per day (for a 30-day month), which is a number that I can usually hit with 45 minutes to an hour worth of work — provided I actually sit down and do it. Frankly, that's the difficult part, and the part I need to work on.

Other than the monumental task of butt-in-chair, this goal should be easy for me. It's essentially a softball I'm tossing myself to set myself up for success. I would eventually like to hit 100k words per month and higher, but I'm not stupid enough to push myself that hard at first.

Also, I've already taken steps to improve my chances. For example, I've slowly weened myself off television by not letting myself watch before 5pm. I've weened myself down to two meals a day, no snacks, so I'm not obsessed with when I get to eat next. I've weened myself off of casual internet browsing by setting up a separate account on my computer with parental controls, locking me out of just about every program aside from Dropbox, Dragon Dictate, Scrivener, Evernote, and Excel, which are the five tools I use to write and track my fiction words.

Additionally, I've spent the last year preparing for this task. I've boosted my word count from around 700 words per hour to 3000+ words of hour (when I'm really in my flow zone). I've written four novels and published three and learned from the feedback. I've studied over 50 books about how to tell better stories and applied it to my writing process. I've refined my process, using productivity concepts like flow, passive barriers, and triggers to boost various metrics that I'm tracking.

I'm not saying any of this to brag. I'm just laying the groundwork for both my process and my approach. I'll touch on more details about these topics as the series continues, so if you're curious about what all of this means, keep reading.

Here is my first day of work. My challenge is actually starting on September 1st, but I'm doing a warm up week to ingrain the habit early.

8:30 am -

Sat down at the computer after getting up and showered. I usually wake up around 7:00 am and spend a few hours moseying around in bed, reading on my Kindle or checking various things like email and blogs on my iPad. I typically don't get up until after P leaves for work, but today is Sunday and I was extra excited for a book I wrote beats for yesterday.

The book is under a pen name, it's the third in a series, and I haven't finished edits on #2 yet, so the only one published is #1. Weird, I know. I'm the type of person who loves to work in bursts of energy but can lose interest quickly, so I've found that the best way to keep working is to have tons of projects going at once. That way, I can work on the one that's most interesting to me at the moment and go until I'm tired or bored, then switch to another one, which suddenly looks fresh and fun again.

Anyway, I honestly haven't written a first draft in awhile. I probably haven't put new words on screen in a few weeks, and I haven't drafted something new in months. (Unacceptable, hence, why I'm starting this challenge.) I could tell that I was out of practice because I felt tons of anxiety as I sat down at my computer.

Luckily, I had already prepared for that fear I was feeling. My laptop was already set to my writing account, with all the files up and ready to go.

BUT... I still felt a ton of resistance. I decided to go make tea before I wrote. I left a red cup full of tea on P's nightstand and made two mugs for myself. I sat back down at the computer.

Then, I realized that because I don't have internet under my new account, I couldn't update my spreadsheet where

I track my word count. That uses Google Spreadsheet, and I couldn't access Drive. So I opened up Excel and created a new spreadsheet, which took another 20 minutes or so.

Finally, around 9:25 am, I was all set up and ready to write. You know how people say the hardest thing about getting something done is starting? I have a trick for getting started on anything I'm nervous about doing: I tell myself I'm going to do one Pomodoro of it, and then if I hate it, I can quit.

So I set my timer for 25 minutes and took off, dictating my first scene via Dragon Dictate, using beats that I wrote yesterday. After 25 minutes, I was feeling okay but still wanted a break. Got 897 words done, for an average of 2150 words/hour.

Not terrible, but certainly not my best. I'm hoping that in the weeks to come, my times improve. But, I can't really beat myself up about it because 897 words is more fiction than I've written in the last two weeks.

Also, it probably seems a little crazy that it took me nearly an hour to prepare for a 25 minute writing session. That's due to lack of practice. Think of it as if you were training for a marathon, but you hadn't gone jogging in 6 months. You're not going to go balls-to-the-wall on your first run, are you? You're going to take a nice and slow jog and try to hit 2 miles without keeling over.

That's how this challenge feels to me. Fear, anxiety, and the lizard brain are real. I've budgeted time to contend with them every day because I know they are my biggest enemies. I also know from experience that they get easier to contend with over time, though they never truly go away.

10:00 am-ish -

The family is stirring, and by that I mean P and our westie. They love to sleep in together, but usually start getting out of bed between 9-10 am. The westie needs to be walked and fed, so I get up from my desk to take care of her. Then, I'm starving, and I hate working while I'm starving, so I warm up my first of two meals for the day, which is leftover takeout. I also talk to P for a little while and deal with some email and internet stuff on my non-writing account.

11:50 am -

I finally stumble back to my writing account a little before noon. I set my timer for 45 minutes and take off again. Why 45 minutes? Because it's a little longer than 25 minutes, and I'm trying to build stamina.

Somewhere in the middle of my writing session, P turns on the TV for the St. Louis Cards game, which completely throws me off. I spend a few minutes searching for headphones and cursing the lack of a door on our office (the perils of living in a one-bedroom + den in downtown Chicago) before getting back to it.

My timer buzzes, but I still have more of the scene to go. My scenes for this series tend to be between 3000-5000 words, which is different from my Socialpunk and Waters Dark and Deep books. Those are typically 1500-2500 word scenes. I have not a single explanation for this.

So, I wanted to stop at the buzzer, but I was decently close to the end, so I kept going. Then, I wanted to stop again when I only had 4 beats left, but I forced myself to finish those too. I completed the scene at 3455 words, clocking in at 1:10 pm, for an average of 1919 words per hour.

I was pretty fried at this point, but happy that I got the first scene done, since it is 1/8th of the total book. I have no idea how it turned out since I don't re-read until the whole thing is ready, but I thought it was a decent rough sketch of what I want the scene to look like. My guess is that I'll add 500-1000 more words to it in my rewrite/edit, so I'm pretty happy with the progress.

1:30 pm -

I came out to watch the Cards game with P. We are both sitting on opposite ends of our couch, on our computers, with the westie sleeping between us. This is a typical configuration for us, and the game makes for good background noise, as long as it's not too loud (I have some sensory perception sensitivities, and baseball games, with the cheering crowd track on, are one of the many social gatherings that trigger my issues). P knows this and lowers the volume when I come into the room.

I play Candy Crush Saga on my iPad for a little bit and check the internet again, including my email and my sales metrics. I also write this post, up until the words you are reading right now.

3:45 pm -

I am still recovering from my writing session and I don't want to push myself on my first day back to the grind, so I switch gears and decide to work on beats for both Unbound and Trinity, which are the second and third books in the Waters Dark and Deep series, respectively. #2 in this series only has a few more scenes to beat out and draft, and #3 is mostly beat out, aside from about half of Kennedy's scenes (she has 12 total). I get all of Unbound beat out, but P gets hungry so we take some time to order dinner.

(By the way, I know that the phrase "beat out" sounds totally inappropriate, but I'm still going to use it. Get your minds out of the gutter!)

5:15 pm -

We get our Chinese and proceed to eat it over a new episode of The Newsroom. Hey, it's after 5pm!

(You're probably asking, doesn't the Cards game break the rules? I don't count it since I'm not actively watching it and it's mostly P's show and background noise for me. I only count TV that has a storyline that I keep up with.)

7:15 pm -

Got back to my desk after dinner and a long walk with P and the westie. I'm ready to do another round of writing, though I have to admit I'm not as excited to write as I was this morning. I equate this to exercise, where motivation to stick to your plan dwindles after the first few gym sessions. Still, I know that while I'm writing, things will feel awesome. I know this.

I still want to get two more sessions in, but I'm not sure how realistic it is at this point in the day. I decided that my waning excitement for writing can be fixed by choosing scenes that I'm really, really excited to write. I choose some Trinity scenes from Rykken's POV.

It took me about 20 minutes to switch accounts and get everything loaded up before I start. This time, I don't bother setting a timer to get myself started. I just start writing and figure I'll stop whenever I get tired of writing in Rykken's voice.

9:30 pm -

I finish up another two rounds of writing with the following stats:

7:35pm-8:25pm - 50 minutes - 1931 words - 2317 word/hour avg.

8:40pm-9:28pm - 48 minutes - 1782 words - 2228 word/hour avg.

Oddly enough, my scenes were nearly the same length (only 150 words apart) and took nearly the same amount of time to write.

I decided to take a longer 30 minute break with the full intention of going back doing another few scenes, since I felt pretty good about what I'd written so far. But when I got back, I looked through the rest of my Rykken scenes and realized I had several half-completed ones. So I decided to quit for the night and instead focus my energy on cleaning up and finishing up some of the scenes I already have 700 or 800 words for, since that will get me closer to finishing up this manuscript.

I also still need to beat out the last 6 Kennedy scenes, so that might be something else to do to kill time tonight.

In total, I've written 7168 new fiction words today, which is not bad at all for a first day back. I had wanted to go really easy today and not push myself aside from the initial fear (if you'll remember at the beginning of the post, it took me nearly an hour of rituals to start writing again).

(I've also technically written just over 3k words in this blog post. So actually, an over 10k day. But... I'm not counting it. It feels like cheating. So we're just going to go with 7k+.)

I'm still not anywhere near where I want to be for words/hour avg., but I did seem to go up a bit in the two evening sessions. I'm hoping that my word count/hour improves significantly over the next few weeks, as I practice and get into the groove. At my peak, I've hit 3600+ words/hour using Dragon Dictate and an outline. So even though 2000-ish words/hour is awesome and much higher than most people, even professional writers, can do, I know I can go a lot harder when I'm in the right mindset.

Also, I know there will be writers out there who want to strangle me for saying that 7000+ words is an easy day of writing. But for me, it felt really easy. I did four short sessions of writing that only totaled 203 minutes. That's less than 3 1/2 hours of actual, clocked work. In other words, Kindergarteners have longer work days than I did today.

Now, granted, most writers aren't going to achieve those averages just starting out, but as I've said, I have spent a ton of time trying to optimize both my word count/hour and my novel-writing process, so I've laid a good foundation for this type of result.

10:30pm -

I go back to the living room and log into my non-writing account to enjoy the internet for a bit. I record my sales numbers for the day, clean out my inboxes, and finish up this post. And by the end of that, P wants to go to bed, so I decide to just call it for the night without working on any more Rykken scenes.

I'm pretty happy with what I've accomplished today, even though I only finished 3 scenes total. I'm trying to be okay with the idea that a little every day is better than a lot all at once, since it's obvious that I burn myself out by pushing the limits of what should be humanly possible in a short amount of time.

Off to bed now... I am reading *The Beam* by Sean Platt and Johnny B. Truant. Really enjoying it so far!

AT ABOUT 10% OF YESTERDAY (LIFE OF A WRITER: DAY 2)

8:00 am -

Got out of bed, showered, dressed. The westie was up so I took care of her with a walk and feeding. I made some tea in hopes that I could get to my computer and start by 9.

When I delivered the tea to P in bed, we started talking about scheduling for this week because we're going to a wedding out-of-town, and there is a ton that needs to happen before that. I had planned to leave this task for later on today, but P had a lot of questions, and I tend to get anxiety over this type of stuff, so I figured why not just get it out of the way so I can free up my mind to write?

Took care of all this, did laundry, got some food, etc. It's amazing how long these little things take.

10:30 am-ish -

Finally back to the computer under my writing account. Today has convinced me that my warm-up pomodoro should be the first thing I do in the morning, before getting roped into all this other stuff. Because then, if the day gets away from me, I've at least gotten some words in.

I picked the Prologue of Unbound, which is from Kennedy's POV. I had visualized the scene in my mind back when I beat it out originally, so I figured it would be an easy get for the morning.

But... I wrote for 30 minutes and got down 719 words, which is absolutely poking along for me. Poking almost always means I don't know what is happening in the scene, even though I had it beaten out. Then it hit me—this scene has a lot of Nephilim world-building, which I haven't done much of yet in my series.

Bleh, I hate poking along. I especially hate it this morning because I wanted to see improved numbers over yesterday. Oh well.

I set the scene aside and probably won't get back to it until later today or tomorrow, in the hopes that my subconscious will do the world-building I need it to.

I need a change of scenery after warm-up and head out into our bookshelf room, which is supposed to be a dining room but isn't because it doesn't have a dining room table. It has lots and lots of books arranged neatly on shelves, and two recliners. I put the westie on one and get settled in the other, then eek out a ton of emails, dealing with freelance client stuff and planning for the wedding we're going to. Coordination is one of my biggest time wasters and least favorite things to do, in general.

1:15 pm -

I look at my fiction to-do list and prioritize a few things that would make me feel like I made progress today (since the day isn't looking particularly productive so far). I decide on 3 priorities:

Finishing up the last beats on Trinity, which will free me up to start beats on the 4th book, Fallen, and also allow me to write the main story of Trinity, which is all from Kennedy's and Thessa's POVs. Kennedy's sections are hard, so I'm not even going to attempt those scenes without knowing where everything is going.

Some clean up on book #2 of my series under a pen name. The draft has been done for awhile but there are some pesky continuity issues that I need to fix before editing.

Drafting up the last few scenes on Unbound, since that will put it into edits as well. These scenes are mostly from Pilot's perspective, and also require world-building, so it might be more of a world-building day than a fast drafting day.

At this point, I honestly don't expect to beat my word count from yesterday, so it feels like a good day to do beating and continuity stuff instead. The continuity will still require writing, but I probably won't keep track of my time, just my word count for these.

Also, to be clear, this isn't my to-do list for the day. Some of it may run into tomorrow or the next, especially if I get really bored or stuck on it. And especially if I start momentarily hating it.

I know a lot of people don't get why I think like this. They think, "push through on the top things on your priority list first. You have to force yourself to do things you hate sometimes."

I honestly don't understand how people live like that, but then, a lot of people hate their jobs and lives because they are unaligned, so it's not completely surprising.

My thought process is: There's not much point in trying to do creative work when you are really hating your story or the task at hand because you are going to go insanely slow at it. Your time will be spent inefficiently. Also, the work is likely going to suck, the same way a run would produce poor results if you were deathly ill and completely out of energy.

To me, it's more efficient to shift gears, make progress on something enjoyable and energizing, then come back to the task with a fresh perspective. Neil Gaiman has a post on this (you have to scroll down to "I blew a deadline recently.") that can maybe explain this phenomenon more elegantly than I can.

10:15 pm -

The day has passed in a complete blur, with little more fiction-writing getting done. I doubt I'm going to get any more in today, aside from some edits I want to finish.

What I did get done during the time period (aside from eating dinner, hanging out with P, doing chores, watching TV, and taking care of my dog) was figuring out the rest of Trinity with beats. I could tell the book was missing something... and wow. What ended up happening was a new storyline that really amps up the whole series to thriller status. Kennedy's character has taken on a life of her own, which both excites me and scares the shit out of me!

So now that there are some big revelations in book 3, I have to consider my plans for books 4 & 5 moving forward. Because the bottom line is, I still have to get to the same place by the end of book 5. The ending can't change. But while I was only going to use Kennedy as a viewpoint character for book 3, I definitely think she might have more story to tell... not sure how to resolve it all just yet.

I also wonder how people will receive her if she becomes too much of a main character. My friend and critique partner, Susan, really likes Kennedy. So do I. But is she a worthy supporting lead? So hard to say. The reality is that I need to take another look at Fallen and Hellfire to make sure I'm tying up loose ends that I've opened in book 3.

Seriously, great fun though.

I'm off to take care of some more client work and chores that need to get done before our cleaning lady comes tomorrow.

1:00 am -

I never go to bed this late. I shipped off a few articles of the 18 (!!!) that I need to send out this week for clients. Now that I've counted them up, I probably need to step up production. I won't make it at this rate.

I'm hoping that tomorrow is much more productive than today was. I read somewhere that Mondays are when you create your to-do list and Tuesdays are when you crank through it... here's to looking at an awesome Tuesday of writing!

Challenge: Develop a Daily Fiction Writing Habit

Today: 719 words

This week: 7887 words

MY SYSTEM FOR GETTING ENOUGH FREELANCE WRITING IN (LIFE OF A WRITER: DAY 3)

9:30 am -

I got up at my normal time and took care of the usual chores with the westie. I also prepped the apartment for our cleaning lady. I am supposed to be out of the apartment by 10 am on cleaning days, but I really wanted to get my pomodoro in before I left, using my mic and Dragon Dictate.

At 10 am, I had clocked 25 minutes with 807 new words completed for an average of 1937 words/hour. Still not where I want to be (my first day I was at 2150 words/ hour) but better than yesterday (1438 words/hour).

I packed my stuff and headed down to the local Barnes and Noble where I quickly cranked out the rest of the scene, using the keyboard input. This gave me an additional 1024 words by 11am (1617 words/hour), which is my fast rate when I'm typing.

My total so far for today is 1831 words. The prologue for Unbound turned out much longer than I had originally thought, clocking in at 2550 words. I'm excited to have it done, because I've wanted to start Serialization Saturday on Wattpad, and now I finally have the prologue and first 12 chapters or so of Unbound to post, one section each week.

So, if you'd like to read the prologue I've just finished today, come back on Saturday when I'll share it on Wattpad.

On a side note, my Dragon Dictate speeds are always much better than my keyboard speeds for two reasons:

I can talk faster than I can type (almost everyone can; the average speaking speed is 150 wpm and the average typing speed is 40 wpm)

Speaking my book helps me separate my writing process from my editing process a bit better, which helps me zip along.

I also try to divide my use of keyboard input and microphone input to avoid injury to either my voice or my hands. I experience sore wrists and fingers after only 3-4 days of major writing (7.5k+ words), so I'm pretty diligent about this. I'm only 29 and I do NOT want to ruin my hands. I try to give them tons of breaks while still getting my work done.

It's a little after 11am now, and I'm a bit hungry, but I'll probably wait until noon and walk back home to eat. In the meantime, I think I'm going to continue to hack away at my fiction priorities from yesterday:

- Some clean up on book #2 of my series under a pen name.
- Drafting up the last few scenes on Unbound, since that will put it into edits as well. These are scenes from Pilot's perspective.

I also have TONS of freelance articles to ship. This is probably a great time to tell you about how I handle freelance work. I am a bit more strict about it in the sense that I have a set expected $$$ goal that I try to ship each week. This comes in the form of:

- Work booked from existing clients
- Work that I find from new clients
- Spec or submission non-fiction work

How this works: let's say I want to make $1000/week from freelance writing. I look at the work I have booked for the week and assign it a value of 100% chance I will get paid for it. Since I drop clients pretty quickly if they don't pay me on time, this is a good estimate. In other words, these are repeat clients who have historically paid me at my usual rate of $0.10/word, on time.

So if I have $500 booked, I subtract $500 from my weekly goal (because $500 * 100% = $500). Now I need to find $500 more for the week.

Depending on what's going on, I either apply to jobs on Craigslist, elance, etc. (only accepting my usual rate, not dropping it for whatever crap pay I can get) or I email past clients to see where they are at and keep myself top-of-mind. I have also done some outbound marketing in the past, though this hasn't really paid off for me. (Which is not to say it doesn't work, just that it hasn't worked in my limited experience, using whatever copy I've emailed.)

Okay, so honestly, often, this turns up nothing or not much. It may turn up something down the road, and it usually does—but it rarely turns up something to satisfy my requirements for that week. I do this step because if I'm not naturally booking my $$$ goal every week, it means I need to do more marketing, plain and simple.

After this, I move on to spec or submission work. Almost all writers in the publishing industry, particularly the fiction publishing industry, work on spec. Think about it—you write your novel, then you try to convince someone to buy it. You write your short story, then you convince someone to buy it. Etc.

Now, we live in a world where you can do those things, and if it doesn't sell, you can put it on Amazon yourself. But it's spec work there too, because now instead of trying to convince one person to buy it for a lot of money, you're trying to convince thousands of people to buy it for a little money.

There is a smaller market like this for non-fiction work. But, like the fiction world, there is no guarantee that your work will get accepted. However, if you're a pretty good writer, the acceptance rate is a lot higher than fiction and the pay is often better too.

You can find an awesome list of links to this world of non-fiction spec writing on the Make a Living Writing website, and my post on how writers need to diversify their incomes may help too.

I use this to fill out my weekly $$$ goal and hopefully convert spec opportunities into client opportunities. For now, I'm pretty confident with my writing abilities, so I assign spec opportunities with a value of 60% chance I will get paid for it.

That means, in my fake scenario above, that I need to write another $833 worth of spec non-fiction this week ($1000 goal - $500 booked work = $500 left to cover; $500/60% = $833). $833 worth of spec work has an expected value of roughly $500.

Sorry for the math lesson. I just think it's important to spell all of this out because there are so many people who think they can't make consistent money as a writer. What they really mean is that they don't have a good system for figuring out how to translate what they need to make to survive into a week-by-week to-do list.

In this scenario, it would take me probably 5 extra articles on top of whatever I've already booked to hit the $1000 goal. (This is because I don't write spec articles for sites that pay less than $100 per article or $0.10/word.) I would write these knowing that some of them might not be accepted, and I would do whatever I could to:

- convert these spec opportunities to client opportunities, where the editor assigns me posts (guaranteed pay for less work)
- improve my expected value assignment by getting conversions up from 60% (also less work)

You can assign whatever expected values you need to implement this system for yourself. The most important thing is that you translate $$$ into tasks, which will make your life so much easier because you can CONTROL what you do on a day-to-day basis.

By the way, this concept is not at all my idea; it's sales 101. Sales seems like a risky business to outsiders, but it's not. Salespeople know what their conversion rate is and translate it back into work. That's why you'll hear, say, a real estate agent say that she needs to book 20 showings a week. She knows that when she does her 20 showings each week, she sells 3 houses a month.

Second, this has nothing to do with cash flow. That's a totally separate topic. Because writers get paid at very weird times and you're always trying to earn money that you may not receive for 2-3 months. This is more about taking a big, big picture and breaking it down to week-by-week, "this is what I must do." Doing things this way should help you hit say, a yearly or a quarterly financial goal, because the risk is spread out over time, but it's not necessarily going to get you a consistent weekly paycheck.

Cash flow is really important for the whole "paying your bills on time" thing. This system doesn't necessarily help you with that, though it points you in the right direction.

Also, you can use this same exact concept to set your fiction-writing goals. I'm not going to run through it right now, because it's nearing noon and I'm getting hungry. But, the concept is the same as above. You have work-for-hire projects, spec projects, and self-publishing projects. You can research the average amounts paid, assign the expected values, and do the math on your own. (At some point, I'll probably break down my math for this, but not today.)

Lastly, I know that the idea of spec work sucks. Writers are more accustomed to it than designers (who throw a hissy fit at the thought of it, usually), but the reality is that all freelance positions are moving more toward this model. More and more, the risk is on the creator to produce something that people want. And you'll have internet marketers tell you that it's not true, you can take money for something before you launch it, but that has its downsides too... primarily, that you have to toil away in freeville for one or two years building an audience to pre-launch to, first.

The way I make myself feel better about the idea of spec work is by creating articles or fiction projects that, even if they aren't accepted, could at least find a home online as part of a paid ebook or other project. I also try to write things I enjoy, that are related to topics I already write about. You'll have to find what works for you, but once you get over this mental hurdle toward spec work, it's a lot easier to earn money as a writer.

10:30 pm -

Wow, the day really got messed up after I got home. There is no other phrase for it. Instead of having a calm day of freelance work and fiction writing, I had mess after mess to deal with.

Which brings me to one of the many downsides of this business: it's a lot easier to get derailed by personal crap than it is when you have an office job.

The nice thing about having to go into work every day is that when you have personal crap, you still have to be at the office and you are surrounded by people who force you to suck everything up and get work done anyway. No, you aren't super productive, but peer pressure forces you to be at least a little productive.

With freelancing/writing, this just doesn't happen. I'm completely bummed that personal crap took over the rest of my day. I'll be looking for better ways to handle this in the future.

Tomorrow the westie has a vet appointment in the morning and I have a writer meeting with Susan, which I'm really looking forward to. Susan is pretty good about getting me back on track with fiction, because we renew each other's energy for our projects.

I also need to catch up on freelance writing tomorrow, because I'm behind. I'm guessing I won't have a big day of fiction tomorrow and will be lucky to get a few thousand words again.

Challenge: Develop a Daily Fiction Writing Habit

Today: 1831 words

This week: 9718 words

As disappointed as I am about progress on the last two days of fiction writing, I'm pleased that I've gotten close to 10k words down this week so far, despite myself. This is definitely not the norm for me. So even though I'm not pulling 10k words every day (yet!), I'm still happy about the challenge and grateful for my progress. Running the numbers is forcing me to make sure I get in at least a little each day, and also examine where my roadblocks are in a really painful, public way.

And hopefully that helps me improve my performance, deal with my crap, and get aligned with my goals.

Still glad this is a practice week though. I've gotten to the halfway point and I think I should set a goal of 20k fiction words before Sept 1st, just to keep me motivated—which means I have 4 days to get another 10k. With the wedding trip this weekend, it'll be difficult to hit this, but it's a stretch goal. And then, I'll be ready for September's challenge.

A LONG DAY WITH NO FICTION! (LIFE OF A WRITER: DAY 4)

9:00 pm -

It's been a long day and the last thing I want to do is keep working. I woke up at 8 am and posted something for Work-In-Progress Wednesday, then got ready for the westie's vet appointment. That went until noon, and after a quick lunch, I hopped on a call with Susan for a story meeting.

We had a ton of fun chatting and also figured out some preliminary details of our first collaboration, which we're hoping to have out sometime next year.

I'm really excited—when I first started writing fiction, I really didn't think I would ever collaborate with another writer. I never thought I'd be able to let go of the story enough, and I definitely didn't understand how two people write one thing. I mean, do they write over each other? Do they divide it up? How do they keep the story straight?

But one of The Self-Publishing Podcasts encouraged me to consider and pursue the idea, and so far it's going better than I thought it would. Of course, Susan and I have been working together for a solid 1.5 years on writing projects, and we've been meeting weekly for 4-5 months now, so we know our styles, our strengths, our weaknesses. That makes it easier. Still, it should be an interesting mix, considering I'm heavy on the fantasy and sci-fi and she's more of a literary writer!

(By the way, I'm linking to the Self-Publishing Podcast about collaborating with other writers, but be warned that this podcast is NSFW and that it takes awhile to get into. The first time I watched the show, it seemed a lot like a few dudes talking about their projects for an hour. BUT, I stuck with it and now it's one of the highlights of my week. So I highly recommend the podcast, but try a few episodes before making a decision one way or another.)

Our meeting ended around five and then I did my afternoon routine: taking the westie for a walk, eating dinner with P over an episode of TV, journaling and working through challenges, and hanging out and wasting some time.

We accidentally watched the first two episodes of Mad Men Season 6, so it took waaay longer than usual. (By the way... so far, I really wish the show had just ended at Season 5. The last episode in that season would have actually made an amazing ending to the show. Not sure if I was just antsy to get back to work, but I was finding it hard to give a damn about a single one of the irredeemable characters in this drama.)

So, now I'm back to my computer, finally. I desperately want to write fiction but I have an insane amount of freelance work to do, and I'm afraid starting fiction will make that work harder. I'm really looking forward to getting back to my normal routine tomorrow... I haven't had tea in two days.

1 am -

I'm exhausted. I cranked out two articles and it's time for bed. I wanted to get at least one pomodoro in at the end of the night, but I just can't.

While writing the articles, I got really distracted for a new idea I have for a series. I both love and hate it when this happens, because the idea takes hold of me and I HAVE to get a sense for it right away. It preoccupies my brain for hours, even when my brain needs to be doing something else.

But, this awesome new idea will be so fun to write, whenever I finally get around to it! (And whenever I finally get some of the current stuff off my plate, because it's just cruel to keep starting series and never finishing them.)

So, it's been a productive day, but not in the way that I wanted it to be. That's to be expected, I guess, with the majority of my morning and afternoon at appointments. Either way, tomorrow is a big catch up day because my end-of-the-week freelance writing deadlines are looming and I must hit those. Luckily, I will be home and have the day to myself.

Challenge: Develop a Daily Fiction Writing Habit

Today: ZERO (it hurts to type that!)

This week: 9718 words

BACK TO MY NORMAL SCHEDULE, BUT CATCHING UP ON FREELANCE WORK (LIFE OF A WRITER: DAY 5)

11 am -

I am so happy this morning. I have my tea, I had a snack, I'm at home with my dog with the entire day in front of me. I slept in for some much needed rest after the last few days. I spent the morning journaling my frustrations and noticed some patterns that I want to get to later in this post (edit at 1:30am: in tomorrow's post). But first, I'm off to get my fiction writing in for the day. Adios.

5:30 pm -

I've gotten four writing sessions in over the past few hours, in between a lot of breaks for cleaning, chores, email, etc. Started out at 1896 words/hour and increased to around 2450 words/hour in the last two sessions, for a total word count of 4871 words. This writing thing is definitely getting easier, and my writing rate is progressing nicely upward without feeling like I'm straining in any way to get the words done faster. I think it'll still be a few weeks until I'm hitting 3000+ words/hour, but I'm building up to it, which is exciting.

In those 4 sessions, I finished three more chapters of Unbound. Only two chapters to go. Hopefully, I'll get to them tonight, but the reality is I have to finish up some freelance work that is due tomorrow first, so that'll be the priority.

I'm off to take out the westie and when I get back, I'm going to switch over to my non-writing account and deal with email, freelance work, and everything else I've been ignoring for most of the day. Susan and I are meeting nightly now to write together, so I'm hoping during our session to get through some of the continuity stuff from the other manuscript under my pen name, which is so close to being in edits.

It'll be another busy night. But with me leaving tomorrow, I don't want to leave any freelance work undone. I'd like to take the morning and early afternoon to get my word counts in, since I'll be on a train most of the evening.

I should admit that I broke my rule and watched a 42 minute show while I was eating lunch today. I realized that the alternative was switching from my writing account to my non-writing account while I ate, which could easily devolve into never switching back. This is part of what happened on Tuesday when I wasted a good chunk of my day on stupid crap.

So I might start watching TV on my lunch break, only one episode, and only on days when I'm working from home. But I might try to find a good 22 minute show instead, since that's about how long it takes me to eat, and why distract myself longer than I need to?

11:15 pm -

I had a productive writing session with Susan that lasted about two and a half hours. I ended up working on client work instead of my manuscript because I have so much due, and I can work on the manuscript tomorrow on the train (no internet access required). The good news is that I've cranked out four more articles and have a good amount of energy left. I still want to get two more articles done if possible, plus my two scenes if I have any energy left after that.

It's another long night for me, but I'm traveling tomorrow and have plenty of errands that will soak up my time before I get on my train. I want to have as much done and shipped as possible so I can focus on fiction between my traveling preparations. I hate feeling the pressure of deadlines and it's easier just to get it done before I leave rather than scramble at the last minute.

1:20 am -

I completed the articles and I'm headed to bed. I still have a bit of energy left for fiction writing, and I contemplated trying to get in at least one last pomodoro before bed and seeing how it went from there, but 1am is too late for me. I'm getting way off my sleep schedule with this challenge, and that's not going to work long term, because I've very protective of my relationship with

P and I don't believe in going to sleep at separate times on a regular basis. So I'm calling it quits.

Challenge: Develop a Daily Fiction Writing Habit

Today: 4871 words

This week: 14,589 words

That means I have 5,411 words left to go if I want to hit my goal of 20k words before week's end. It will be a challenge to get this in before I leave tomorrow, but I'm hoping to take a chunk out of it at least. Then, I can finish it on Saturday morning if absolutely necessary.

I'm really surprised that I've been able to hit this fiction goal with honestly, very little effort compared to what I thought it would take. Today, for example, I only worked 123 minutes on fiction, which is hardly a tough day of writing. Yesterday I wrote zero and the two days before that, I had fewer than 2000 words each. This challenge is making me realize what's possible.

If I were to do 20k words of fiction per week, for example, I'd easily hit 80k for the month, which is significantly more words than my original September goal of 50k words for the month.

But even then, I feel like 20k words is too... easy. I feel like I've completely slacked off this week, and if I could just tune up my productivity each day, plus increase my word count/hour, I could pretty quickly double this amount. Per week. That's astounding to me.

Of course, I won't have any definitive answers until I try. But I'm excited for the possibilities, especially since I've seen my productivity skyrocket with non-fiction just through sheer practice at cranking out articles. It has to be possible with fiction too. It has to be.

See you tomorrow!

SLEEPY BUT PUSHING THROUGH END-OF-THE-WEEK WORK (LIFE OF A WRITER: DAY 6)

9:30 am -

I've very, very sleepy. The problem is I wake up between 6 - 7 am every day, no matter when I fall asleep. I wake up with the sun, which is wonderful, except when it isn't. So going to bed at 1:30 am gives me only about 5 or 6 hours.

This weekend isn't going to do me many favors in the sleep department, but I'm hoping that by Sunday night I can get back to my 10:30 pm bedtime. I miss reading a few chapters of fiction before bed. I want my routine back!

Starting on my fiction writing. I'll get a few sessions in, finish up some last minute freelance work, do some preparation for my trip tonight, and hopefully get a few more sessions in before I get on the train. That's the plan at least. We'll see if a nap derails it all!

12:45 pm -

I'm back from a long lunch with P. So far, I've done one session and gotten the next scene of Unbound completed. 2133 words at about 1729 words/hour. Not a great time, but not terrible, considering that P is working from home today and kept coming into the office to ask me questions. He also had a meeting via Google Hangout in the living room, which completely broke my concentration for several minutes. Things are a bit scattered in our household today, since we're both trying to wrap everything up before getting on the train tonight.

P has another meeting in about 45 minutes, so I'm going to get another writing session in, then start my last minute freelance work during his meeting.

1:51 pm -

Done with the first draft of Unbound! I'm really excited. There are still a few rounds of editing to get done, but I'm pretty happy with how things turned out for the book. Plus, I now have two things to work on on the train this evening, this, and the other manuscript.

My next bout of fiction will be on Trinity and the third book in my other series under the pen name. I'm a bit more excited about Trinity right now, so I'll probably get back to that first.

11:30 ish -

On the train! So relieved. I did NOT get those last two articles completed before getting on the train. I got home after dropping the westie off at boarding, sat down on the couch, tried to work, and fell asleep instead.

I finished the articles up on the train and sent them off to hit the deadline. Trains have wi-fi now, by the way. Signal was excellent almost the whole way there.

In between writing the articles, I read a book called Over the Edge that Susan recommended to me. Pretty good! And fast-paced. I don't typically read thrillers, but I like that they move along at a nice clip.

I'm trying to get back to loving reading, but wow, being a writer has messed me up there. No matter what, I always find myself with an editor hat on, critiquing how I would change this or that. Do other writers feel this way? I think being the one in charge of every little decision in my books makes it difficult for me to turn the reigns over for other books.

12:30 -

At the hotel, ready for bed. (Past ready for bed.) Did not get in any additional fiction today on the train, though I didn't expect to. Unfortunately, I also did not get into editing mode on my books... so I will have to step that up on Sunday's train ride.

Tomorrow or Sunday, I want to do a wrap-up of my first week before going on to September goals.

Challenge: Develop a Daily Fiction Writing Habit

Today: 3334 words

This week: 17,923 words

A little over 2,000 words left to go... round up? Just kidding. I'll have to pick up a new scene or two in Trinity tomorrow to make the goal, but for now, it's beyond bedtime.

Again, watching these numbers makes me feel like a complete slacker. It's awesome to see how quickly they add up, but all I can think is, if I just applied myself each day... could I double, triple, quadruple what I'm doing now?

It's clear that a 50k goal for Sept. is too easy. At this pace (which again, was surprisingly easy for me this week since I only spent 1-3 hours getting my words in each day), I would already have an 80k word count for one month. That's a novel (or almost two for me with the way my books are structured). A challenge is supposed to push you, right?

I'm torn. I would like to see myself keep this pace for a few more weeks before committing to it... then again, now that I know what's possible, shouldn't I commit and push myself a little? Will decide when I can form a complete sentence again. (Note that the last one wasn't.)

HAPPY WEDDING DAY! (LIFE OF A WRITER: DAY 7)

9 am -

I don't expect to get much writing done today because one of my best friends from college is getting married! We are here in St. Louis to celebrate with her. Fun!

Since there won't be much updating today, I thought it might be a good time to talk about productivity and pattern matching. Keeping this record of my daily output has been eye-opening and helpful in identifying major problems in my work day. Keeping this record publicly has forced me to push myself a little more each day, because I don't want to look like a loser-idiot who can't get things done.

In examining my record over the last few days, there are some things I've noticed:

1. SCHEDULING

On days where I get my fiction writing in early, I'm really happy and much more productive for the rest of the day.

I seem to prefer getting fiction done in the morning and in the evening. I'm ready to stop writing fiction by about noon so I can grab lunch, and I don't seem to get back to it until later that evening, 6-or-7-ish, if I do get back to it.

I have no idea if these blocks of time are optimal for writing fiction, but I'm curious what protecting them would do for my output. (By protecting them, I mean, saying that I will not do any other work except fiction then.)

I also wonder what would happen if I actually got out of bed when I wake up and started right away. I don't seem to get to writing until 9:30, at the earliest. I'm wondering what I could accomplish if I pushed that time up.

Working to this schedule would leave me with a set morning of sessions and a mostly set evening of sessions. I know that sometimes I will not be able to do the evening sessions due to plans with P or other people.

It would also leave me with the afternoons to get my freelance work done. Although I hit all my deadlines this week, I didn't get to my spec work, which is kind of a problem. I can't let that keep happening. But I get the sense that right now, my afternoons are full of empty crap and goofing off. So I would need to buckle down big-time during the afternoons to stick to this schedule.

A BIG part of the "afternoon of crap" problem might be because I switch over to my non-writing computer account during lunch. I had been doing this because I wasn't watching TV until after 5, but now I'm thinking that's a mistake. I have two accounts to make use of passive barriers (definition: something, like closing out all your programs and switching user accounts on your computer, is so much work that you decide not to do it when you get the urge). When I get the urge to check internet under my writing account, I know that I would have to switch, and it stops me.

The problem is, while having a writing account creates an awesome passive barrier to me checking the internet while I'm on the account, it also creates a passive barrier when I'm in the non-writing account, in that I don't want to switch back to the writing account because I'm waiting on this email or I need the internet for research, etc.

Then it's five hours later and I've derailed myself.

So, I'm wondering if a TV break would work instead... of course, that can easily get way out of control for me too. I love TV, that's why I was avoiding it in the first place.

The real problem is, I need to get shit done in the afternoon, in the 1pm-5pm time block. That's the bottom line. My freelance work tends to flow into the evenings, and that is lazy. So next week, I'll try to figure out how to make afternoons = freelance work, because I have a feeling that when I solve that problem, everything around it will fall into place.

The other thing I need to balance is taking shorter breaks between sessions. For example, on 8/29, I end a scene at 1:22pm and don't start the next one until 3:40pm. (!!!)

What was I doing for over 2 hours in-between? I know I wasn't eating lunch. I know I wasn't working on something else for a client. And if I had been writing during that time, I would have gotten another 2 sessions in, and probably another 3000-4000 words.

When I'm in fiction writing mode, I need to be WRITING. Breaks are fine. But they should be 10-15 minutes at the most—enough to go to the bathroom, make some more tea, or pet the dog. 2 hours of no output is too long.

2. WRITING

I'm loving writing my fiction work. I'm getting that antsy feeling, when I don't get to write, where I need to feed my soul with a little word count. It's a good feeling when for awhile there I saw writing fiction as a chore that I had to drop everything else for. Now, I see that it fits in between my other obligations.

That said, I also feel the urge to push myself harder with writing fiction. My love for optimizing things gets in the way of my passion for creating stories. I still need to work out a balance for that.

I'm nervous to push on my word count/hour. I want to go at a higher rate, but not at the expense of making writing not fun. I don't want to burn myself out. My thoughts are, that I'll keep track of writing rate for September but I'll focus on getting my schedule right. Once I hammer out problems with my schedule, I can circle back to writing rate and see what could be optimized there.

For now, though, I think getting more hours of fiction writing in will boost my word count much more than writing an extra 500 words/hour would.

3. SLEEP

Sleep is so important to me, and I just didn't get enough of it this week. Next week, I have fewer freelance deadlines, so I'm going for a hard stop at 11pm, which is about my normal time for bed. No more 1am evenings... it's just not worth it to me.

If I need the extra hours of awake time, I want to tack them on to the beginning of the day, not the end. That means getting more done in the afternoons. Again, that seems to be the main theme of what I'm seeing—optimize the afternoons for freelance work.

4. GOALS

20k words was awesome this week. Next week, since I don't have anything major on the calendar, I'm going for 30k words. That means that I need to get roughly 5k words a day, which will mean getting up a bit earlier and leaving the evenings for play + a little extra word count.

30k should be more than doable, even though it's 50% more than what I accomplished this week. If I were at 100k, I wouldn't be all, "I should do 150k next week!" But since this is only 10k words more, I don't think it's too hard of a push. It'll be a challenge, but a reasonable one.

At the end of the day, the words are not the problem. Now that I'm on a roll, the writing is coming easily. It's the schedule that isn't. I need to:

- Convert "afternoons of crap" to "afternoons of freelance work"
- Work on getting into flow during the writing time I do have

There's so much left to improve and a lot of word count being left on the table. I can do better. I'm sure of it.

Headed back to bed with a book now. Hey, it's a vacation!

10 am (the next day!)

Whirlwind of a party! Updates in the Sunday post!

THE BLUR OF NOT WRITING (LIFE OF A WRITER: DAY 10)

12:00 pm -

The last few days have been a blur of not writing. I can't explain why, only that it has been incredibly difficult to readjust to working after a few days off. I tend to be a "burst of energy" person, but for whatever reason, I fall off the wagon very quickly when I take a break. Consistency is key to my success.

Not that I haven't done anything at all the last few days. I sketched out the plots to Fallen and Hellfire, which was useful. I cleaned up a few scenes from Unbound. I did a lot a longer story meeting with Susan yesterday to figure out our project. That story requires a ton of research, so I spent several hours on that.

I ran errands. I took care of my dog, who always gets a little anxious/sick when she gets home from boarding. I recovered from an intense weekend of traveling.

BUT... no writing. Today, our cleaning lady came over, so I had to clean up the pigsty that is our apartment this morning and also had to spend the morning away. No microphone, so I didn't get writing in this morning.

That seems to be another pattern of mine. Generally, I prefer to write brand new drafts via microphone, because it hurts my hands otherwise. It seems like when I don't have access to my microphone, I come up with more reasons not to get writing done. It's very frustrating, especially when there is SO MUCH stuff I can (and prefer to) do without a microphone—clean up problem sections, revise rough drafts, finish up half-written scenes, etc.

I am extremely frustrated with myself right now, especially since I was all cocky at the end of last week and so sure that I would get 30k words this week. In reality, I didn't technically finish my 20k words from last week (I was 2k words shy). I meant to write them on Saturday, but then we had an issue with transportation, which took an hour to resolve... blah. Excuses. I am full of them.

So I will be WRITING tonight. I have the whole evening blocked off for it. In the meantime, I STILL have to clean up two drafts (Unbound and one under a pen name) so I can get them edited and published. I had wanted all of this to happen last week on the trains, but those rides were surprisingly unproductive, especially the one home, which I spent "recovering" from the night before.

There is a silver lining to all of this... I have 14k words for Trinity done, 18k words for Fallen done, and 22k words for Hellfire done. Each of those books will likely end up between 45-50k, but I don't have to write all those words in the drafts. That means that the drafts will take less time and I'll hopefully have them close by the end of September.

Also, although I've sorted out my to-do list for fiction, I'm still not sure where I stand with all my freelance stuff. I think it's something I'm going to push off until tomorrow.

I know I don't have any deadlines coming up, but I want to get some of that spec work done that I didn't get to last week. Also, I want to make sure that I've got my September goals outlined and planned for.

It feels like I'm attempting to do a lot, but I'm still aiming for 30k words this week. I know it will require more words each day, but I also have a lot of goals for September in terms of what I want drafted and published. I'd like to keep building my writing abilities until I hit a true max where I'm uncomfortable producing any faster. I definitely don't feel like I hit that max last week (in fact, I felt like a complete slacker).

Something else I've realized — I haven't left much time in my schedule for cleaning up drafts and editing them. By focusing on word count, I've de-incentivized myself to clean up written words. I need to figure out how to combat that, because having two complete manuscripts just sitting on my hard drive, not making people happy or putting money in my pocket, sounds like a very stupid business plan.

10:30pm -

The evening got away from me again. It does feel like an explanation is in order, but the reasons are personal and not important at the end of the day, since we all have personal stuff that can derail us. I did get some freelance work done, and I watched a documentary that was important for research for another book set I'm working on, but I didn't get much fiction writing in.

The only reason I got any in (to be clear is because I absolutely FORCED myself to do a short session in the evening. Didn't even make it 25 minutes. 746 words later, it's time for sleep.

Challenge: Develop a Daily Fiction Writing Habit
Today: 746 words
This week: 746 words

GAINING MOMENTUM AFTER A FEW DAYS OF NO WRITING (LIFE OF A WRITER: DAY 11)

11:45 pm -
Wow! I completely forgot to write my entry for today. I have to wonder if I'm tiring of this exercise already.

No worries, hopefully it just means that I've been productive.

I don't know the exact times on everything, but I can say with certainty that today I've:

billed nearly all of my clients (one I'm still waiting on the correct email address)

written close to 4k words (wanted to power through a few more scenes tonight, but I'm too tired)

talked to Susan about the research we need for our new project (which took about 1.5 hours)

planned out my freelance writing for the month. Exhausting!

It's been a moderately productive day, which reassures me that I just needed to get back into the swing of things after leaving town for a few days. It also reminds me that I need to add a few days buffer every time I leave, even if it's just for a bit. Maybe the key is either not leaving, or budgeting time to work (and sticking to it) when I do leave.

Off to bed. Goodnight!

Challenge: Develop a Daily Fiction Writing Habit
Today: 3988 words
This week: 4734 words

WRITING IS LIKE SPORTS, MAYBE (LIFE OF A WRITER: DAY 12)

4:15 pm -

I just got finished with a 3-hour story meeting with Susan. Between that and talking into my microphone all morning, I'm all spoken out.

For the next few hours of the afternoon, I'm switching to typing, and maybe taking a short nap at some point.

My writing rate was a lot slower yesterday (around 1800 words/hour), but today it's picked up to around 2400 words/hour. It seems like whenever I take a day off, it's a long push upward to get back on track.

6:05 pm -

I am done with all of Rykken's scenes in Trinity! There were eight, total. I'm going to tackle either Kennedy's or Thessa's scenes tonight, though I'm not sure which.

Surprisingly, my word count is still unbearably low for today: 1780 words. I think this has a lot to do with finishing tons of half-written scenes. I really only get the word count roaring when I am completing brand new scenes.

I may need to rethink the way I'm looking at my achievements. Maybe I should focus on scene count instead of word count? Or both? I'll have to think about this more.

11:00 pm -

People probably think that writing is not a physical activity, but I have gotten a slight injury almost every time I've gone on a daily writing binge.

Writing can cause injury, just like sports do! (The difference is, writing is more fun.)

I've solved a lot of my RSI/arthritis/carpal tunnel problems by alternating between keyboard and microphone (dictation) inputs, but now I'm facing an issue with eye strain. It probably doesn't help that we run the AC all day, which tends to dry out eyes. Either way, I've been trying to give my eyes adequate breaks, because I am experiencing some mild dry eye symptoms, blurry vision, and headaches.

Sigh. No additional words done tonight. But it does make me very happy to be over 1/3 through the draft of Trinity.

At this rate, I haven't even hit 10k words for the week yet, and I only have two days to go. I'll be surprised if I get to 30k, especially with this new eye strain challenge, which is going to affect my abilities to do reading, writing, editing, and just about anything else that is part of my job. Plus, this weekend I need to get a few finished manuscripts ready for publication, which will cut into my writing time.

This weekend, I'm going to dedicate some time to rethinking how I want to work things, given the setbacks I've encountered this week. I still believe I can push my word count per week sky high. As with any goal, there will be setbacks that require tweaking and reworking of "the plan." We'll see how the rest of this week shapes up in terms of word count, fix the problems, and try, try again next week.

Challenge: Develop a Daily Fiction Writing Habit
Today: 1780 words
This week: 6514 words

APPARENTLY, THE KEY TO SUCCESS IS PUTTING IN THE HOURS (LIFE OF A WRITER: DAY 13)

11 am -

I'm going to start writing in a few minutes. I found a sort-of workaround for my eye issues, which is closing them and looking away from the screen while I'm using my microphone. I can also keep them about half-shut while I'm typing, which is mildly annoying, but I'm pretty good about not needing to look at the screen or keyboard while I'm typing, so the "looking" part is just to spot check anyway.

So, if you see a mistake in this entry, it's probably because my eyes are closed as I type.

I've been strategizing about the future of my writing career. Although I've been self-publishing since 2009, it's becoming more and more obvious that I need to start writing for traditional publications, in addition to telling stories my own way. I've been reading up on short story markets and compiled a list of all the good ones for sci-fi/fantasy/horror.

I'm not sure when I'm going to start actively writing for them. Most want stories that are 5000 words or less. That's 2-3 hours of work for me, provided I already have a story idea. It seems stupid not to take the opportunity, especially when there are so many markets to query and I can just self-publish whatever doesn't sell (which I'm guessing would be a lot of it). There's not much waste. And the benefits include:

- formal recognition for my writing
- a chance to build an audience for each of my pen names; potential additional sales of my self-published work
- payment ($0.05 a word and up, which is about half my non-fiction standard rate of $0.10 a word)
- admission to writing organizations (places like SFWA require professional sales for membership)

- opportunity for awards (usually only professional sales are eligible)

Technically, this applies to novels too, though writing a novel takes quite a bit longer than writing a short story. My thought is that standalone novels are a better fit for traditional publishing at this point, since trilogies are a hard sell, and since the financials on series are significantly better in self-publishing.

Also, I feel like querying traditional publishers with a novel is almost like "wasting" a project. Like you have to essentially write off any potential profit outside of the advance, and consider it a marketing expense. With a solid audience under any pen name, I would probably be able to make back an advance of $5k (which is the average) in 6 months to a year. With traditional publishing, I likely won't see any royalty checks. That's just the business.

The thought of going the traditional publishing route for a series is just... stupid. I don't know how else to say it. Unless you are writing the next Twilight, there isn't much sense in signing over all your rights to something, probably forever or at least for several years.

So, in my mind, a standalone novel is a promotional tool, nothing more. It's hard to self-publish a standalone novel, so it seems reasonable to throw it away at marketing.

The problem with knowing that all of this is smart career strategy is, it doesn't come naturally to me. I'm not much of a "standalone novel" type of writer, in the same way I'm not much of a "short story" type of writer. My stories are insanely big, always, and then they grow even larger. I'm just a huge idea person.

But it would be good practice to learn how to have smaller ideas and littler stories. So far, I have one idea for a standalone novel (out of, like, hundreds of story ideas), but it's for a romance, which I wouldn't do under Monica Leonelle anyway. So maybe I'll test the waters with that book?

Either way, I sense this is one of those things that would be good for me, but that won't pay off for a solid 3-5 years into my career. I guess my goals right now are to:

- get my schedule and writing process under control and predictable each week (which is what this current challenge is about)
- get enough books out to build a predictable income (either a full-time income or an income that only requires freelance writing occasionally to fill in the gaps)
- Then, the next steps are:
- incorporate short story writing into my workflow (without disrupting my regular production schedule)
- learn how to query, who to submit to, etc.
- sell something to someone, repeat

THEN, repeat the process above with standalone fiction novels. (I doubt I'll even circle back to this until sometime in 2014, so don't expect to hear about it again anytime soon.)

Anyway, this seems like a great strategy, but there are a lot of steps to get there. I'm thinking that having traditionally published short stories and novels is a goal for 2015, 2016 timeframe. Short stories maybe a little sooner, in 2014. In researching all of this, I'm pretty excited to move forward, but also wary of throwing another wrench into my toolkit, especially when I'm still struggling with getting a weekly word count in.

Yes, I have big plans. In reading about all these different opportunities to earn income as a writer, my natural inclination is to immediately fit it in to my plan, even when I haven't gotten something else figured out. I tend to take on too much at once.

10:50 pm -

P had to borrow my computer for most of the afternoon today, so I spent that time mapping out my writing plan for the rest of the year. Wow. I am not going to get as much done as I hoped, even if I work like crazy over the upcoming months.

The good news is that my writing rate for today jumped significantly over what I've been seeing since this challenge started. I hit between 2500-3300 words/hour for nearly all of my sessions today, which is so exciting. Finally! Looking forward to hitting in the 3000's for all sessions—it feels possible.

Also, I'm at the halfway point for Trinity, so in a few more days (or by the end of next week, unless something goes horribly wrong), I should have a first draft of it. Another exciting benchmark, since I just finished up Unbound at this time last week.

I was able to get down 7539 words today with 5339 of those happening between 8:30-10:50 pm. I haven't been using a timer for my scenes, but I started doing pomodoros again, and that seemed to motivate me somehow. I credit pomodoros for much of my word count gains in general. Even when I was typing everything (no microphone or dictation software), I easily went from 1000 words/hour to 1600-1800 words/hour, just by doing 25 minutes on, 5 minutes off.

I'm going to try this pattern again tomorrow. I seem to only be able to do about 2.5 hours at a time before I feel beat, but I'm hoping to up that to 3-4 hours as I gain stamina. That's 6-8 sessions in a row. But, if I were able to do it, I'd clear 10k words in that timeframe, which would be HUGE for me.

It'll be interesting to see what happens tomorrow. I don't intend to spend the whole day writing, because I try to spend a portion of the weekend with family. I definitely won't hit 30k words like I'd hoped, and probably won't even hit 20k unless I really power through in my morning session. But, I'll probably end up around where I was last week, so at least I haven't regressed. That means next week I have a fighting chance at beating my current pace.

My eyes are still acting up a bit, but the break from the computer helped. For now, I'm keeping them shut as much as possible so I can still get my work done.

Challenge: Develop a Daily Fiction Writing Habit

Today: 7539 words

This week: 14053 words

SATURDAYS ARE FOR REST (LIFE OF A WRITER: DAY 14)

10:30 am -

I got up early today, but didn't make it out to my computer until about 9 am. I bummed around the computer for a bit, and I'm kind of just waiting for P to wake up so we can go to brunch.

I feel a bit tapped out on the Hallow world, but that said, I'm not particularly excited about my other manuscript either. I can't tell if I'm just tired from the writing I did yesterday, or if I need a few more manuscripts ready to go to avoid this waning interest syndrome.

6:30 pm -

I tried to work on some freelance stuff this afternoon, but hit a wall. I did, however, get my other manuscript compiled to edit on the Kindle, and I think I'll work on Unbound now for the same purpose.

11:45 pm -

I got a few chapters of Unbound into edits, but still have 7 more to go.

My word count is pretty pitiful today, but that's due to me wanting to implement a new schedule where I take Saturdays off from fiction writing. Like I said earlier, today is the end of the week, and I really wasn't that interested in any of the manuscripts I was working on. A day off from writing (and by that I mean, writing whatever I can but not worrying about hitting any sort of target) is needed, from what I can tell from the last two weeks.

I'll talk more about my new schedule tomorrow!

Challenge: Develop a Daily Fiction Writing Habit

Today: 839 words

This week: 14892 words

August total (for the last week):17,923 words

September total (so far): 14892 words

Challenge total (so far): 32815 words

DISAPPOINTING PROGRESS (LIFE OF A WRITER: DAY 15)

8:00 am -

It's a brand new week!

After going back through last week's numbers, I've decided to make a few changes to my work schedule.

First, I've decided that from 8:00am - noon-ish is fiction writing time. I'm going to do whatever it takes to wake up and get to the computer by 8:00am. I got here on time, with a few minutes to spare, by getting out of bed around 7:25am (wake up time: 7:00am).

I refuse to wake up to an alarm, but I naturally wake up around 7am as long as I get to bed before midnight.

I'm also going to set aside 8:00pm and beyond for writing. "Beyond" is the operative word, since I try to go to bed before midnight and there is preparation required for that. It's not clear how much I will get done in the evenings.

I'm only running this schedule from Sunday-Friday each week. On Saturdays, I want to be able to relax, bum around, watch TV, and hang out with P. I'll probably still write a bit, but I want to keep those days free for fun (and just give myself a break overall, without completely derailing myself).

I'm also switching to 40 minute pomodoros. I checked out my stats from the last two days and noticed that 25 on, 5 off is not the most optimal timeframe for me. Most of my scenes take between 35-45 minutes to complete, and the 25 on gives me 50 minutes of work time, which is too much. It's no surprise that when I finish early, I end up taking the extra time as a break instead of starting another scene.

I'm considering upping my pomodoro times to 40 minutes a session, with a 5 minute break. That would give me 4 writing sessions in 3 hours, and the opportunity to (hopefully) finish 4 scenes, one per writing session. I finished 3 scenes in 2 hours and 20 minutes on Friday night, with several 5-10 minute breaks, so this seems like a reasonable pace.

I'm committed to this schedule for a week only. By committed, I mean, "intending to follow it." If it ends up being too hard, I'll keep track of that here. If it ends up being unproductive on some days, I'll keep track of that here too.

I don't think I'm setting a word count goal for this week. I haven't hit it in the past two weeks, so I've abstracted it out to butt-in-chair hours instead. If I stick to this schedule, I'll get far more words in than a mere 20-30k.

I'm considering tracking instead the number of scenes I complete, since that's a more accurate representation of how far along I am in the book, but I don't even want to mess with that for this first week on the new schedule. I'd love to see what the schedule produced and then see where I can tweak it to optimize scene count.

In many ways, I feel like I'm starting over with the whole challenge this week. But I want to acknowledge (mainly to myself) what I've accomplished so far:

I've gotten in 32815 words of fiction in the last two weeks. This is freaking phenomenal for me, and proves that there's something about this challenge that is working.

I've moved one manuscript into edits, and have another close to edits. I'm still focusing quite heavily on new words, but I'm hoping Saturdays and afternoons become the times when I move first drafts into something publishable.

I've come to enjoy writing, not just having written. Writing scenes no longer requires me to drag myself to a computer and force words to come out. The work feels good as it's happening, which is a beautiful thing.

While I'm falling short of my goals and expectations, I'm still making progress. That feels good. It gives me hope that I will get to something that works really well in the next few months.

It's 8:30 am now and time to start writing fiction.

11:51pm -

I got in 2342 words in my morning session before my Dragon Dictate software started acting up. So, I spent some time fixing that and then got to work on Unbound edits. I got another 4 scenes done and only have three to go now. One of them requires some decent reworking, one needs a few paragraphs added, and the last just needs a mild read-through.

The television was really tempting today. P pretty much watched television the entire day, both yesterday and today, and it was impossible to stay away when I've barely watched any TV for the last two weeks.

I also looked at my planned books for the next few months, and wrote out a probably-too-aggressive plan for what I think I can accomplish from 2013-2014. I researched a bunch of industry changes on the Kindleboards, especially a Netflix-like startup called Oyster. I'm holding out on publishing any sort of public opinion on it until it launches, but I'm surprisingly optimistic about the opportunities it presents.

So I got a lot of fiction-book-related stuff done today, but I didn't get enough words down for my liking. I'm a bit disappointed in myself.

Also, I completely missed my evening session of writing, though I planned for those to be more of "maybe" sessions. I'd ideally like to get 3-4 evening sessions in per week. Of course, since I didn't get the morning one done in full, I wish I had gotten the evening one in. I meant to, but instead, I procrastinated, thinking I had plenty of time to do a little more today. Then, I got hit with a ton of time-sensitive chores around 10:30 pm and didn't get back to the computer until now, which killed the extra 3000 or so words I could have added tonight. Boo. I hate it when I could have done better and it's completely my fault that I didn't. Lesson: don't procrastinate those words.

I thought about writing a little more tonight, but then I realized that might screw me up for tomorrow. I think it's smarter to go to bed and start fresh in the morning, at 8am. The morning session is definitely more important to me than the evening one.

Then again, maybe I'm just kidding myself as far as this schedule goes...

Or maybe Sunday just isn't a great day to start?

I'm not sure.

At least I got more words in this Sunday than the last...

Challenge: Develop a Daily Fiction Writing Habit

Today: 2342 words

This week: 2342 words

August total (for the last week):17,923 words

September total (so far): 17234 words

Challenge total (so far): 35157 words

BREAKING 10,000 WORDS, FINALLY (LIFE OF A WRITER: DAY 16)

8:18 am -

I'm so excited for today! I have 11 Kennedy scenes left to go before I'm done with the first draft of Trinity, so I'm wondering if I can get through a good chunk of those today.

I was right to go to bed when I did; I woke up naturally around 7:45 am today. Not my usual time, because I usually go to bed at 11:30ish or earlier.

I have a bit of raw energy, so I might try writing while pacing today. My highest word counts per hour have been when I did this, so I'm curious what might happen.

Of course, I can't pace all the time, just like I can't use my mic for every word I put on the page.

So by the time I got that set up, it was about 850. I had a couple problems with the mic set up, which stalled me, but 30 minutes now is not a huge sacrifice if I can start writing a lot faster while facing.

2 pm -

My pacing is working pretty well so far. I wish I could do this every day, in fact, because it's so efficient and I really love the way the first draft of Trinity is going. Granted, I love Kennedy, who is the character I'm writing right now. She cracks me up, which makes her really entertaining to write about.

I'm consistently at a little over 3000 words/hour and I've gotten in 6420 words over the course of about 123 minutes (with tons of breaks, of course). P is gone for the rest of the day and I'm going to take advantage of having the apartment to myself and try to get in more words.

Unfortunately, that means pushing off some freelance stuff for another day. I don't have any deadlines to hit, so at least there's that, but freelance work is also starting to feel as pressing and urgent as finishing the first draft for this book. Still, I don't think I can squander my time alone in the apartment. I can write articles anytime. Writing this manuscript is easier when I don't have any distractions.

4 pm -

Completed another scene—only 7 left to go on this draft. It's very exciting to be moving so quickly through the draft. I'm at 8648 words for the day, but starting to get a little worn out by it. I'm wondering though if it has more to do with the pacing than the writing. Either way, I'm going to take a little break from it all and watch some TV while I edit a scene from Unbound.

11 pm -

I'm exhausted. I made it to 10,154 words before I had to call it quits. It feels wonderful to have written so much today, but I have to admit that by my second to last session, I was sitting down rather than pacing, and by my very last session (squeezing an extra 400-ish words in the break 10k for the day) I was typing. My voice was tired from speaking so much today.

Either way, I think I certainly pushed the limits a bit. Since tomorrow is the day my cleaning lady comes, I'll probably take it a little easier on the word count.

Plus, I need to get back to freelance writing. I'm excited to push some non-fiction work out to clients tomorrow.

Aside from writing fiction I also chatted with Susan for about an hour and half today. So far, our writing sessions are heavy on the talking and extremely light on the writing. Actually, non-existent on the writing. We agreed that tomorrow we will actually get something done. During our Tuesday session, I plan to work on the last of the Unbound rewriting needed so I can get that manuscript into edits, soon.

I'm pleased with today's progress. I'm going to reward myself for a hard day's work with a little doodling tonight about a new series I want to start at some point... :)

Challenge: Develop a Daily Fiction Writing Habit

Today: 10154 words

This week: 12496 words

August total (for the last week):17,923 words

September total (so far): 27388 words

Challenge total (so far): 45311 words

FULL OF THOUGHTS AND NEEDING TIME TO PROCESS (LIFE OF A WRITER: DAY 17)

10 am -

I slept in this morning! Just a bit. Today is when our cleaning lady comes, so I had to be out of the house by 10am. Anyway, I woke up around 7:15 am and felt sleepy still. So I slept in a bit and wasn't ready until 9 am, which is when I start my pre-cleaning for the cleaning lady. (I know, pre-cleaning is stupid. But if you've had a cleaning lady, you understand that they are much happier when you've picked up dirty socks from the living room and loaded the dishwasher already.)

I'm not sure if I made the right decision. Is it bad that I put sleep above my writing schedule? Part of me feels like it's lazy. The other part of me feels like being cranky will, in the long-term, be a detriment to my writing goals. I try to feel myself out and push myself just a little further when needed, but I don't think I'll ever be the hard-core, finish-it-at-all-costs type.

So, this morning I feel incredibly refreshed. But I haven't gotten any fiction writing done yet. And now that I'm sitting at Barnes and Noble, I really don't think it'll be the most productive use of my time because I don't have my mic.

I have 6 scenes left of Trinity to finish the first draft. I'd love to get them done today, but I doubt it will happen, especially having missed my morning session. The first 6 Kennedy scenes were nearly 12,500 words total, and since I haven't cleared that amount in one day at all in this challenge, it's probably a definite no on finishing today.

That said, I will finish in the next few days, and my original plan was to keep plowing through the series and work on Fallen and Hellfire next. The problem is, I haven't done beats for them. Which means I need to work on beats at some point this week so I can keep going with the series, or else I need to write my other manuscript for my pen name.

As I look at my schedule, I've noticed that I really haven't done a good job of scheduling time or setting goals for the other aspects of my writing. Beats, for example—also, redrafting, edits, proofreading, publishing. I'm thinking of just setting weekly goals and spending an hour or two a day trying to get there. For example, this week I need to:

- Get pen name manuscript into critique (I send the manuscript to Susan for feedback) and proofreads
- Get Unbound into critique and proofreads
- Get Fallen beaten out (probably by Wednesday)
- Get Hellfire beaten out (won't get to it until next week)
- Next week I need to:
- Get Trinity into critique and proofreads
- Write Fallen (partially write it this week; include the 8 scenes already written)
- Write Hellfire (include the 12 scenes already written)
- Publish Unbound
- Publish pen name manuscript
- Get some pen name manuscripts beaten out (I'll be writing for my pen name for a few weeks after wrapping up WD&D drafts)

The question is, when does all this work happen? I definitely don't want to to stop my daily writing habit to accommodate this work. Am I naive to think it can happen around my daily writing, during the breaks?

I'm not sure. But here are some numbers: even yesterday, during my 10k words, I only spent 176 minutes actually writing. That's just under 3 hours. Of course, I wrote on and off each day, so it's not like I woke up at 8am and was done before lunch.

Also, I watched 6 episodes of Scandal yesterday. I know—I swore off TV, and I was doing really well, but this weekend I got sucked back in again. TV is seriously so, so good. I've missed it.

I watched Scandal earlier this summer already, but that was a marathon, so it all blurs together. I wanted to watch it again to better break down the storytelling elements, since I remembered them being pretty impressive at hooking me. (By the way, "storytelling research" is frequently my rationalization for watching TV.)

So—there's all that time too. I mean, I'm still not working hard per say. I don't think most people would say they had a hard day's work, but managed to get 6 episodes of a 42 minute show in. No, most people would be shocked to get anything done with a day like that.

I'm going to see if merely stating my goals for the week magically makes them happen, without worrying too much about a particular schedule for them. This seems like productivity suicide, but... ??? One thing at a time, I guess. I refuse to sacrifice my word count gains for all this other stuff—it needs to happen more in the in-between time.

While I'm being random and rambly, I have so many more things to talk about.

#1 - I'M ADDING A SMALL CHALLENGE TO THESE CHALLENGE POSTS.

I mentioned a few days ago that I'd been researching the short story fiction market. I want to incorporate short stories into my writing career plan, but I've never been an avid short story reader. So challenge #2 is to read one short story every night before I go to bed. If I do this until the end of the year, I'll have read over 100 short stories from a variety of sources, which seems like a decent start to tackling how to write a short story.

To do this, I've subscribed to a few monthlies through Kindle. Right now, I have Asimov's, Analog, Clarkesworld, and Apex—all sci-fi/fantasy markets for the Monica Leonelle pen name. I'll probably add more from other genres as I find new markets that I'd like to submit to. I also downloaded the Best Of ebook for the last 5 years of short stories on Tor.com (another sci-fi outlet). Plenty of material to read, but I do want to find some good romance and mystery/thriller periodicals to add to the rotation.

#2 - MY BLURRY VISION CLEARED UP.

After several days of thinking I was going blind, had glaucoma, had diabetes, had cataracts, was going to die, etc., I finally diagnosed my blurry eye problem as dry-eye. I noticed that P had a lot of the same symptoms as me, and read up on how to fix it. The issue was that we live on the 22nd floor of our building, which is basically the same temperature as hell during the summer (you know, because heat rises and all). We run our AC like crazy, and that sucked the humidity right out of our apartment. We turned the AC off and used windows and fans for a day or two, which immediately cleared up the issue. Then, P ordered a humidifier from Amazon because he loves the AC and wants to turn it back on.

#3 - WRITER'S MARKET IS ON ITS WAY TO MY HOUSE.

I can't wait to get my hands on the 2014 edition. I don't know what I'm excited about most—the non-fiction section, the literary agents section, the short story section... it all sounds useful to me. I guess right now the non-fiction section will be the most beneficial, since I'm quickly running out of places to send my work to.

#4 - OYSTER AND MATCHBOOK

I don't have much to say about Kindle's new Matchbook option, aside from it being a cool new feature for self-published authors.

Oyster, however, is interesting news. I wrote a post about it today.

11 pm -

I absolutely, positively did NOT want to write this evening. I don't know if it's because I wrote so much yesterday, but I was seriously thinking about skipping altogether today.

Then, I bucked up and forced myself to write one scene. I phoned it in, big time. But actually, the scene turned out just fine. Funny how that works.

1609 words later, I'm ready for bed.

Challenge: Develop a Daily Fiction Writing Habit

Today: 1609 words

This week: 14105 words

August total (for the last week):17,923 words

September total (so far): 28997 words

Challenge total (so far): 46920 words

FEELING WEIRD AND CONFUSED (LIFE OF A WRITER: DAY 18)

9:45 am -

I have such a weird feeling about today. I woke up around 7 am and read in bed until about 8:15 am, when I finally rolled out and started getting ready. I couldn't find anything to wear. Then I couldn't stand how messy our living room was. Since we live in the city and don't have cars, we get almost everything mailed or delivered to us— books, furniture, toilet paper, even groceries. This creates a lot of packaging that is just... everywhere. It makes me nuts. We have ordered a ton of stuff from Amazon this week and it's coming in small shipments, and there are boxes everywhere.

I cleaned for awhile this morning. Now, it's time to write, but my mind is still preoccupied with other things. For example, I want to get my publication schedule together for the next four months, since December is essentially a race to the finish for getting stuff published this year. Publishing is a seasonal business; you get high sales December-March, and then things taper off through the spring and summer months. I'll do better if I have a lot of inventory in December. So I'm trying to figure out my breakdown with the time I have left to write.

I'm also worried about pen names and have decided to condense the four that I had planned down to the two I already have. I realized that at the rate it takes to grow a pen name, I might not even be able to launch my other two until late next year, at the earliest. And even when I did, I would have to make sacrifices each month on new releases— because it's smart to release new things for each pen name regularly, but it's not like I can have 4 new releases on a regular schedule, every month. It's too crazy. It gives me, like, a week each month for each pen name. To readers, it would seem like each author never released, or released so infrequently that they shouldn't even pay attention.

Four pen names was insane. Two pen names is still ambitious, but I already have everything set up for both, so I might as well go with it. and that leaves me with half the month for one pen name and half for the other. Plenty of time to get a few releases drafted under each name, especially if I write several shorter works for each.

This restructuring required moving all my ideas from the discarded pen names into one of my two remaining pen names. So now I have a huge list of ideas for each pen name, and they're not all as related as I want them to be.

And THIS, got me started on brand expansion—how do you become "known" for something when you want to experiment with lots of other things? I think celebrities do this so well, and what they do is focus on one very specific style for a little while, become known for it, then kill it within a year or two.

Like Katy Perry—she did that bubblegum candy queen thing for a few years, and now she's moving on to something else, I'm assuming, though I can't totally tell what because all anyone is talking about is Miley Cyrus, and I can barely remember what Katy Perry's latest song is called.

So, I think that even with combining pen names, I need to focus Monica Leonelle on something very specific at first. To me, that's sci-fi, fantasy, and horror for young adults. I have a ton of contemporary thriller ideas, but I think that's for later, for an expansion. I have a ton of romance ideas too, but... idk. I feel like romance needs to be under my other pen name. I can see how sci-fi/fantasy/horror can go with mystery/thriller, but I don't see where something like historical romance fits in with all of that. And I already have some romance-ish work under another pen name. So I think that's where my division is.

I'm not totally sold on the idea of fewer pen names, but at the same time, I don't want to manage 4 (or more) identities. It's too much for me. It alleviates confusion, but also obstructs cross-promotion of titles for readers who do read widely from a number of genres. I write things I like to read. And I like to read from at least 10 different genres, from romance to YA to all types of fantasy to middle grade to hard core sci-fi.

I also can't stop thinking about short stories. Susan informed me last night that she had over 20 short stories sitting on her hard drive, and I made her send them to me. I think she should create collections of her work and get it out there. I'm so interested in short stories, but I had planned to have multiple pen names so I could submit them like crazy to editors (many don't allow multiple submissions from the same author). But having fewer pen names affects my ability to do that. So I'm torn, again.

All of these decisions are floating through my mind as I figure out what my fiction schedule is for the rest of the year. I don't mean publication dates; I mean drafting dates. I'll probably finish up Trinity today, but since I don't have Fallen beats worked out yet, I'll shift to my other manuscript next and finish that up for the rest of the week. I still need to figure out how editing and publishing fit into my workflow, too.

11:00 pm -

I didn't write today. I had too many thoughts swirling in my head, plus I received Writer's Market and spent the evening poring through that.

I don't feel bad though. I am glad I took a break, because it means that something is wrong. So I'm reevaluating that tonight so that I can fix things tomorrow.

Challenge: Develop a Daily Fiction Writing Habit

Today: 0 words

This week: 14105 words

August total (for the last week):17,923 words

September total (so far): 28997 words

Challenge total (so far): 46920 words

FINISHED ANOTHER MANUSCRIPT DRAFT (LIFE OF A WRITER: DAY 19)

3:15 pm -

Not writing yesterday made me realize how bored I am with the current draft I'm working on. Trinity is a great story, one that I've looked forward to writing, but as with all of the Waters Dark and Deep books, the way I have it broken up into three perspectives, makes the book more difficult in many ways. The books are broken up into 25 scenes, with:

- A prologue or epilogue
- 12 scenes for the A perspective (main character of the book)
- 8 scenes for the B perspective
- 4 scenes for the C perspective

I write each of these perspectives in a marathon, out of actual scene order, to maintain voice.

But so far, I have gotten stuck on writing the A perspective for every single book. I get bored. I get too comfortable. And while Kennedy is a funny character, it can be exhausting to be stuck in her head for 12 scenes straight, especially when I'm trying to get those scenes done quickly.

I think my issue is that I need variety. It can't possibly be better for me from a voice perspective, but I tend to get more done when I "procrastinate" on one thing by doing a different project.

I can feel myself growing weary of the Waters Dark and Deep series. That's okay, because I'm already three books in, but I was planning to go straight into the last two next week. I don't think I'm going to do that now. I've been working on Trinity so far today, and I only have one scene left. I think I'm going to finish that, jump into my manuscript under another pen name (since it's the only other thing I have beaten out) for the rest of the day, and try to beat out something completely new and different in my off hours.

So far I've gotten in a little over 6,000 words today. I had an epiphany last night about my work schedule that I'm testing for the next two days. I'll write about it later in this entry if it works out.

My goals for this upcoming weekend are pretty simple: I need to get my manuscripts out, and I need to prepare more scenes (beat them out) for the next week of writing. I need to shift gears a bit on projects to make the writing come a little more easily for me, so I'm going to look at what's next and what I can move around from my schedule for the rest of the year. My thinking is, the priorities are still the same until December, but when I actually handle them will be different. So I'm looking at projects I planned for later and trying to figure out how to start them now, so I have enough variety and can switch manuscripts whenever I'm feeling heavy resistance.

11 pm -

I completed 7810 words today, and also completed the first draft of Trinity! I feel like I should be happier about this, to be honest. But with this daily writing habit, I'm realizing it's on to the next thing.

Also, I wish that I had written more. I hate ending the day like that, but it's a reminder to work harder tomorrow.

From now on, though, I'm focusing more on minutes spent than word count. I know that the more writing minutes I get in a day, the more words I get. And right now, 7810 words feels like a lot... but 158 minutes spent does not. I can do better than 158 minutes. I'd like to work my way up to 200 minutes per day, then move up from there.

I would eventually love to be at 2000 per week, which is 33.3 hours. It seems reasonable. That said, I'm only at 452 minutes of writing for the week, so there is a lot of room for improvement.

The good news is that this week I actually surpassed 20,000 words! I still have tomorrow and (maybe) Saturday to keep adding. I'm not going to hold my breath for 30,000, because I don't want to disappoint myself.

But the challenge is working. I'm very happy that I've written over 50k in fewer than three weeks... that's a NaNoWriMo completed already.

So far, I've read exactly two short stories as well. Heading off to read some more, in keeping with my goal of averaging one per day (30 per month).

Challenge: Develop a Daily Fiction Writing Habit

Today: 7810 words

This week: 21915 words

August total (for the last week):17,923 words

September total (so far): 36807 words

Challenge total (so far): 54730 words

Short stories read: 2

Minutes spent writing today: 158

Minutes spent writing this week: 452

GETTING BACK AFTER FALLING OFF (LIFE OF A WRITER: DAY 25)

7:30 pm -

I fell off the rails. I thought I could take a nice little break on Friday and Saturday, then resume writing on Sunday. I was wrong.

It's now been 5 full days since I've written anything.

I've been doing other stuff during that time, though. I outlined 5 books in that time period (all under the other pen name). I created lots and lots of covers. I did some freelance work all day yesterday.

But no fiction.

I can tell you now that it feels terrible not to write. It is absolutely depressing, but also a vicious cycle, because being depressed over not writing makes me feel sad, which makes me not feel like writing.

It seems like one day off here and there is okay... but two days in a row leads to a binge of television, note-taking, sketching, and planning.

It would be different if it led to editing and publishing... but so far, it hasn't. So my focus on writing has nothing to do with my lack of editing and publishing. Which is actually kind of a relief, because it means I need to get that done in between writing.

P left today. He's in St. Louis until Saturday, so I have the apartment to myself for the next several days. And there are no excuses—I have to write because what else could I possibly do to pass the time? It's too boring otherwise.

11:45 pm -

I'm very sleepy. I've been working on a few outlines and want to keep going with them. I wish that I had written tonight, but I feel like I'm working my way up to it, like I did the first time.

I've decided to start tracking other metrics, too. I think I'll talk about it tomorrow though.

Getting this post out seems like the silliest, smallest step in the right direction. I think it will help motivate me to get back on the horse, though. I'm proud of myself for putting this out there. Because tomorrow will be a better writing day for it.

Challenge: Develop a Daily Fiction Writing Habit

Today: 0 words

This week: 0 words

August total (for the last week):17,923 words

September total (so far): 36807 words

Challenge total (so far): 54730 words

Short stories read: 6

Minutes spent writing today: 0

Minutes spent writing this week: 0

September total (so far): 862 minutes

Challenge total (so far): 1406 minutes

Scenes beaten out this week: 1

Scenes revised this week: 0

Scenes edited this week: 0

Books published this week: 0

I WROTE TODAY! (LIFE OF A WRITER: DAY 27)

11:30 pm -

So, two days after my last entry, I finally wrote actual words. I had planned to spend the entire time P was gone writing, but that probably would have worked a bit better if I had been writing this whole time.

I'm relieved I got some words down today, and in fact edited the one scene I worked on to the point that it's pretty much done. It's the start of a new series under my pen name, and the first scene went slooowly. It's okay though, because I was doing character development, setting, backstory, and everything all at once. I started out using my mic, but switched to typing after a 25 minute pomodoro.

The scene is 2355 words long, which is the perfect length because the thing I'm working on is supposed to be around 20,000 words total, and there are 8 scenes.

I've done a lot of other stuff the last few days, specifically a huge story meeting with Susan and a TON of outlining for various stories. One of those is the Socialpunk series, which I got stuck on about a third of the way through the first draft of the second book. I think I've figured out the new story lines for the trilogy, but still need to flesh out the details. I want to start a serial in the same world (but maybe with different characters), but I don't think it's fair to release that until I get the trilogy out.

Another story is also under Monica Leonelle, and it's a collaboration with Susan. We've been talking about it for awhile and I'm a bit nervous to say, "Yes, we seem to definitely be doing it," but I guess I'm going to come out and say that, with the stipulation that it could all fall apart still, since we don't have the full outline of the series done and there is still plenty that can go wrong.

Susan and I have two ideas that we want to get out in 2014, and I'm really excited about both of them. Collaboration is something I never expected to do because I'm a control freak over my books, but Susan brings a lot to the table and there is no question that I would never be able to do either of these ideas on my own. They both require a ton of research, details, and subtlety, none of which I'm great at. Susan is great at all of these though, so I'm pretty thrilled to be working with her on them.

I think tomorrow I'm going to get back to a series that I know pretty well, probably still under the other pen name. I feel the need to race forward on something. Starting something new is always fun, but I forgot how difficult first books in series can be. Sometimes you just want to go back to the familiar.

Challenge: Develop a Daily Fiction Writing Habit

Today: 2355 words

This week: 2355 words

August total (for the last week):17,923 words

September total (so far): 39162 words

Challenge total (so far): 57085 words

Short stories read: 6

Minutes spent writing today: 89

Minutes spent writing this week: 89

September total (so far): 951 minutes

Challenge total (so far): 1495 minutes

Scenes beaten out this week: 9

Scenes revised this week: 1

Scenes edited this week: 0

Books published this week: 0

STILL NOT COMPLETELY BACK ON THE HORSE (LIFE OF A WRITER: DAY 31)

10:00 am -

Wow, I've been at this for a full month now. Incredible. In that time, I haven't written nearly as much as I had hoped, but I'm going to push myself to the end of the month so that my first full month of results (September) is where I hoped to be at.

In August, I set myself the goal of hitting 50,000 words written in September. Right now, I have a week left and a little over 10,000 words to go.

Last week I was horribly unproductive in terms of word count. I only hit 2355 words total, which is terrible for me! The weeks before that I managed between 15-20k per week.

I have a lot of challenges to address going forward, that I'll try to tease out as much as possible in this post.

PROBLEM #1 - I'M NOT GETTING ENOUGH WRITING DONE.

Last week I wanted to write but couldn't get myself to just start. I believe this may be because of a few things:

I didn't have anything new outlined or beat out

I had depleted my inspiration after three weeks of consistent writing

I was overwhelmed with everything else I could be doing to get books published, like outlining, beating, revising, editing, proofreading, creating covers, and more

I was procrastinating until too late in the day. I stopped writing almost immediately after I realized that I was only writing a few hours worth of the day. This made me think subconsciously that I could put off writing all day and still get 3 hours of writing done, which is simply not true. I need to start writing early in the day and take lots of breaks to do other stuff in-between. This is what gets the words done.

I reset my goal from word count to time. This has been a terrible idea, I think for psychological reasons more than anything else. I'm going to try instead to set a goal for # of scenes completed and word count from now on, since word count seemed to be working pretty well for me before.

PROBLEM #2 - I AM OVERWHELMED BY THE PROCESS OF GETTING OTHER PUBLISHING TASKS DONE.

While writing a first draft is insanely important, it's not exactly a publishable piece of work. I currently have three manuscripts that need to be revised, edited, proofread, and published. To be published, they need covers, descriptions, front matter, back matter, metadata, and compilations into various formats. I hadn't budgeted time for any of this, which made it feel like I was stuck.

My only solution is to set a scene goal for editing as well. The problem is, I don't know much about how long it takes me to edit something. I have tons of data on how I write, but very little on how I edit.

Enter... spreadsheets! I have a new spreadsheet to track my editing time. Fun, I know. So we'll see what I learn over the next few weeks of tracking.

PROBLEM #3 - I'M NOT DOING A GOOD JOB AT PUTTING MARKETING MECHANISMS INTO PLACE.

So far, my plan has been, "Get a ton of work out, put some of it on permafree to open the sales funnel, then start marketing when I have enough product to make it worthwhile." I've had this idea that I'm going to automatically be successful when I have a certain number of books out, but the more I think about it, the less it makes sense. I read an ebook on growth hacking today and it took me back to my marketing days of trying to grow a product slowly, steadily.

I have tons of ideas and realized that if I implemented 3 growth hacking techniques every week, I'd have over 100 ways to bring new readers to my books with 6 months. That's huge.

To be clear, I'm not talking about promotions of any kind. I don't think I'm ready for a marketing calendar, which is where I would lump all of my promotional activities. There's definitely a place for that, and I'm confident I will get there eventually, but right now that is a lot to manage for a one-time hit of sales.

I'm also not talking about ongoing interactions, like starting a Facebook page or a Twitter profile for my characters. Anything that requires consistent, ongoing work is not sustainable, especially if I am starting 3 new things every week. I can see doing this if I had a staff who could maintain the content, or if I had a ton of fans who wanted to interact with each other. But right now, it's not a good fit for me. I need to be writing, not playing on Facebook and Twitter.

So what am I talking about? I'm talking about effective one-time techniques that keep working long after I put them in place. An example would be putting a book on permafree—it just keeps getting downloaded, drawing people to my work and my series. Or, putting a call-to-action to my email list in the back of every book. I already do this, but I can optimize it in so many different ways. Or, creating landing pages for specific actions I want readers to take. Like sharing the books with friends, or writing a review. Or, building an optimized Facebook campaign that can run with very little ongoing input.

So in about a month or so, there will be a little section in these entries called Growth Hacking. Look forward to that.

11:45 pm -

Gah! I didn't write any fiction today. I HAVE to change that tomorrow.

Challenge: Develop a Daily Fiction Writing Habit

Today: 0 words

This week: 0 words

August total (for the last week):17,923 words

September total (so far): 39162 words

Challenge total (so far): 57085 words

FIRST STEP IN GETTING BACK TO FICTION WRITING IS GETTING THESE ENTRIES OUT (LIFE OF A WRITER: DAY 34)

10:45 pm -

I have done a terrible job of keeping up with this diary, but the good news is that I've written for the last two days. That is, after another 5-day dry spell, following the 8-day dry spell. I feel like the fact that I wrote 2355 words in a 14-day period deserves an angrily screeched F-word, especially when I was hitting a 15-20k average for the 3 weeks before that, but I'll spare you the vulgarity and just say that I suck, I suck, I suck.

Yes, I started writing again. But it's still slow-going:

Wednesday (two days ago) - 2459 words

Thursday (yesterday) - 1567 words

Overall, just a little over 4,000 words so far. Not terrible for two days, but horrible for this week! Especially when I only have tonight (which I'll be able to squeeze a bit of writing in, but not a ton) and tomorrow (which is a Saturday, aka "not a day I have historically hit huge word counts").

Still, I beat last week, the week from hell. And I am still within reach of hitting over 50k words in September. As of this minute, I have fewer than 7k to go and I still have 4 days to do them in. Of course, I'm hoping to make at least a dent in that tonight...

GROWTH HACKING

As I mentioned in a previous entry, I am really excited about the idea of growth hacking and how it can apply to my books and websites. I realized over this last week that the best opportunity I have to growth hack my author career is through my email list. So I am slowly building a list of 100 or so small ways to grow my email list (things that preferably don't require one-time promotions or heavy ongoing maintenance).

I'm not sure about getting 3 things done per week, yet. I feel like the best thing for me in the next month or two is to get more product out. That in itself is a growth hack. I'm still sitting on 3 manuscripts (though I plan to publish 1 this weekend) and I have other pieces partially done, and lots of new ideas outlined and beaten out. Plenty of material to go.

That said, I've made a short list of calls-to-action that I want to include at the backs of all my books. I would love to get these mostly right now, so I don't have to redo them later (because realistically, later might never happen). Getting those calls-to-action together will take at least a small amount of effort, even if it's just setting up a page with an email opt-in.

GETTING BACK ON TRACK

I think I need to get back to the basics of this challenge. My fiction writing has definitely slowed down in the last two weeks, and it's been an uphill battle to get back in the groove. Often, that can be attributed to simply not getting the small things done, like this diary entry.

In fact, when I first started preparing for this challenge, I did it by cleaning up my inbox. Stupid, I know, and seemingly unrelated. But I've found that taking care of the small things each day helps build discipline for the big things, like this challenge.

Also, without question, the days that I write this entry serve as a reminder of my goals, a record of what I'm accomplishing, and an accountability of my stats. I haven't wanted to write the Life of a Writer series lately, because I haven't gotten a lot of fiction writing done lately... but then, maybe the higher word counts will come from getting this blog post out each day. Even now, I feel the urge to write fiction, because I see a big fat ZERO staring at me below.

GETTING CHEAP COVER ARTWORK

There is one other thing I've been working on the last few weeks: covers, covers, covers. I've been searching through Shutterstock and using my monthly plan (I bought 1 month of 25 downloads per day) to snatch up all the images for as many series as possible. I highly recommend this if you are trying to get out a lot of content and need images. You can purchase a monthly Shutterstock plan for a little under $175 (with a 30% off coupon that you can Google for—I've never failed to find one, it seems like they are always running a special), cancel the automatic renewal, and then download 25 images per day as needed for 30 days straight.

You lose your opportunity every 24 hours, so you have to be extremely disciplined about this to make it work, but if you pick a time each day to get your downloads in, and if you keep a document with links to all the images you've found, you can maximize your monthly subscription. This is how I get all my covers done for basically pennies each (plus my time). You can get 750 images total, which is enough to keep you in covers for years and years at a time.

There are many more things I want to write about, but I'm going to have to save them for another entry. Now, it is really time to write and get some words in. See you soon!

12:52 am (on the 28th) -

I had some trouble with my mic and had to take care of some evening chores with P, but was able to squeeze in a paltry 1651 words in the last 40 minutes or so. I had to type some of that, so my speed wasn't that bad.

I'm headed to bed. I have 3 days in a row of writing under my belt. I'm posting this entry. I'm going to call that a win for the day.

Challenge: Develop a Daily Fiction Writing Habit
Today: 1651 words
This week: 5677 words
August total (for the last week):17,923 words
September total (so far): 44,839 words
Challenge total (so far): 62,762 words

STRUGGLING THROUGH LOW WORD COUNTS, BUT DETERMINED NOT TO BREAK THE CHAIN (LIFE OF A WRITER: DAY 35)

3:20 pm -

I spent the entire morning and part of the afternoon coming up with freelance topics to pitch to various paying blog outlets. As I've mentioned a few times, I make the most money writing technical content for various sites. September was actually a horrible month for me with freelancing. I spent a good portion of my time trying to make it work with this client who had too specific a field to be quickly researchable. My hourly rate was going as low as $20/hour. I finally had to tell him that I couldn't work for him anymore, because there just wasn't enough money in it.

Also, there was a lull in work with my two main clients. These slow-downs (famines, as freelancers call them) always seem to come out of nowhere for me, but I think it's because I don't prepare for them the way I should. Ideally, you do freelance work whenever you can grab it and work on your own stuff in-between, during the famines. But, in September, I blew off nearly two weeks of famine by doing very little writing. Boo to me.

So, I really need to get some more freelancing work started. I need to budget time for it during October. I'm not making enough with my fiction to do anything otherwise, though I expect that will change when I get some work out this month.

Other than that, I'm trying to figure out my goals for October. I am pushing myself to get as much work out before Christmas because that's when things hit big for ebooks. This involves having writing goals, editing/publishing goals, and freelance goals (because I still need to pay bills). It also means trying to capitalize on the assets I do have, which are primarily my fiction. I need to do whatever it takes to get that content into multiple formats with as little input from me as possible, so that each little stream can start earning.

I'm also trying to figure out some other little goals I have. I strongly believe that consistency is something you practice. I've been trying to develop other little habits, particularly around the house. For example, every morning I load the dishwasher while I'm brewing my tea. Every Wednesday I start running loads of laundry. Every Sunday I want to start putting a Peapod order in.

I also want to create healthy lifestyle goals. Like cooking 3-4 meals at home every week, and getting 10,000 steps in every day (surprisingly difficult to do when you work from home).

I used to use Basecamp and Remember the Milk to track things like this, but I'm thinking of switching to Trello's free solution. It has a really fun iPad app that I've already started using. And I love the idea of keeping track of all my ideas and projects, even if I never get to them.

6:40 pm -

I'm really tired. I have somehow managed to drain all my energy for the day. I feel like I'm making progress on several projects, but I want to write more and don't completely have the energy to do it.

I've so far written 1462 words today. Must. Write. More.

9 pm-ish -

Got some energy back after eating dinner and typing about 480 words into the next scene I'm working on. I'm going to attempt to write some more with the mic for the next few hours to take advantage of this second wind.

Midnight -

I pushed myself after my short burst of energy. My total for today is 3487 words, which is not terrible, considering

I normally take Saturdays off from fiction. Of course, I've taken off a good portion of the last two weeks from fiction, so it's no surprise it's not a huge strain to write today. I'm proud of getting some work done, even if I'm still crawling along at a snail's pace for writing.

In at under 10k words for the week; not the greatest! But closing in on my 50k goal, as long as I keep up the same numbers (1000-3000 ish) over the final two days of September.

Challenge: Develop a Daily Fiction Writing Habit

Today: 3487 words

This week: 9164 words

August total (for the last week): 17,923 words

September total (so far): 48,326 words

Challenge total (so far): 66,249 words

GEARING UP FOR OCTOBER (LIFE OF A WRITER: DAY 36)

12:45pm -

I'm really excited today for a few reasons.

One, is that I was inspired by Trello and decided to start a Lose Weight Slowly challenge. It's pretty simple—I have a list of things to do for the week and move them to "Done for the Week" as I complete them.

A lot of them are really simple things. Like "Walk up 5 flights of stairs," which is a fairly simple thing to do in my building. I live on the 22nd floor, so if I'm coming inside by myself, I can simply do the first 5 flights, then catch the elevator back to my apartment.

This seems like a small change, but it's actually huge. I am so used to living or working in buildings where I do stairs regularly (second or third floor office, for example).

But since I started working from home, I rarely do stairs in my daily routine.

I've posted a new page on my site called "Goals" which is here: http://proseonfire.com/goals/. I'll probably start keeping track of other Goals on this page as well, and you can see my progress each week as I tackle little goals for myself.

I like Trello a lot. It is very visual, which is good for the way I process ideas and progress. I'm thinking of other ways I can use Trello to visualize my progress on other goals, especially my writing ones. And the coolest part is I can share entire boards publicly, which makes it easy to post updates on big projects I'm working on.

Here are some other boards I'd like to set up:

- Book Status board - I'd like to move all my books through a series of lists called Outlining, Writing, Editing, Publishing.
- Scene board - I'd like to move all my scenes through a series of lists called Beating, Drafting, Revising, Editing, Critiquing, and Proofreading.
- Growth Hacking board - I'd like to move all my websites through a series of tasks for growth hacking (this one is harder to visualize right now, since I don't totally know what those "tasks" are and how I want to present them)
- Freelance Writing board - I LOVE the idea of a board with article #'s and $$$ that have lists called Pitching, Writing, Editing, Submitted, Published, Invoiced, Paid. This would help me keep track of my weekly goals and also help show others that freelance writing is a viable way to make money. My only issue is that I wouldn't want to share too many details about each

article, since many of them are ghostwritten, so this may have to stay a Private board.

Anyway, I have lots of ideas for this tool. But I've spent way too much time playing with it today, so I'll have to start some of these other boards later this week!

The great thing about this new challenge to get a bit more healthy eating and exercise in is that I am walking a lot more. I love walking but hate being bored while walking. So I set up (as I've been wanting to do for awhile) a voice recorder on my Android (I'm using Smart Voice Recorder, which has a Pro version I can upgrade to eventually) so I can write my books while walking. Dragon Dictate can transcribe my voice recordings and turn my words into pages and pages of text, just like it does while I'm at my computer.

I tested the setup today and it works reasonably well, though I still get the most accurate results using my AT2020 Audio-Technica mic. It may just mean that I need to improve my Android Mic profile through Dragon Dictate, though, so I'll keep testing and trying to improve that process.

I'm excited to try this out because whenever I pace, my writing speed shoots up to 3500-4000 words/hour. I expect that will happen here, too. So, I could potentially get more words done or perhaps just free up some of my time when I'm home in front of my computer.

It'll be interesting to see how this goes, either way. Experimentation is fun for me.

Now, I'm off to run some errands, get dinner started (in the crock pot), and give the westie a bath. Then, writing. Hopefully.

5:45 pm -

Well, I just got back from running my errands. I decided to test out my recording setup on my way to Jewel-Osco (a midwest grocery chain) and recorded about 7 minutes of a scene from a book under my pen name.

I'm pretty disappointed with the results. I checked in on the transcribed file (after also typing out my version of the file, based on listening and typing), and it had only picked up about 73% of what I said. Very frustrating. Now, I was in a crowded area, and my test before just walking around my bedroom did much better... but yeah, I'm disappointed.

There are a few things I can change:

- my setting (quieter)
- the mic I'm using
- the recording software I'm using
- the audio quality I'm recording at
- the way I speak (with command)

All of those things may help get my transcriptions up to the 95% plus accuracy I'm currently enjoying by typing at my computer. Still, it's going to need a change in dictating style for me, and I'm not as happy about that part of it.

The good news is that I recorded 468 words in 7 minutes of speaking into that mic, which is a speed of over 4k words/hour! And I had A LOT of pauses due to random distractions and people walking by (I am not an overly self-conscious person, but I did feel slightly silly dictating to myself as I walked by random groups of people who could hear exactly what I was saying).

Anyway, this could be very good, if I could get the transcription part of things working a bit better.

7:30 pm -

I just got back from a walking with P and the westie, and I'm pretty exhausted. Looking forward to a few hours of delicious dinner and the Breaking Bad finale.

I tested the issues I was having with the recorder again tonight. I changed the audio quality and my mic. I'm not sure it made a huge difference, though I did notice that when I speak in a quieter setting, I don't have those huge gaps in content. It's more like a few words here and there, but as I was listening I started to understand why it wasn't picking those up.

I think the biggest improvement I can make is speaking more fluently, with more diction and volume. This is exactly the change I didn't want to make, but I'm going to test it tomorrow to see if it helps.

11 pm -

Man, I'm exhausted. I'm not completely sure why. I completed 4 items on my Lose Weight Slowly List, which were to cook dinner, take a long walk with Mia, walk up 5 flights of stairs, and put in a Peapod grocery delivery order. I'm wondering if the sheer added pressure of checking these things off my list, plus the physical strain on my body, is part of it?

I also got in over 11k steps today, which is surprising, especially when I didn't even take one of my long walks. The walk with P and the westie was unexpectedly long. P doesn't typically go with us, but we spent an hour or so out and about because he was there.

But no more words, and I have no more in me for today. Tonight I might put together a few more Trello boards or just go to bed.

I'm still pondering over my October goals where writing is concerned.

Challenge: Develop a Daily Fiction Writing Habit

Today: 721 words

This week: 721 words

September total (so far): 49,047 words
August total (for the last week): 17,923 words
Challenge total (so far): 66,970 words

50,000 FICTION WORDS IN SEPTEMBER (LIFE OF A WRITER: DAY 37)

11 am -

Last day of the month! I'm really excited. I have about 1,000 more words to do today and I've hit my September goal of 50,000 words!

This morning, I've been messing around with the transcription software again. I was really disappointed and also slightly relieved to realize that the issue is almost entirely with my microphone and android setup, and not with the transcription itself. This is good because I can record my words and transcribe them now, rather than dictating them directly into the screen (which sometimes causes data loss). It's bad because it means I have to get my mic + android setup up to the level of quality I'm enjoying with my awesome audio-technica mic, or else I can't record on the go.

The other option I'm looking into is how I can use my audio technica mic to record on the go, since that would be the optimal solution.

Of course, I need to actually get around to working today at some point, too.

4:30 pm -

After hours (pretty much all day) of looking for a solution to this on-the-go recording problem, I may have finally found something that'll work. I don't want to post it publicly though in case I'm an idiot and it doesn't work.

Either way, it's coming to me from Amazon and should arrive tomorrow night at the latest.

Big sigh of relief, at least for now. I'm bummed that I can't test it right this second, but glad that I can move on with my day.

First, I need a serious break. Then, I'll come back here and get to work on my manuscript under my other pen name so I can hit my 50k words goal for the day. Tomorrow will be a big day for freelance writing, so I won't have as much time to do the stuff I love before then.

10:58 pm -

The hunt for the adapter I needed exhausted me for the day. I'll admit that when I sat down at 10:36 pm, I didn't want to write. But I finished my scene from yesterday and got 1167 words in 21 minutes.

Done and Done! 50k words in a month. Awesome.

I know it's actually not that many fiction words. Most writers can do much more. But as a writer who for a long time didn't write very often, I'm really proud that I've stuck to this challenge for 37 whole days and hit a goal I set for myself at the beginning of the month, one I've never actually completed before.

One other thing I will say, on a pretty unrelated note—I am SO GRATEFUL for my awesome Audio Technica AT2020 XLR mic. After using a ton of other mics to test my on-the-go setup, I now remember and appreciate how dreadfully awful Dragon Dictate worked with them. There are still some minor errors using the AT2020 (primarily because I'm a soft-spoken mumbler when I'm sitting at my desk speaking), but it is damn good at dictation with my current setup.

I am so, so grateful for this easy way of getting my ideas and stories into text. I seriously question if I would still be a writer without these amazing tools. I would probably want to be, but I'm not sure my hands or my patience would hold up without this incredible program and my awesome mic.

Off to bed now. Tomorrow starts October, and I'm really excited to talk about my goals for the next month.

Hint: I'm going to set a goal higher than 50k words. Shouldn't be a surprise, when I hit 50k while basically goofing off half the time. Needn't I improve?

Challenge: Develop a Daily Fiction Writing Habit

Today: 1167 words

This week: 1888 words

September total (total): 50,214 words (HELL YEAH)

August total (for the last week): 17,923 words

Challenge total (so far): 68,137 words

Short stories read this week: 0

Scenes beaten out this week: 0

Scenes revised this week: 0

Scenes edited this week: 0

Books published this week: 0

September Insights, October Resolutions (Life of a Writer: Day 38)

11 am -

It's a new month! I'm so excited. New month means new possibilities and improvements.

A big part of making this month successful is understanding where I failed last month. So I've put together a few charts to capture some of the data I've collected.

As you can see, my word count per day leaves a lot to be desired. Certainly, it varies wildly. I got most of my writing done in the first two weeks of the month (over 2/3rds of the total) and the last bit spread out mostly toward the end of the month.

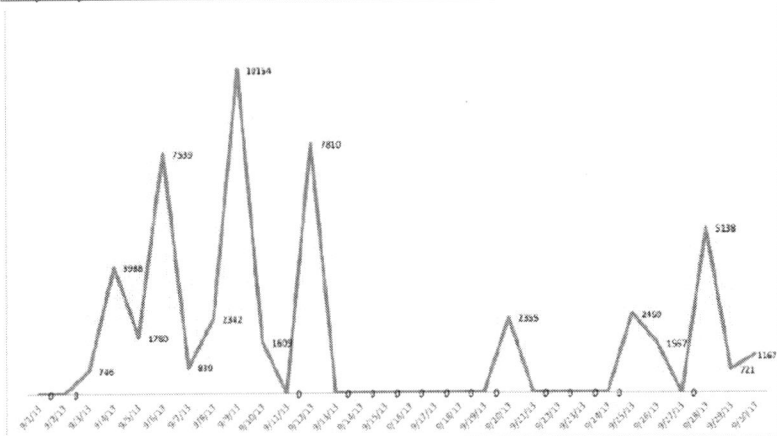

Word Count Per Day

My minutes writing per day looks about the same as the word count chart. What this tells me is that they are highly correlated (duh) and I need to pick one metric and stick to it.

I believe a big part of what messed me up this month was switching to the mindset of "putting more hours in."

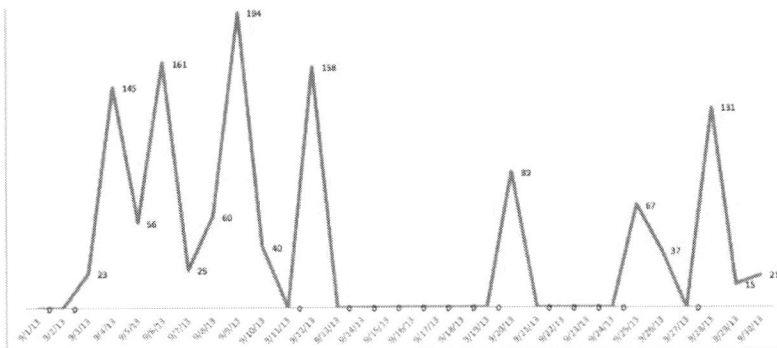

Minutes Per Day (Writing)

For whatever reason, that dulled my interest in writing more, which is when I fell off the horse.

So I think I'm going to stick to word count for now. The number of minutes I worked each day is interesting, though, when looking at the average number of words per hour for the day.

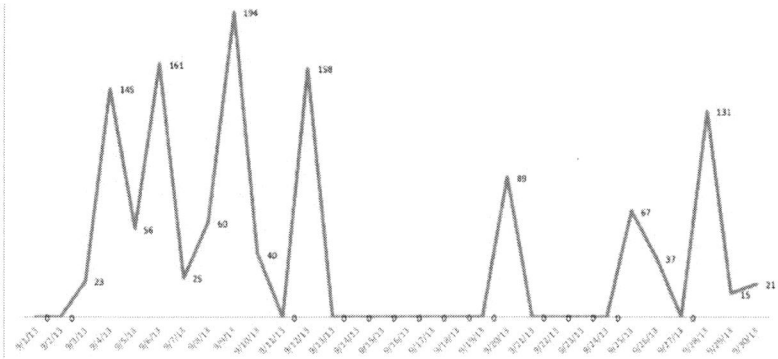

Average Words Per Hour By Day

The data is really limited, but what I did notice was that the stretches where I was writing more regularly, my writing speed seemed to pick up. After the long stretch, it was abysmal (1588 words per hour). By the end of the month, I seemed to be doing higher numbers on average, though again, the data is extremely limited and not indicative of much at this point.

I also charted the data next to each other on the same graph, which didn't provide much. (Red is word count, orange is avg. word count)

Again, the data is limited and this analysis isn't honestly that analytical—I'm hoping to collect more data in the coming months and use R to draw insights from it.

What I did notice (anecdotally) is that there may be lower and upper thresholds with word count. It seems like on days when I write "a lot" (which I would classify as 7500 words or more), my speed went up significantly. On days when I wrote "not much" (which I would classify as 2500 words or less) I also seemed to see a boost (more so toward the end of the month).

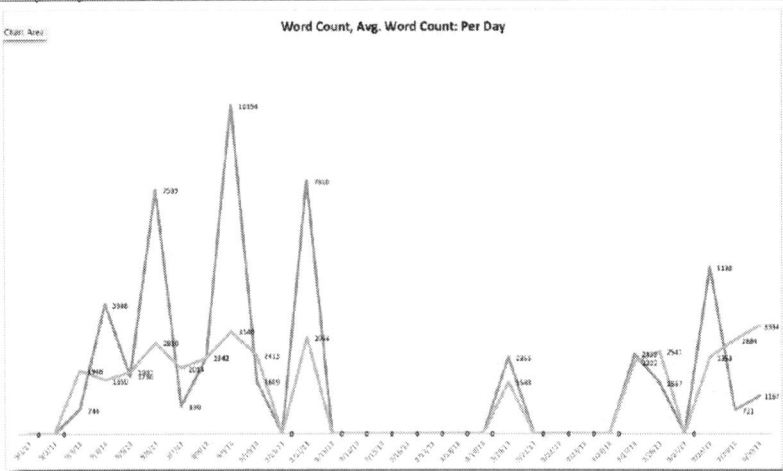

Mashed Up Chart

I'm not as interested in the lower-end boost, but I am interested in the spikes in speed for higher word count days. It seems like the optimal thing to do on a per-day basis is try to hit 7500+ words.

Whether that's optimal on a day-to-day basis in terms of energy is still not clear. That's a ton of words!

My September totals are: 1222 minutes, 50214 words, 2465 words/hour (average).

Not terrible for one month. Though the fact that I only wrote fiction 20 hours out of 720 hours of time during the month of September makes me feel pretty lazy.

The three days that I wrote over 7500 words, I spent 161, 194, and 158 minutes writing. It seems like the optimal amount could be 2.5-3 hours, though again, this data is incredibly limited.

I used Excel to chart all of this data, but I think I will probably use R next month. I didn't do it today because I have to install it and set it up on this computer, and I didn't want to spend a ton of time on it today when I have a number of other things to do.

So, it's time to look at goals for October. I've already talked a bit about my Lose Weight Slowly goals, and that's going well enough for the week so far (you can check my chart under proseonfire.com/goals/ to see my progress). I'm cooking dinner again tonight, and then I'll be starting my longer walking periods when I test my mic setup. I also walk to and from P's office sometimes, which is the equivalent of about 40-45 minutes each way (about 4.5-5 miles total). I count that as one of my laps. One thing I noticed is that I keep missing opportunities to hit the 5 flights of stairs. I talk the westie out three times a day and have forgotten nearly every time the last few days. I'll need to work on that to get the stairs in this week.

My October writing goals are a different story. There are a few really important spots I want to focus on:

Drafting Goal: 100k words for October

I want to continue drafting every day, like I have been for the last 6 days. I don't think breaks suit me. Getting a little done every day makes me happy, so even if it's something small, like 15 minutes two days ago, or 21 minutes yesterday, it seems to keep my momentum and interest going. Plus, the numbers do add up, slowly.

My goals for drafting this month are:

MAINTAIN THE CHAIN

Even if it means writing for 20 minutes at 11:30pm at night, I want to put some words on the screen every single day. My lowest days this month (outside of the zeros) were days that I got 746 words and 721 words. I'm going to set the low-end threshold at at least 500 fiction words to count as "writing." Since that takes me about 10-15 minutes to do, it's completely reasonable to hit this threshold every day.

INCREASE WORD COUNT/DAY IN GENERAL

I know I'll have off days, and I know there will be days when I just don't want to write as much. But I find the 7500 word/day threshold fascinating and want to try to get my average to at least half of that. My average for this month was 1674 words per day, which means I'd need to more than double it to get there. Double it would be 3348 words, while halving the 7500 words/day would be 3750. So, I'm going to settle on between 3000-3500 words/day average for October.

INCREASE MY TOTAL WORD COUNT FOR THE MONTH

This means my total words goal for the month needs to be around 100,000. Which is a HUGE amount. I'm more than doubling my goal from this month, and that makes me crazy nervous. I'm counting on two things to get me there:

- writing every day without breaking the chain
- figuring out my mic situation so I can dictate while walking (killing two birds)

The biggest thing I must avoid is days that I don't write at all, I think. In September, that was exactly half the days, or 15 days total.

If I had called it in on all those days and written even 1,000 words per day, I would have an extra 15k to add on to my total. And, the fact is that writing begets more writing, so that number would probably be much higher.

So, 100k words. Yikes. Can I do it this month?

PUBLISHING: GET SOMETHING OUT EACH WEEK

I have not done a good job of moving my fiction drafts to published content. I talked about this a lot during

September but honestly haven't found a great working solution to it that I can follow.

I feel like this needs to be the next big priority for me, similar to how I started this month with the goal to get 50k words done. Yes, I need to double the drafting goal, but I've figured out a lot of my processes for that already. Now, it's just about maintenance and improvement.

Publishing, on the other hand, is a habit I need to get started. There are so many elements to it, including revising, editing, critiquing, and proofreading, that I don't have a great handle on getting done. But I'm going to do what I did with the drafting goal, which is take it one little piece at a time.

After all, with drafting, I figured out outlining and beating too to get to where I am. So I just need to apply that same thinking to the publishing portion. I have a few ideas of how to get it done:

OUTSOURCING

This is the best option because it frees my time. But who to outsource to, and how to pay for it? That's part of the equation. I currently outsource to my critique partner, I suppose, but outsourcing more of these processes would be better.

One idea I have is to outsource the revising and proofreading portions of the work. For me, revising is simply going back through the Dragon Dictate version of the work and correcting the little mistakes it makes. If I could provide an audio file plus the output for each scene, someone else could go through it and get it done.

Proofreading is basically what it sounds like, checking grammar and punctuation and the likes. I've looked into online tools that allow someone to check a manuscript against grammar rules and much more, but there's still the process of going through all the changes to get a cleaner text. If I could provide the check + the manuscript, I may be able to pay someone else to go through it and return the text to me.

I would probably prefer to build a small team to get this done, but the costs will add up. I've also thought about using Amazon MTurk, which would require me to split up the work into smaller pieces than scenes. I'm not totally sure what I want to do, but I'm looking into each and trying to figure out a pricing model I can live with.

Editing, I have to do myself. I look for consistency and setting the right tone and mood here, and I often rewrite small chunks of the book here to better represent what I meant to say.

CUTTING DOWN ON EFFORT

Getting a better first draft has been part of my strategy from the beginning, because like any piece of art, it's easier to get it right from the beginning than to go through and try to fix something that is broken.

We'll see if it pays off when I work on Trinity, which is the first book that really used my optimized outline-beat-drafting process.

I haven't come up with a great way to measure this, but I am going to keep track of my editing time, the same way I keep track of my drafting time, so I may have more results for next month.

LITTLE EVERY DAY

Just like with the drafting, little moments of editing add up to published pieces. I believe I need to develop some sort of habit, just like anything else. For example, I could see myself editing while I watch the westie play with other dogs at the park. Or I could see myself editing over my morning tea, or in the evenings over a cup of coffee. I haven't quite come up with that perfect thing yet, but I know the key to unlocking this daily habit is associating it with something I look forward to.

Given these ruminations, it seems like the action items are:

- figure out how to easily/cheaply/quickly outsource the revising and proofreading portions
- find a way to incorporate editing into my daily schedule, similarly to how I do drafting in my daily schedule

As far as publishing something every week goes, the fact is that I have 3 drafts of books ranging from 20k-50k words done. By the end of this week, I may have 2-3 more (two are over halfway done, and one is not started but is really short). I have plenty of content to publish this month and could get one thing out each week... if only I could crack the nut on the whole "editing" thing.

The goal is reasonable, but experimental at this phase. I hope to have more insight into it over the coming month as I collect data on what I'm currently doing.

FREELANCING: 10-15 ARTICLES A WEEK

I slacked off so much on freelancing work this month, and I really regret it now. I honestly didn't even notice that my work was drying up, even though I've been doing this for nearly two years now and there are always periods of feast and famine. I just got out of a feast and the famine hit hard this time... especially since I was so distracted by how productive I was being with my fiction work.

I need to get back on track though. The one good thing I did this month was spend a ton of time researching new markets I can tap as far as the pitch-write-invoice piece of it goes. I'm pretty excited to gear up for some of them, and it will be interesting if I can turn any of them into regular clients.

I don't think I want to get into this too much now, but throughout the month I'll probably write more about it. I'm still trying to figure out how I want to work this, but I do know that I want to write at least 50 articles this month.

Sounds like a lot, but remember that some of these will be 500 words, which, even with research, can be done very quickly at my writing speeds with Dragon Dictate.

Still, it will be a lot of work to implement this daily habit too, and I have to admit that I'll probably fail a bit more here than with the other two. I have big goals, but I don't think it's realistic to tackle them all at once. My priorities have to be in:

- Maintaining and improving on my daily fiction writing habits
- Starting up a weekly publishing habit

Freelancing is already part of my workflow, so this will be all about taking a more rigorous approach with the help of Trello.

That's it. Three major goals and one goal area where I am starting from scratch, basically.

Additionally, I'm still doing the Lose Weight Slowly challenge and my Clean Apartment challenge, the latter of which I haven't written about because I've been implementing it since July and have made a lot of progress on habitualizing what I need there. These challenges are a bit easier since I don't have as much riding on them and am really just trying to reign in the chaotic nature of life with them and make my life with P much more tranquil and happy.

And, I didn't forget about two other challenges I've talked about here. One is the Short Story challenge (which is to get traditionally published with my short stories) and the other is the Growth Hacking challenge. After thinking about what was really important for me to accomplish this month, I decided that these two had to be cut for now. That doesn't mean I won't do any preparation for them, or that I won't circle back to them, because I will. It just means that I'm not ready to put them front and center. They'll have their spotlight moment in the coming months, though, I'm sure of it.

It's about 3pm now (I took an hour break for lunch). I'm going to get started on some Trello organization for these challenges, so that tonight I can get going on the real work that needs to be done. I'll be testing my new mic setup with a few scenes from a book under my pen name. If it works out, I'll be able to get some pen name stuff wrapped this week and start a few new books for the Monica Leonelle pen name.

Overall, I'm really excited about this plan and the progress I'm making. While I strive to do more all the time, I am really appreciative of the progress I made during September. I learned a lot, I got some real work done, and I built many good habits that now require nurturing to maintain.

I'm both excited and nervous going into month two of this diary. Nervous, because I've made a commitment to writing about my own failure in a genuine way, and there's a lot of opportunity for failure in this plan. Excited, because there's a chance I could succeed at everything I want this month. It's a blank slate. And that's a beautiful thing.

5pm -

I know this update is forever long for a single day, but I don't care. I'm so excited to share my Trello board for moving scenes through the entire process.

Trello Publishing Board

One of my favorite things about Trello is how visual it is. As you can see from my screenshot, it's really easy to identify where my gaps and bottlenecks are. Hopefully this chart makes it obvious why I need to prioritize editing and publishing this month!

The second thing I discovered is that I need to get a few more scenes beated out, because I'm running out pretty soon. This is especially true if my word count starts taking off in the next month due to my on-the-go recording and my Lose Weight Slowly goals.

The third thing I realized is that I can get my work critiqued really quickly by Susan when I send her the scenes one at a time. The only reason I realized this was that I sent her a scene last week from this new series I'm putting together, and she got back to me within 12 hours about it. This actually speeds up the process significantly, since the instant feedback is exciting and she doesn't need to do much or put much effort into it, aside from reading and commenting back on anything she feels strongly needs to be changed.

We've done it other ways, like sending each other full works, and that does take a ton of time and effort on both of our parts. I'm going to suggest this to her in our next meeting (tomorrow) so that we can breeze through the feedback process faster (and also not feel the need to comment so much on each other's work, which I think is unnecessary since we've worked together a lot, and we kind of know what the other person thinks on basic issues).

The reality of critiquing is that it's got to be an exchange, and it's got to stay fun. Without those two things, it becomes a huge chore for the person reading the stuff. Also, I'm not going to let critiquing hold up my production schedule, because that is silly. Seeing as I can't even keep up with the amount I've produced in the last month, I can't expect anyone else to.

Ideally, I'd like to get this board evened out this month. I would love if every column looked like the Beat column, which only has about 10 things in it. This visualization makes it painfully apparent that right now I'm not running lean, like I should be, and dedicating too much time to certain columns while leaving other columns neglected.

It's going to be a huge challenge to balance this with the idea of writing more. At 50k words a month, I'm not handling my production process very well. Doubling this will exacerbate the problem, but that's all part of what makes the challenge fun and exciting.

By the way, the titles listed in this Trello are under both pen names. I don't see any harm in sharing it this way, since nothing is really listed out and since the pen names aren't a secret by any means. I'll probably make this public at some point, but I'd like to think it through a bit more before making that decision.

I've also come up with a few fun places to get some editing done:

- Barnes and Noble (there's a huge DePaul campus store near my apartment)
- The Park (any of them)
- The Atrium at the Library (also right next to my apartment)
- On the Train
- The Beach (.3 miles from my apartment)
- Gleacher Center (U of C downtown campus)
- Harper Memorial Library (U of C)

I'm an alum of University of Chicago, so I still have access to many of these buildings. One of my bff's is at the Harper Center campus, so it would be fun to be down there more often.

The parks and beach may soon be less appealing thanks to horrible Chicago winters, and I rarely ride the trains.

My best bet is probably B&N and the library atrium. Going to the Harper Center could also be amazing, because there's a bus ride to and from, an awesome salad bar on the campus, and lots of walking and pretty buildings.

The biggest issue is getting out of the apartment. I'm way too comfortable in my own home to read for more than pleasure... and it probably doesn't help that I use evening reading to fall asleep.

Now, the issue is putting in the time... how do I force myself to go? I still don't have a great answer to that question. I need some serious incentive to make it happen, that doesn't have to do with buying books. Maybe checking books out at the library? Exploring the bookstore (which I love to do)? Who knows.

10:30 pm -

I worked on my setup for on-the-go again today, and... it works! It's NOT as good as a regular dictation session would be. There is a bit of feedback from the adapter I'm using, which is affecting the recording, and thus the accuracy, but overall the solution is significantly better than what I had before.

I'm still missing some words, particularly when there is a ton of wind (or artificially created wind due to putting the mic right next to the fan). I have to try to speak louder and/or improve my abilities to use this, but it's definitely a major step in the right direction compared to how bad things were.

I might test it tomorrow, though I'm hesitant to do a huge run with it when it's still unproven. Maybe I can just walk for an hour or something. That way, if the recording is terrible, I can just listen with headphones and speak it into the mic, and I've only lost an hour of time. (Or get it transcribed, which is probably the more efficient solution.)

Now, I need to get cracking with a TON of other stuff—taking out the dog, downloading some images from Shutterstock, getting this post in, and most importantly, getting some writing done. Will not break the chain! But frankly, I'm going to use my computer setup because the recorder setup is slightly more annoying.

12:30 am -

48 minutes, 2638 words.

I had fun writing tonight, but the late hour reminds me that I really want to start getting my writing done earlier in the day. I am not loving the 1am bedtimes right now.

It's time for sleep, after I post this and finish up my Shutterstock downloads. Goodnight!

Challenge: Develop a Daily Fiction Writing Habit

Today: 2638 words

This week: 4526 words

October (so far): 2638 words

August total (for the last week): 17,923 words

September total: 50,214 words

Challenge total (so far): 70,775 words

WRITING ON-THE-GO, FINALLY (LIFE OF A WRITER: DAY 39)

11 am -

I'm tearing through my 5 flights of stairs, now that I'm remembering to do it. It's not bad at all. It takes only a few minutes, but forces me to get extra steps in.

The most interesting thing about the Lose Weight Slowly challenge is that I genuinely feel more energetic. I got SO much done yesterday without feeling sluggish at all. Is this really all it takes to see more productivity?

For example, when I was writing last night, I maintained a 3298 words/hour speed over 48 minutes straight. That's unusual for me, especially since a portion of that time was past midnight. My typical speed for nighttime writing is closer to 2500 words/hour.

I started Lose Weight Slowly for a number of reasons (the largest one because I need to lose weight), but a big motivation for me starting now was the idea that I could boost my overall energy and get more done. I'm already starting to see some of those results, which is really cool. I'm curious to see if my results are imaginary, ephemeral, or the real deal over the course of the next month.

This morning, I thought of a few more things I probably need for my on-the-go setup to work—a wind screen for my mic (I'm using the pouch it came with for now), a 9V battery charger and spares—so I need to make some more purchases on Amazon pretty soon. I may head down to Best Buy today and see if I can't get the second item on the list.

I'm very excited to test my setup today, but also nervous. What if it doesn't work? What if I run out of power, or mess up the recording? All that writing effort will go to waste.

2 pm -

It works! I'm pretty thrilled. The setup actually works and I got great results on my first (albeit short) run at it.

I walked down to the Chicago riverfront and tested it for about 18 minutes before I had to come back for a meeting, which didn't end up happening. While I was walking back, I listened to the recording, which was pretty good, considering all the crap that was going on around me. Then when I ran it through the transcription, it decoded pretty well. I captured 1081 words in 18 minutes for a rate of 3603 words/hour. I was especially surprised by my speed, because listening back to the recording, I was speaking soooo slowly. I wanted to tell myself, "Spit it out already!" It probably didn't help that I knew what I was about to say, almost verbatim.

7 pm -

I talked to Susan for about two hours and crashed short after that. I was so tired without even realizing it! I think my exercising high just came down after so many hours. A big part of that is I haven't been sleeping well at night— going to bed at 1am, waking up at 7am... it's just not good for me. I'm making a list now of everything I want to get done before the evening so I can get to bed at a decent hour tonight.

I think I'm going to skip writing more words tonight, unless I get a real urge in the next 4 hours or so. I have all day tomorrow to go outside and write, and now that I know my solution works, I'm really excited to get started! That puts me a bit behind on my word count for both today and yesterday, but I believe I can catch up. Or, if I get everything else done tonight, I can add another couple thousand words to the manuscript I'm working on, but I have a feeling that isn't going to happen, realistically.

At 3500 words a day (which is a slight overestimate needed to hit my 100k goal for the month), I need to be at 17500 for October by the end of the week. That's 13781 words in the next three days. And it's completely doable, if I write outside on a few long walks.

10:25 pm -

I feel like I haven't gotten enough done today. I would normally stay up and get a ton more done, but the reality is I need to go to bed earlier. That means cutting myself off at 10:30pm.

Which means, getting stuff done earlier, if necessary! It didn't help that I napped for a good portion of the afternoon.

Goodnight.

And okay, I'm probably going to sneak in some editing if I can.

Challenge: Develop a Daily Fiction Writing Habit

Today: 1081 words

This week: 5607 words

October (so far): 3719 words

August total (for the last week): 17,923 words
September total: 50,214 words
Challenge total (so far): 71,856 words

FIRST FULL DAY WRITING ON-THE-GO (LIFE OF A WRITER: DAY 40)

8:30 pm -

I'm so tired tonight. I got three scenes off to Susan today and I got two more scenes done on a manuscript I'm working on for my other pen name. And... those were actually the last two scenes of this manuscript, so I'm done with it! Since this challenge started, I've finished drafts for 3.5 books, each between 20-50k words. Pretty exciting.

I did my walk today with my mic, and it was pretty fun! The only thing that sucked was my back started hurting after awhile. I think it comes from lack of posture and/or not enough strength in my back/abs, but I'll have to watch that since I am carrying quite a bit of equipment with me as I walk around. It would be nice to spread the weight out a bit more on my body, but for now my solution is a purse with a cross-strap.

I ended up getting 4,270 words done today, which is not terrible for a daily, but not really what I was expecting for a walk that long. I could have honestly walked for much longer, but I had to come back and deal with something for P, so that cut my walk short. Ideally, I want to walk a bit earlier in the day, when it's less crowded and when I have more freedom over my time. It rained for most of the morning, so I was lucky to get out at all, I suppose.

I also realized that walking north is a bad idea... the sound from the highway and the people is just too loud. South is a better option. But not too far south, so I need to plan my route out a bit.

I am also happy to just walk up and down the trail, right across from Grant Park. That stretch is so quiet and peaceful. And I got a lot more words in doing that, anyway.

My speeds for today were 3196 on one scene and 2975 on the other. There are a few minutes added to those recordings due to adjusting equipment, but I decided to leave it in the final total, since the whole point is to get better at recording with this equipment. These aren't terrible speeds either, but certainly not what I was originally expecting for my first big day out.

16,400 steps and counting for today though. Can't complain about that! For reference, I (or anyone) can burn about an extra 500 calories a day when I walk this much. So, about a pound a week, as long as I watch what I'm eating.

I'm at a point in the night where I put in a good day's work, but I still have a bit of time left. I can't decide whether I should work on freelancing or do the thing I'm more motivated to do, which is either beat more scenes for Fallen or edit more scenes from the book I'm currently working on. Of course, that's what got me into trouble in the first place last month! Maybe I should get the freelancing stuff done.

9:30 pm -

I was researching some stuff for one of my freelance articles when I realized why I'm so disappointed with my 3000-ish words/hour today. I've seen myself hit 3500-4000+ words/hour walking, so now my expectations are set pretty high. But the awesome thing is, even though my rate was a bit slow today, I still hit 3k words hour, which has been my goal for awhile. Awesome. I know I can get in the 3.5-4k range, but today is a good start. Time to build up!

I'm going to go ahead and post this now, since I don't have any plans to write more words or send off more scenes. I may edit a bit more tonight, but I won't send it out until tomorrow.

I'm happy with today, but I still need to bump up my word count/day if I'm going to hit 100k by the end of October. At 3 days in, I should already be up to 10,500, and I'm only about 3/4ths of the way there. I really want to hit 7500 words on my walks, at least a few days a week. I just think it would be cool. And for me, that would only be an extra one, maybe two scenes. I completed two scenes today, and a third one would have brought the total to around 6500-7000 words. I could have done that, if it weren't for my obligations at home.

I have 9511 words to go to catch up by the end of the week. With two days left, if I can hit the same amount each day that I hit today, I should be pretty close.

I'm disappointed that I'm only at just under 10k words for the week, and it's already the end of Thursday. I'm historically bad at writing on Fridays and Saturdays, so I'll have to make sure I stay on task and get the work done.

Challenge: Develop a Daily Fiction Writing Habit

Today: 4270 words

This week: 9877 words

October (so far): 7989 words

August total (for the last week): 17,923 words

September total: 50,214 words

Challenge: Develop a Daily Fiction Publishing Habit
Scenes beaten out this week: 0
Scenes revised this week: 0
Scenes edited this week: 3
Scenes proofread this week: 0
Books published this week: 0

GETTING INTO A WRITING GROOVE (LIFE OF A WRITER: DAY 41)

4:20 pm -
Sigh! I got 7273 words done today between 10:30am-1pm. Which was awesome! The bad part is that the last file was corrupt for some reason, I think because the Gain on the IRig got messed up in the middle of it. I really have to watch that more carefully.

Otherwise, though, I got 20k steps and 7000+ words, and I'm pretty thrilled. I think I could have gotten a lot more, but I had to skip certain parts of the manuscript that were, uh... inappropriate to speak out loud. I'll have to finish those parts at some point, probably tomorrow when I'm feeling a bit more willing to write than I am now.

So, I fixed the scene that had been corrupted. I had a feeling that the Gain might become a problem if it accidentally moved around, so maybe I'll just find a way to tape it into position next time. Luckily, I created separate recordings for each scenes and check the recordings at the beginning of each session for Gain levels, so I won't lose much work this way. But today, I lost about 15 minutes of recording, which costed me a little extra time, but mostly extra frustration.

But, it's all a learning process. I'm learning how to make this walking work for me, and it's surprisingly good so far.

I switched from my heavy Coach purse to a lightweight Incase backpack, and that helped immensely with the back soreness I was experiencing yesterday. Made a world of difference, and was also more convenient to work from, so I plan to stick to that.

I also walked south instead of north and it was significantly less crowded and quieter. It's feeling like a winning route to me, though I still want to make sure I'm safe on the path, especially with all that equipment on me.

Other than that, not much else to update with. I haven't done any other editing and I'm all out of beats, almost. I need to work on more before tomorrow if I want to venture out again.

I need to get some freelance stuff done, now, so I'm going to get back to it before P comes home for the evening and things get busy again.

11:10 pm -

It's Friday, right? I haven't gotten anything more done. But the truth is, I need to if I'm going to do a long writing session again this weekend. I probably won't be able to, due to P being home. Still, I've run out of scenes to write, which is unusual for me. Gotta fill up the coffers again, plus keep pushing those other scenes through the later phases of the process.

I have soooo much I want to get done this weekend, there's no way I can cover it all. I need to figure out what's most important and get that done first. In my mind, that's beats, some drafting, lots of editing, and freelance work. I may stay lighter on the drafting than usual to pick up some of the rest of this stuff, editing especially.

Challenge: Develop a Daily Fiction Writing Habit
Today: 7273 words
This week: 17150 words
October (so far): 15242 words
August total (for the last week): 17,923 words
September total: 50,214 words
Challenge: Develop a Daily Fiction Editing Habit
Scenes beaten out this week: 0
Scenes revised this week: 0
Scenes edited this week: 3
Books published this week: 0

NEED TO GET BACK TO WORK TOMORROW (LIFE OF A WRITER: DAY 43)

1 am (Monday morning) -

I am writing just to say that I haven't been writing! It's been a busy weekend. I'm excited to get back to work tomorrow, but I spent the entire weekend working on growth strategy and covers.

A big part of that is because I ran out of beats, which makes it extremely difficult to get more writing done. But, I've also slacked off on editing this weekend.

Still, I'm determined to get back to it tomorrow. That's why I'm writing this entry, as a public reminder to get back to work. Breaks aren't a bad thing, unless they last too long. I would love to take weekends off from writing eventually, but I need to develop enough discipline to get back to work come Monday.

Very excited about my covers though, and I needed to sort those out because my Shutterstock account expires in 10 days.

Lose Weight Slowly Challenge Going Well, But Way Behind On Everything Else (Life of a Writer: Day 44)

9:45 am -

Good morning! I'm writing this because I want to make sure I get back to work today.

I'm still working on my Lose Weight Slowly Challenge and took a snapshot of where I ended up for the week.

LOSE WEIGHT SLOWLY WEEK 1

I did surprisingly well. The only things I missed were a few 5 flights and eating enough salad. The salad part had to do with not starting early enough in the week—I got to Wednesday or Thursday and realized I needed to step up my salad eating to get through everything.

Technically, I got in all the 5 flights I had set out to do at the beginning of the week. Being the silly person I am, I noticed that I was almost out about mid-week and decided to add a few more to the list. Then, I didn't get them done. Good job, right? Oh well.

Either way, it's a brand new week, and I will be trying to maintain what I have on my to-do list. So far, I'm a bit behind, because I took a lot of the weekend off from these goals and challenges to take care of stuff I had been neglecting.

This week, ironically, I've so far walked up 5 flights of stairs and eaten a salad. I'm hoping to make more progress today.

I did a horrible job at both my editing and my freelancing goals, but did pretty well with the writing goal. I am behind again, having never fully caught up last week and having not written yesterday. Today is the 7th, which means I should be at about 24,500 words by the end of the day. I'm starting out at 15,242 words so far for the month, so it's unlikely I'll catch up today. By the end of this week, I should be at 42,000 words, so I'll likely aim for that over the next 6 days instead (26,758 words, or about 4500 words a day for the next 6 days).

I can hit this if I walk every day. The biggest issue I have right now is that I don't have any scenes beat out for walking. So my first task will be to beat out more scenes, about 25 for the week. I'm probably going to try to do at least some of that this morning.

I've also done terribly at freelancing. I am not completely sure why, aside from just not finding it as interesting as what I'm working on with fiction. I've decided that no matter what, I need to pitch 3 articles per day during the week, Monday-Friday. That's 15 articles pitched, which should get me at least 10 articles accepted. There's no way I'm going to hit the original 60 article goal I had for this month, considering I have zero after the first week, but I know that when the articles are assigned I get them done. So I need to get over the hurdle of getting them assigned, and not worry about when I actually write them.

And editing—well, I'm ramping up slowly on that too. Five scenes a day is probably the ideal amount here, but I would be happy with three as well. Any regular progress is probably better than sporadic process because little by little adds up faster in my experience.

So, maybe the trick is that I literally can't go to sleep unless I have at least 1 done in each of these three categories—writing, editing, and freelancing—per day. That seems fair. I have a goal, but if that fails, I have to do at least a little to make progress.

We'll see. I am trying to be patient with editing and freelancing, because it took me so long to get moderately consistent with writing. I've had a lot of ups and downs and false starts, and it takes daily effort to stay on top of my goals.

10:30 pm -

I just had an odd revelation, because I feel so stuck on editing right now. What if I alternated between manuscripts the way I do with writing? Right now I'm stuck on scene 4 of this book under a pen name—but I could easily edit a few scenes of Unbound from the Waters Dark and Deep series.

Something to try today.

In the meantime, I need to get back to writing. And beats. And see if I can't get some editing done today, too.

11:40 pm -

I didn't make it as far as I wanted through the one scene I have left that is beaten out and ready to draft. But, I still snagged 1630 words. Every little bit counts. I'm hoping to make up some big word count totals in my walk-n-talks over the next few days. I need to complete four to meet my Lose Weight Slowly challenge, and that's likely all I'll have time for this week.

I would genuinely love to be able to do these walks every single day, but it's a large chunk of time—3 or more hours—and it's really not plausible for a regular week, with everything else I have going on with P.

This also requires me to get a ton of beats done, which will take a large chunk of time too.

I moved Unbound onto my Kindle so I could start editing it. Those scenes won't count for today, but it's a step in the right direction.

And freelancing? Sigh. Try again tomorrow.

Challenge: Develop a Daily Fiction Writing Habit

Today: 1630 words

This week: 1630 words

October (so far): 16,892 words (out of 100,000)

August total (for the last week): 17,923 words

September total: 50,214 words

Challenge: Develop a Daily Fiction Editing Habit

Scenes beaten out this week: 0

Scenes revised this week: 0

Scenes edited this week: 0

Books published this week: 0

Challenge: Pitch 15 Articles a Week

Pitched: 0

Assigned: 0

Completed: 0

EVERYTHING IS FIGURE-OUT-ABLE, BUT NOT TODAY (LIFE OF A WRITER: DAY 45)

11:45 am -

I was thinking last night about how I haven't explained some of my thought process for these journal entries.

I was reading about weight loss and noticed that of the people who actually lost weight, it was much harder than they made it look. They had a lot of false starts and stops, despite having excellent progress overall.

So, that's how I feel about these goals. It is incredibly embarrassing to write posts like the one I did yesterday, for example. I not only had to admit I took two days off (when just last week I said no breaks in writing) and it was also embarrassing to post that I'm making zero progress on my editing and freelance goals. I'm doing this for two reasons:

1) To shame myself into actually working

2) So that when I or anyone else looks back on my journey, it is painstakingly obvious that I struggled, screwed up, and was overall human during the process.

So yes, it is not cool to have all those zeros next to those goals. But I'm patient with myself, because I know that this is the hard part about developing a habit. Because I know that I'm playing the long game, not the short one. Because I know that the only way to move forward is to forgive myself and listen to what I need.

Maybe you can do better than me, which is awesome! I hope you do. Right now, my only competition is myself: am I doing better this week than last? That's how lasting habits form, in my experience. So I am starting with absolute crap habits and need to push myself to turn those zeros into something, anything.

I'm confident I will do it. Someday it will feel easier, and then even later, it will feel like such second nature that I don't need to track it. Right now, writing daily fiction falls into the "easier" category. So I will succeed at this, too, in time.

I'm stuck in an office all day, which means no writing (though I did get my long walk in by coming to the office in the first place). I think I'm going to hit the freelancing and editing goals hard today. Might as well, since I'm stuck!

11:30 pm -

Today has not been great on the goals front again. I did get some freelancing done with one of the companies I work with, which is good. I also got a pitch for 6 articles outlined, and fixed up my blog so I can use it as a reference (not this one, my ML.com one).

But, no words, not a ton of edits (though I got part of a scene done). I'm headed to bed to edit some more. As for writing, I realized that my idea of writing every single day is probably not necessary, as long as I do my 4 walk 'n talks a week. During these sessions, I can easily get around 7500 words, which totals about 30,000 by the end of the week. Plenty of room for error there, when I only need 25,000 a week for this month.

I think that would make these goals easier. I realized earlier when I was writing this entry that I've optimized my writing to death, and found that the walks are, plain and simple, the most productive way to do this job. There's genuinely no reason to write outside of the 4 walk n talks a week unless I am really excited and want to get something down on the screen. Time to work smarter, not harder. Optimizing my writing process was a huge investment, so I should take comfort in the idea that I've found a good system. It might be time to go into autopilot with it.

That would then leave my daily to-dos at freelancing and editing. I believe that these too can be done in bulk rather than daily, but I'm not completely sure of the configuration yet. I just know that trying to juggle three daily goals is overwhelming me and tearing my attention in all different directions, which is leaving me with not much to show at the end of the day. I can tell, because I've been watching a lot of TV lately, which is always a sign that I'm shutting down due to overwhelm.

So, one thing at a time. I'm still working out the best way to get it all done, and I do think it's possible, but I realize now that it's not as simple as slow and steady on each goal, every day.

I feel a bit defeated. But also, I'm trying to remind myself that this is part of the process. I read back to my beginning entries of this challenge and saw how much I struggled to get to this point. The process is a struggle. Maintaining is a struggle. But I've beaten the struggle before, and I can do it again.

I have 25,000 words to draft, 21 scenes to edit, and 15 articles to pitch every week for the rest of this month to hit my goals. I still think it's possible. It'll just take some experimentation to figure out the right combination of work, that doesn't make me miserable. It's figure-outable. Time to figure it out.

Challenge: Develop a Daily Fiction Writing Habit
Today: 0 words
This week: 1630 words
October (so far): 16,892 words
August total (for the last week): 17,923 words
September total: 50,214 words
Challenge: Develop a Daily Fiction Editing Habit
Scenes beaten out this week: 0
Scenes revised this week: 0
Scenes edited this week: 0
Books published this week: 0
Challenge: Pitch 15 Articles a Week
Pitched: 0
Assigned: 0
Completed: 0

IRIG PRE BROKEN ALREADY (LIFE OF A WRITER: DAY 47)

1pm -
Yesterday was a bad day. I went on my walk (25k steps, woohoo!) but my audio adapter blew out. I lost a chapter of work and also wasn't able to record more.

From there, things went downhill. I feel a bit defeated right now. But a few things I learned yesterday:

I LOVE the walk 'n talks. They are also critical to my workflow. That means I need to have backup equipment so that when something breaks, I can get back up and running that day, rather than 2-3 days later, from ordering new equipment.

Walking is a huge chunk of my time, so any of that wasted is not good for my business. I need to bring backup work in case my audio fails. That means bringing some editing work to do, even though editing is not as natural as dictation while walking.

So, I took the rest of yesterday off to handle some personal things and regroup.

Today, I'm going to work exclusively on freelance stuff and continue to regroup. I can't explain it—the loss of that work really hit me hard. I think because I found something that was so perfect and productive, and it just isn't working the way I planned. I am not in the right emotional state to work on fiction in any capacity, and I just need to take a personal day today.

I know this entry is depressing, but I want to be real about the ups AND the downs of this job. I am not always good at handling wrenches in my plans. For whatever reason, this one hit me really hard and I just need some time to process for now.

I did get some words in yesterday, but I haven't gone through the recordings to see exactly how much. I lost a lot of words too that I hope I can recover in some form.

I'm not sure if I'll be writing for the next few days... I'm just not in the right place at the moment.

I'm trying to remember this is just a setback, that I can recover from. I can still get in my 100k words goal for this month if I figure things out and work hard over the next few weeks. I'm still fighting, I just need a breather.

11:30 pm -

I checked out the files, and they are all bad. I'm so bummed. But I'm getting a replacement iRig PRE and will try again Saturday. I'll probably just redo these files, because I don't want to try to salvage what I have.

I'm DESPERATELY hoping that iRig PRE is not just a shitty product, and that I got a bad one. I really, really, really want this setup to work. PLEASE PLEASE don't suck.

Bleh.

Bummed about this + some personal stuff. I'm taking a few days off. So I'll catch up on Saturday or Sunday, when I'm back and ready to work.

GETTING SOME FREELANCING PITCHES DONE, FINALLY (LIFE OF A WRITER: DAY 49)

12:00 pm -

So, the last few entries of the Life of a Writer series have been really depressing. It's time to get back up and excited for work!

I have my new iRig PRE and I haven't tested it yet, but I'm hoping that it performs as well as it did the first day I went out. There's another product on the market that does the same thing if it doesn't, that I may also try.

I also have my rechargeable batteries now, so if this is a working solution I know I won't run out of battery juice.

I am insanely behind on my goals for this week. In fact, and especially since I lost two scenes from my last walk 'n talk, I've made almost zero progress on any of them.

So, I'm starting over and recalculating everything needed to be done per day starting from Oct. 13th to Oct. 31st. It seems like the most reasonable thing to do, since I can't recover the lost time, I just need to play catch up.

WRITING GOALS

So, for my writing goal, I need to average 4,375 words a day, which is, honestly, a HUGE goal. The only way I can see realistically hitting that is with the walk 'n talks, which are sort of in flux right now since I don't know if I can actually do them anymore.

But I'm thinking if I can do 12 more walk 'n talks this month at 7k words each I will hit this goal still. That's only 4-5 per week, which was what I was planning to do anyway. There are a lot of breaking points in that plan, unfortunately, which really scares me, but I gotta go with what I have for now and quickly duplicate my setup over the coming weaks for points of failure, just in case.

EDITING GOALS

My editing goals are a bit blurrier, but right now I have 5 manuscripts that need to get through editing. I tell Susan almost daily that this is ridiculous, especially since my goal is to produce a few more this month!

I would be happy if I got through even the manuscripts I currently have by the end of the month. That is a total of roughly 75 scenes, which is only an average of 4 scenes per day. I originally wanted to 5 per day, but I still need to figure out just exactly how to get it done.

I've thought of abstracting it out to a specific location, similar to how I've done with the walk 'n talks. My only hesitation is that having two outings per day on most days is not realistic for me. I can handle one at most. So I believe editing needs to get done at the desk, one scene at a time.

FREELANCING GOALS

I wanted to get 60 articles placed and completed this month. That's obviously extremely unrealistic at this point. Then, I wanted to get 15 articles pitched per week. I think it's possible to get this done every week, but I definitely didn't get it done this week. I technically still have time. One of the tactics I'm taking is to pitch the same publication multiple ideas in the hopes that 3-4 will stick. I'll have to update this as the tests for that tactic go along.

I still want to get 40-50 articles pitched this month. There are roughly 3 weeks left in October and I will have some of this goal done today. So we are still looking at about 15 articles a week for the next 3 weeks. I think the goal is good and realistic, the problem is dedicating a day to doing it (rather than doing 3 a day or something—which doesn't seem to work for me).

I'm thinking about this schedule: send pitches on the weekend, since they are these small little packets of work, and do most of my writing and editing during the week.

This would give me a few days off from pushing forward on fiction (which is what I consider the more difficult work) and I can spend the weekends planning, reevaluating, and experimenting (which is essentially what a pitch is to me).

People will get back to me throughout the week and I can schedule articles as they get assigned.

I can also work on beats over the weekend, since they are essentially prep work for drafting throughout the week.

So that's what I'm working on today. I don't have many expectations; again, I'm just continuing to experiment with getting work done. I'd like to think that someday all of this will get easier and I will have my system down, but who knows?

3:00 pm -

I just tested the iRig PRE and I'm getting decent results with it. I've noticed that the Gain is just a problem with this, so I put some tape over it and put it on a low setting. For some reason, the recording sounds better on the iPad than on my Android, so I might start using that while I'm out and about.

I'm going to work on pitches and beats for the rest of the day, and probably tomorrow too (though I might do a walk to test my setup, sometime in the afternoon since the Chicago Marathon is going on all morning). The challenge is to get about 15 pitches out today and tomorrow, and to get all my scenes for next week beat out as well. I'm working on one manuscript from my other pen name (which I wrote and lost 2 scenes of already, boo), and then I think I'm headed back to the WD&D series. I feel excited about finishing books 4 and 5 of the first cycle, and I have a good chunk of those drafted already so it seems like a worthy goal to get the rest drafted by the end of the month.

I was planning to start two other small series for the month, but I think I'll push them off until next month. It's just much easier on my mind to draft scenes from series that are already established with characters and settings and everything else. It's harder to create the details of something all new.

Midnight -

I finished off the day with 6 pitched ideas to one publication. I also made a list of the other articles I plan to pitch this weekend so there's not as much thinking to do as I go along.

Once at least one or two of my articles to the one publication is published, I can leverage that article to pitch other websites in the same niche (the ones that I've confirmed are paying sites, that is).

There's a second site in this same niche that accepts unsolicited submissions, so I'm going to pitch another round of articles there too.

And I want to submit a few articles about writing fast and my dictation setup to a some sites as well.

It's really a relief to have gotten that big submission done, and I think it gives me confidence to move forward with more submissions. The pipeline will be full soon, I hope!

I have SO MUCH FURTHER to go with the rest of these goals. This week has pretty much been a wash, it feels. Yes, I got a little done, but not nearly what I wanted to, and that's a huge bummer.

Tomorrow is the beginning of a new week, and that means shifting gears. If I can get some more pitches done for tomorrow I'll feel better moving forward. I actually really like the idea of doing pitches on the weekends—it fits with my natural inclination, which is to sit and watch TV for a good part of the time. Research and pitching are easy multi-tasking items to check off the list.

Challenge: Develop a Daily Fiction Writing Habit

Today: 0 words

This week: 1630 words

October (so far): 16,892 words

August total (for the last week): 17,923 words

September total: 50,214 words

Challenge: Develop a Daily Fiction Editing Habit

Scenes beaten out this week: 7

Scenes revised this week: 0

Scenes edited this week: 0

Books published this week: 0

Challenge: Pitch 15 Articles a Week

Pitched: 6

Assigned: 0

Completed: 0

I'M BACK, SORT OF (LIFE OF A WRITER: DAY 50)

1:30 pm -

I'm back! I'm feeling better than I have in awhile. Maybe because it's the beginning of the week again, and life feels fresh.

After the snafu from last week, I have a ways to go with my goals. Before I talk about that, I wanted to share an update from my Lose Weight Slowly challenge.

LOSE WEIGHT SLOWLY CHALLENGE WEEK 2

It seems like when I take time off, everything suffers. I did less on my Lose Weight Slowly challenge than last week.

The laps around the loop are understandable, but I also didn't do enough cooking or stairs. For cooking, P made dinner one of the nights last week, and I ate tons of leftovers. Overall, I still didn't eat out, which makes me realize that I may not need to cook any more than 3 nights a week, ever, especially if I'm eating lots of salad too.

For whatever reason, I struggled with walking up the stairs this week. A part of that is the westie hates doing it, so she gets up two flights of stairs and then makes me carry her the rest of the way.

That said, I want to do this. I consider it moderate exercise that's good for the heart, and climbing 5 flights of stairs 10 times a week burns an extra 600 calories a week. It's not a ton, but it's a simple habit that takes a few minutes each day and burns nearly an extra pound every single month.

So I'm going to make a better effort at climbing stairs this week.

As far as results, I am losing weight, especially now that I'm in my second week of this new routine. I started out gaining several pounds that first week (this is common whenever starting a new workout routine), but the weight is coming off now. Since the beginning of the month, I've lost 1.5 pounds, nearly all of which was body fat rather than lean muscle mass (according to my Fitbit Aria scale).

I probably would have lost an extra half pound if I had done all the work on my list this week, but there's always tomorrow. I'm honestly not in any huge hurry, hence why I'm doing it slowly. I don't want losing weight to take up a ton of time or effort, because it's not sustainable for me.

But, I like the idea of losing an easy 4-5 pounds a month, so I think if I can build the habits I've laid out on my Trello over the next few weeks, I'll start adding more tasks to this list so I can solidify my weight loss. I'm sure I'll hit a plateau at some point, and I want to keep switching things up to combat that.

My overall goal is to lose about 30 pounds of body fat. That's actually the dream goal; if I lost 15-20 of those 30 pounds I'd be pretty happy. I'm not that overweight and wear the extra weight I have reasonably well (it goes to my curves), so it's not even really about looks. I'm more concerned about my health, especially since I'm turning 30 and need to come up with a reasonable routine to keep my weight down.

11:30 pm -

A day of freelance work. I'm hoping to submit and bill soon. It was a pretty easy day, with a lot of breaks, but it is the weekend.

Challenge: Develop a Daily Fiction Writing Habit

Today: 0 words

This week: 0 words

October (so far): 16,892 words

August total (for the last week): 17,923 words

September total: 50,214 words

Challenge: Develop a Daily Fiction Editing Habit

Scenes beaten out this week: 0

Scenes revised this week: 0

Scenes edited this week: 0

Books published this week: 0

Challenge: Pitch 15 Articles a Week

Pitched: 0

Assigned: 10

Completed: 0

WALK 'N TALKS ARE BACK! (LIFE OF A WRITER: DAY 51)

9 pm -

Yesterday, I said I was back, but I really took the day off. Today, I got back to my walk 'n talks, and wow! I feel awesome again.

I completed 4 scenes that were each close to 3000 words. My total word count for the day is 11,645 words. I'm so happy!

I also managed over 30,000 steps today, which is an awesome new achievement for me. Part of this is that I hit a parade on the way over to the lakefront trail, which forced me to backtrack until I could find a way through. The other part of it was that I took the westie on one of her long walks this morning, which gave me an extra 3000 steps.

So, I'm pretty thrilled that I got half of a manuscript under another pen name drafted. On Wednesday, I'll go out and do the other half, and then it's probably on to another WD&D book.

This is exactly what I desperately needed to kick off the week.

I tested my setup again, and I really can't tell if my iRig PRE was the only problem. I was having some weird crackling using both iRig PREs that I have, and then I realized my mic wasn't connected correctly. Once I fixed that, I had no trouble using the second iRig PRE with my iPad, which for some reason gives better sound while recording.

So, in short, I really have no idea what's going on. I just know that what I did today worked, and I'm happy with the dictation and the word count I received back.

I'm also happy with my speed, which fell between 3100-4100 wph. My writing occurred over 4 hours, from 1pm to 4:57pm, which is nearly 2911 words per hour. That's astounding for me. Hitting a true 3000 wph is an absolute dream for me, and I know that the longer I use my setup, the better I'll get at it.

The bad part about all of this is I'm exhausted both physically and mentally. I think I need to start the walk much earlier in the day. I got home at about 5:40pm and did a bunch of random stuff, took care of the dog... and by the time I sat down to watch a little TV and veg out, P was home. Not exactly the calm day I wanted. I didn't hit the road until 12:20 pm, and frankly, I need to start sometime between 9-10am. That would put me home much earlier, which would give me a few hours to de-stress and then get to work again later in the day.

Still, I'm pretty pleased with myself. Now, I need to do this 3 more times this week. That would put me at around 60k words, which would make me feel a lot more confident about hitting 100k for the month!

I would be happy doing this 4 times a week—after all, with these numbers, I could get over 40k words a week, which is over 160k words a month. The thing I need to work on now is controlling energy, because that's what would let me do more work after the walk 'n talks.

And editing and freelancing goals are still in the pits. I've really got to figure out my system for each of those, and fast.

Tomorrow is my editing and freelance day, since I'm out of the house for client meetings. I think I'm going to post this now—if I get any more work done tonight, it'll probably be more beats for Fallen.

Challenge: Develop a Daily Fiction Writing Habit
Today: 11,645 words
This week: 11,645 words
October (so far): 28,537 words

August total (for the last week): 17,923 words
September total: 50,214 words
Challenge: Develop a Daily Fiction Editing Habit
Scenes beaten out this week: 0
Scenes revised this week: 0
Scenes edited this week: 0
Books published this week: 0
Challenge: Pitch 15 Articles a Week
Pitched: 0
Assigned: 10
Completed: 0

BACK TO BASICS (LIFE OF A WRITER: DAY 52)

8:25 am -

I thought about my problems with getting editing done this month and I realized I need to get back to basics with developing a habit. I pulled out absolutely every trick in the book to develop my drafting habit, yet I've tried to skip steps for this editing habit.

No more. It's time to unleash hell on developing this editing habit. So here are the rules:

Do a tiny bit in the morning, before anything else. This should get me "on a roll" for the day.

Use triggers and rituals to ingrain the habit. With writing, I used tea. I think it makes sense to use tea again for editing, along with a specific chair in my reading room.

Do it every single day. Consistency on a daily basis is really a key. So I need to make it a priority to edit every. single. day. I don't plan on doing this forever, and would eventually like to get to the same point I am with the fiction goal, where I've found an efficient way to chunk the work into just a few days a week.

- Make it a priority. I've let this goal compete with freelancing and to some extent, writing, and it loses every time. So for now, this has to be my number one goal I'm trying to hit. I need to have faith that my writing goal will take care of itself with walk 'n talks and my freelance goal will take care of itself with external deadlines (provided I hit the 15 pitches per week).

- Start small. I've had in my mind that I need to get 5 scenes done every day. But that's a lot of scenes and a lot of time spent. One scene per day is probably enough to gain momentum on this.

- Schedule it. I have a conflict because I want to make walk 'n talks a part of my morning too. I think I'm going to have to decide over the next few weeks whether editing should start the morning or writing should. I know yesterday I felt pretty stressed when I got home at 5:30 and didn't get to sit down and unwind. But I think part of that could be because I didn't get to eat anything beforehand. So a better schedule might be wake up, do a few hours of editing over early lunch and tea, hit the road by noon, home by 5pm or so.

- Break it up. I have a two-step editing process—read on Kindle and add comments, then make changes in Scrivener. I've now broken that out into two steps on my Trello board to better represent progress.

I really want to make editing a habit; it feels so critical to my workflow and very much like the missing piece that would help me get my work into print quickly. It's a crucial piece of being a successful indie author.

This, of course, means I'll have to cut other things out. All the TV I've been loving lately, for example. I think I'm finally ready to make that sacrifice though.

I remember a point with writing where I felt amazing as I was writing. I move from loving "having written" to loving writing itself. I need to get there emotionally with editing, too.

Once I'm there, I believe that batching will work and I can chunk down to editing 4 days a week. I really want to get to a point of weekends off. I don't think that will be possible for at least 6 months to a year, but that's where I want to be eventually.

11:50 pm -

I didn't have a particularly productive day today in terms of goals. I didn't write because today is not a writing day, which is weird for me. It is weird to purposely take a day off from writing rather than being a slacker.

But on the other two goals, no progress, aside from getting a few more articles assigned from my freelance client. I guess that is progress? I'll count it in my goals.

What held me up otherwise? I have just a day left on my Shutterstock account, so I have been looking for the last of the cover images I need all night.

I have a few closing thoughts for the night. A big part of why I'm getting drafting done is because I have figured out a really efficient process for doing it. I have not yet found that for either freelancing or editing.

I suppose I can apply fast writing to the freelancing process, that just requires habit.

Editing is a bit harder, because it feels right now like it takes as long as it takes. If I could get it done faster, I'd be really excited. Is it possible? I don't know. I'll have to do some additional research.

The second thought I had for the day is that I really, really want to start putting everything I've learned during this process into a more permanent form. The information I have could help people, so why not put it out there? I want to start with ebooks, but would like to eventually create short video courses to accompany some of the topics.

I have a few concerns, such as whether it will take away too much from my fiction and freelance goals right now. There is an opportunity to generate income from this, but will the money come in time to make it worth the opportunity sacrificed on the other projects? If these little non-fiction projects are fairly easy to get out, it might be worth it. For example, if I could do one walk and get a rough draft for one of the books, then clean it up in another run and publish, that would be fast enough for me.

So, I'm pondering whether I want to pursue the non-fiction path right now, and also what I would charge to make it profitable for me.

The third thought is that I really want to start blogging again, on my other blog. I want to write short posts about random topics that interest me at the moment. I don't think I'll have time for that until I generate enough income from my fiction to be full-time though, so that idea is definitely on the back burner for now.

Challenge: Develop a Daily Fiction Editing Habit

Scenes beaten out this week: 0

Scenes revised this week: 0

Scenes edited this week: 0

Books published this week: 0

Challenge: Pitch 15 Articles a Week

Pitched: 3

Assigned: 13
Completed: 0
Challenge: Write 100k Words in a Month
Today: 0 words
This week: 11,645 words
October (so far): 28,537 words
August total (for the last week): 17,923 words
September total: 50,214 words

STARTED MAKING SMALL PROGRESS ON EDITING TODAY (LIFE OF A WRITER: DAY 53)

5:19 pm -

I went on another one of my walks today, which went really well again, for the most part. I realized while I was already out that I had accidentally drafted five scenes last time, not four, which meant that I only had 3 scenes left to go to finish my manuscript. This would be fine if I had brought something else to work on, but I didn't. I was done with my manuscript about 65% of the way through my walk, so I started ad-libbing through Fallen. I got through two scenes really quickly (Fallen scenes are much shorter, for some reason) but the battery in my mic died without me realizing it, so I ended up losing most of those scenes. Which was okay, since I probably want to think through them a bit more and I can redo them pretty quickly tomorrow.

I learned two lessons today. My batteries need to be recharged after every walk 'n talk, and I need to always have a few extra scenes beaten out in case I finish early!

But, tomorrow will be better. Either way, I got another 25,000 steps, 6812 words, and another manuscript drafted!

So now I have 6 manuscripts drafted, and before we go any further, I should mention that I did get a bit of editing done yesterday and this morning. So I'm starting that habit, slowly but surely too. With any luck, I'll have some of these books out and earning soon.

As happy as I am about the words, I am wondering if need to do an extra session this week. It's halfway through the month, and I'm still only at a third of where I need to be for word count. I know I had some technical difficulties and have a solid plan for catching up, but there is something that makes me nervous about writing 60k+ words in just 15 days.

11:20 pm -

I had just enough time tonight to beat 5 scenes, but I still want to do more. I think it's more important, though, to switch to editing for now. Plus, it's bedtime.

I'm not completely satisfied with what I've accomplished today, but it was an okay day overall. I would say that I'd like to see 10k-ish words as the norm for my walk 'n talks, and still make more progress per day on editing and freelancing.

I'm starting to wonder if I really just don't have enough time to do it all. The idea of that is extremely frustrating, so I hope it's not true. A part of me thinks that if I just keep optimizing every little process, I can have and do everything I want. It's a pipe dream, but I don't want to settle for being ordinary, either.

There is the thought that, if I ever become a full-time fiction writer, then I won't have to freelance anymore. The thing is, even if I was a full-time fiction writer, I'd still want to have time for blog-building, which will take the place of freelance writing if and when I get there financially.

I'm really interested in building a major topic blog in the coming few years. I want to do something that's more career-related, since my blog made me so happy at one point and helped me meet so many new people without really having to try or network. I have an exciting idea for a blog that I've been toying with for awhile, and finally decided I'm going to devote some time to at the first of the year, when I'm hopefully a bit more settled with writing and editing.

Speaking of which, I've decided that I'm maybe going to end these updates on December 31st of this year. I'll probably still do a weekly update, but not a daily one. The reason I started these updates was to hash out my habits and share what I've learned, but I think if I can get all of these habits worked out by December, it will be time to move on to other non-writing habits and goals.

But, I'll still be writing daily, just on my new project. I have to figure out the rest of my writing schedule first, of course, before I can even think about tackling that. So all of this is still up in the air, and I may very well change my mind, but that is the tentative plan for now.

Challenge: Develop a Daily Fiction Editing Habit
Scenes beaten out this week: 5
Scenes revised this week: 0
Scenes edited on Kindle this week: 1
Scenes sent to Susan this week: 0
Books published this week: 0
Challenge: Pitch 15 Articles a Week
Pitched: 3
Assigned: 13
Completed: 0
Challenge: Write 100k Words in a Month

Today: 6,812 words
This week: 18,457 words
October (so far): 35,349 words
August total (for the last week): 17,923 words
September total: 50,214 words

THE EDITING HABIT IS HAPPENING, FINALLY (LIFE OF A WRITER: DAY 54)

10:40am -

I was planning on a walk 'n talk today but it's raining outside, with no signs of letting up until about 3pm, which is too late to leave. I live in Chicago and it gets dark pretty quickly in the evenings; that will only get worse as winter sets in.

P suggested that I instead do a walk 'n talk in our building's stairwell. Not a bad idea, but for me, I just really don't enjoy going up and down stairs (nor is it easy for me). I can't see myself productively writing while huffing and puffing up and down those stairs.

I feel a bit of relief for the rain, to be honest, not because I don't enjoy my walk 'n talks, but because I desperately need to get some editing and freelancing done. I'm at 35k words for the month with drafting, which means I have 65k to go—but, with walk 'n talks, that's only 7 sessions at 10k each, or roughly every other day for the rest of the month. Still completely doable.

I'm hoping to go both Friday and Saturday this week, just to hit at least 50% of my goal. It would make me feel more confident that I can succeed. Then I'll have 12 more days to hit the other half of the goal, which is plenty of time to get 5 more 10k sessions in.

I've gotten some more Kindle editing done between last night and this morning. I'm surprised at how easy it is. I remember when I started out writing a lot, I went through this period where I felt like what I thought was hard was actually easy, and then through another period where what I thought was easy was actually fun. I can see myself going through the same thing with editing. It's not fun yet, but I will learn to love it, eventually.

I've also realized with freelancing that most publications want to read an entire article before agreeing to it. Part of me thinks that's so frustrating and inefficient, but I have to remember that most people don't understand the writing process at the level I do.

(I realize how snotty that last sentence sounded. But it's true; I have written a lot more words over the years than the majority of people, even if they work online. The details of a post can be fixed to suit a publication; the concept, theme, and general outline of it cannot, so that should be the point of negotiation that people start from.)

Either way, working on spec is the way to go, even if I don't enjoy it. What that means to me is that I need to have a secondary purpose for every article I write in case it's not accepted by the publication. That could be a number of things:

- pitching it to a different publication
- self-publishing it for $$$
- self-publishing it as a lead-in for one of my series (one of my growth-hacking strategies)

I'm just... unsettled about this. I think because some of my niches are not ones that I'd explore if I didn't need the money. So it feels like a wasted effort to write about something if I can't get money for it. Silly, I know.

There is also the matter of... well, then why not write and try to sell articles in niches you do want to write about?

The easy answer is they don't pay as well. Though I do want to get some non-fiction going for Prose on Fire, since I believe that the information buried in these posts is actually very valuable and could really help other writers.

Oh, well. Instead of pondering this, I need to move on and just get to writing! I should assume that some of it will hit, some of it won't, and anything that doesn't can either be re-pitched or self-published.

I'm starting to realize that my mind can maybe only handle two major tasks per day. Like writing and editing. Freelancing and editing. Freelancing and writing. I wrote last week about how the weekends might be for pitches and beats... but I am still considering just doing 4 days of writing, 4 days of editing, and 4 days of freelancing every week. Pick two a day, that's roughly 1 day off. (Or 2 days with only one focus, which is just as good.) Something about that schedule feels right to me. The beats easily fit in to my workflow on a day-to-day basis, since most scenes take just a few minutes to beat out.

So today I'm working on beats, editing, and outlines for several freelance articles I need to submit this week. I also want to work on those Prose on Fire ideas I have, and figure out how to incorporate a Daily Non-Fiction Writing Habit. I know from experience that it's easier than writing fiction! Is it worth starting up another word count challenge?

It would be so awesome to get some Prose on Fire guides up. I have passed on this idea before because I didn't know how to market non-fiction without blogging a ton to build that audience. But then I realized, I could probably do the same thing I do with fiction—provide something extremely related for free. So I could write a (short) book on how I write 40k words a week (of course, I need to actually do that) and then create an article about the top 3 things that helped me write faster. The article could be free, with a strong call to action to get the full story in the book.

Challenge: Develop a Daily Fiction Editing Habit

Scenes beaten out this week: 14

Scenes revised this week: 0

Scenes edited on Kindle this week: 8

Scenes sent to Susan this week: 0

Books published this week: 0

Challenge: Pitch 15 Articles a Week

Pitched: 3

Assigned: 13

Completed: 0

Challenge: Write 100k Words in a Month

Today: 6,812 words

This week: 18,457 words

October (so far): 35,349 words

August total (for the last week): 17,923 words

September total: 50,214 words

SHOULD I RAMP UP ON PROSE ON FIRE? (LIFE OF A WRITER: DAY 55)

1:27 pm -

I woke up this morning with so many ideas for the Prose on Fire content I've had on my mind this week.

I'm not sure why, but I have been getting this feeling lately that I want to build a few passive income blogs.

287

No, not the spammy, disgusting kind that try to sell you diet pills and such. And passive income is probably the completely wrong word, since I plan to post regularly, maybe twice a week.

I want to build them because a part of me will always be an entrepreneur, a media lover, an entertainer, and a marketer. There is so much fun to be had with creating non-fiction, and I am craving some artistic exploration there.

I was supposed to go on a walk 'n talk today, but I got so distracted by my ideas that I missed my deadline for leaving (remember, I have to leave before noon so I can get home before it's dark, for safety reasons). Oops. I think that is going to be the new challenge of these walk 'n talks, that it's hard to get up and go to them every day.

But, I really only have to do one more to complete my Lose Weight Slowly goals, and there is tomorrow for that.

Today, I'm going to keep working on my Prose on Fire ideas and also get some freelancing stuff done.

I may also have to write tonight to assuage the guilt of skipping. After all, I do still need the words...

11:30 pm -

Editing in the morning is not working. I've done nearly all my editing in bed before I go to sleep or when I get up right away. Editing time with tea has turned into brainstorming and dreaming time, which gets me sidetracked for the day.

What makes more sense is walk 'n talks during the day. I need to leave early, in the morning, since that time is wasted anyway on dreams and plans.

A challenge is that when I'm done, I get home and have more work to do. And Im pretty tapped out on creation at this point. I need to save the easier work for after walk 'n talks. That means I just can't do freelancing after walk 'n talks, but maybe I should be doing it during walk 'n talks? The whole walking and writing thing works insanely well... I need to put more stuff through the process that seems to already work.

I'm changing my freelancing goal from 15 pitches per week to 25,000 words per week. That is roughly enough for 10 articles. It makes sense to me because my original goal was to pitch 15 and get 10 assigned, but it's clear that pitching just isn't working for me at the moment.

I was looking at my blog-building goals today and thought to myself, why not start now? I strongly believe you should do what you're inspired to do when you're inspired to do it, at least for a few hours a day, because passion can be fleeting. My main roadblock is that I'm still making slow progress on both my editing and freelancing routines... Plus I'm playing catch up on my fiction writing word count for the month too.

Part of me thinks I should get a handle on everything I'm trying to juggle now. Another part of me thinks I am close to a solution for freelancing (if I can put it through the walk 'n talks) AND editing (if I can stick to my few in the morning/evening routine), so I should go for it and get the sites ready for a hard-hitting January of activity.

Something to think about more this weekend... because something has to change.

STILL STRUGGLING, BUT THANK GOODNESS FOR GOOD FICTION WRITING HABITS (LIFE OF A WRITER: DAY 57)

2:30 pm -
I did my walk 'n talk today and feel pretty good about myself. I went a bit earlier, around 8am or so, and it was

really nice. There were still a ridiculous amount of people outside going north, but it's also Sunday, so I'm hoping that things are better during the week.

I still haven't gotten my audio onto my computer, but once I do and get it transcribed, I'll have a better idea of how many words I got for the day.

4:21 pm -

9,234 words today! And 7 scenes total from Fallen, the fourth book in Waters Dark and Deep.

I'm happy, but I don't like the level of accuracy when I go north vs. south on the trail. That said, the north part of the trail is a bit safer, at least... it's just much closer to the highway, and that part is really loud.

Oh, well. I can improve it in the revisions.

I felt great this morning, so I want to outline a bunch more stuff today so that I can go again tomorrow. Woohoo!

11:20 pm -

I have so much stuff to outline, and I can tell I'm getting back to that overwhelmed place. I'm not sure if it's because I'm not totally keeping my goals with editing and freelancing, or if it's because I'm also trying to add in some of this Prose on Fire stuff and getting overwhelmed with my ideas. The great thing about writing fiction is that there's a sequential order to follow; write book 1, then book 2, and so on. With non-fiction, there isn't anything like that.

I have A LOT of ideas for Prose on Fire, and it's all starting to get out of hand. I need to pause and take it small chunk by small chunk, remembering that when I started out, I wanted to grow Prose on Fire slowly, in my spare time. That's still the case.

The first thing I created was a framework that I'm still thinking of a name for. It's essentially like Maslov's

Hierarchy of Needs, but helps fiction writers build a career using foundational stages, then going up. I looked at a number of success stories for both new and older writers and saw the same patterns emerging, which inspired me to create a structure that showed how the most successful authors seem to accomplish what they want.

I think that is the place to start with the content. After that, it would make a lot of sense to begin at the lowest stage of needs, but I believe most of my exciting content (like everything I'm learning with writing faster and developing daily habits) actually falls under Stage 2. I might start there, since I want to be known for writing and producing books quickly to begin with. After that, I might look back to some Stage 1 topics, which mostly revolve around learning the art of storytelling.

It's still in its wee early phases right now, and to be honest it's overwhelming on top of everything else I want to get done with editing and freelancing. I'm not sure if it should take a backseat for a bit while I develop true habits with everything else. I'm finding it particularly difficult to get my freelance writing done. I'm just really uninspired to work on it, for whatever reason. I hate myself with each passing day that I don't make any progress on it.

And that means that I need to just suck it up and get it done already, so I don't feel bad anymore. I mean, today I wrote nearly 10k words of fiction, which would have made me ecstatic a month ago; but bleh, I actually just feel awful this evening about how "little" I accomplished because I didn't get any articles done.

Boo. I still have a long way to go with hitting these goals.

And I hate feeling so disappointed with myself.

On the Lose Weight Slowly front, I did pretty well last week. I did end up removing the 5 sets of stairs cards from my list because I just wasn't enjoying doing them. It didn't make sense to force it, when they don't burn a ton of calories (700 for the week if I do all 10 sets), and I get plenty of incline when I complete my walks for the week.

LOSE WEIGHT SLOWLY (OCTOBER 20TH)

This week, I'm hoping to get in 5 walks to make up for the one I missed. I don't mind missing a few items on my list, but missing a long walk is a threat to my calorie-burning, since each one accounts for so many (about 700-1000 calories burned per walk).

I also wanted to report that as of yesterday, I'm down 2.9 pounds from the beginning of the month. Three weeks in, so that's roughly a pound per week. Not bad at all! I was hoping to lose 5 pounds a month, but for the amount of effort I'm putting in (not a ton, aside from walking a lot), I really don't think I can complain about losing 4 pounds instead.

Challenge: Develop a Daily Fiction Editing Habit
Scenes beaten out this week: 0
Scenes revised this week: 0
Scenes edited on Kindle this week: 0
Scenes sent to Susan this week: 0
Books published this week: 0
Challenge: Pitch 15 Articles a Week
Pitched: 0
Assigned: 19
Completed: 0
Challenge: Write 100k Words of Fiction in a Month
Today: 9,234 words

This week: 9,234 words
October (so far): 44,583 words
August total (for the last week): 17,923 words
September total: 50,214 words

ANXIOUS, EXPECTANT, POTENTIALLY OVERWORKED (LIFE OF A WRITER: DAY 60)

8:15 am -

Wow, I've forgotten to post something for 2 days now. I think what's happening is that my posting habit was tied to my Shutterstock habit, and now I don't need to deal with Shutterstock in the evenings anymore.

Also, the last few days have just been weird. I don't now how to describe them. Let me try to tease things out as much as I can to see what's going on.

Freelancing is holding me up, big time. It's one of those things that wouldn't be so bad if I just sat down and did it. But I'm so uninspired.

The thing I am inspired by? Prose on Fire plans. I made one that I'm happy with, but now I need to figure out how to put it into action. I'm not completely sure where to start.

I haven't gotten any fiction writing done in the last several days. Part of that is because I feel guilty about not freelancing (despite never getting freelancing done when I stay home) and another part is because the only thing I have beaten out is Fallen, which I enjoy writing, but which is so far ahead of where I am with edits (back in the middle of Unbound, book 2). It occurred to me this morning that I might be a cycler with editing, which is weird, because I'm not one with writing.

I'm a bit stuck on editing. I've gotten as far as I can with the two books I have on Kindle, and now need to apply those edits in Scrivener. I could probably keep going on Kindle if I had my other books revised, but I don't. So something psychological is holding me up there, too.

So, I haven't gotten much done this week so far, aside from 10k words of fiction. Based on what I've written, it seems like the priorities are:

- Somehow get some freelance work done, even if I have to use pomodoros to force myself
- Beat out some more fiction to write on the walks
- Get some new books revised and ready for Kindle editing
- Get Kindle edits into Scrivener so I can cycle through and move forward on editing

I have to admit, none of these really screams fun to me right now, which may be why I'm feeling stuck. I guess if I had to pick a few, I would pick beating out more fiction and getting books revised for Kindle. Maybe that's what I should focus on for now?

Plus the freelance stuff. Ugh, the bane of my existence. Why can't I just be happier about that?

Let's talk about something more fun: Prose on Fire stuff. I have been doodling and brainstorming (and dreaming) for the past several days and came up with a framework for the 6 stages of successful fiction writers. This is the order in which writers become mega authors during their careers. I am, unfortunately, only at Stage 2 out of 6, but I realized something while creating the framework, that I could move through the other stages quickly if I follow them in order, since each stage only requires systemization before moving onto the next stage.

For example, Stage 2 is being able to produce books on a consistent basis. I'm not 100% there yet, but once I get a handle on this editing thing, I should be able to move on to Stage 3, which is all about streamlining the sales funnel.

The stages are actually very quick to move through, but what I'm more excited about is having a framework that I can share with others and become known for. I didn't do this intentionally, but now I have some cornerstone ideas that can set POF apart from other writers who write about writing.

I also mentioned before that I wanted to launch POF being known for one very specific thing, then expanding into other topics, and the most obvious thing is writing more, faster. Between upping my writing speed and upping my word count per month, I have a lot to share there. Plus, Prose on Fire lends itself well to this idea anyway.

I'm excited about getting started, but also unsure of where specifically to start. And unsure of how much time to invest when I still have so much other stuff going on with freelancing, writing, and editing. It's not like I don't already have a ton of work to do. How realistic am I being with this idea?

I've done some cost calculations and don't expect to be seeing any dough for awhile, but once I get everything set up, I believe I have a decent way to monetize that should be worth my time and efforts. That's a relief, but in the meantime, I have bills piling up and not a ton of immediate income coming in. I HAVE to get some freelancing done. That is just the reality.

My second priority going into the end of the month is getting books out. I'm really questioning if my drafting goal is what I should be focused on right now, but I also don't want to lose momentum completely with either drafting or my Lose Weight Slowly efforts. I checked again yesterday and I've lost nearly four pounds this month. Things are working, and I don't want to ruin that.

I CAN DO IT ALL! Or at least that's what I keep telling myself. Am I being unrealistic?

8:55 pm -

So, I did the exact opposite of everything I said I was going to do today. I woke up with an urge to walk and had to get it done.

I completed the last seven scenes I had beaten out for Fallen, and got 7,394 words. Not a bad amount, though not as many words as my last outing. For whatever reason, a lot of my scenes in this book are short, and they are also coming out slower on a words/hour basis. That's okay though; Waters Dark and Deep stuff always seems to come out slower, and it's not a huge deal to me.

I still have a long way to go to hit my 100k goal. I'm currently at just over 50,000 words. I probably need to go walking twice more this week, then at least 3 times early next week to hit the monthly goal.

I'm not sure how I feel about it. On the one hand, I want to do what I said (to myself) that I was going to do. I want to follow through. It's pointless to set a 100k goal, then say, well, 80k is still good enough.

At the same time, 100k just isn't quite as important to me as it once was. With the walking, it's clear to me that I can maintain a steady writing pace with 3 walks a week. That feels good enough to me, in some way.

I want to finish the Fallen draft, pick up the Hellfire draft (WD&D #5), and pick up another two drafts from my other pen name (8 scenes each) before the end of the month. It's a stretch goal, but close to within reach. And this amount should be just enough to help me finish out the month.

As for next month... part of me wants to hit a writing goal, but part of me doesn't. It's important to me to hit 25k or more each week. But outside of that, I'm not particular about the numbers. I think I've proven to myself that I can make progress on drafting. The important goal now is editing and publishing progress.

And that's where I'm still failing, despite an entire month of trying to work on it. I've made a bit of progress and not much more. I want to hit it harder, but I'm stressed out about freelancing and money and my lack of getting anything published so far this month, despite having some of this stuff drafted since the summer.

I think next month, I probably need to pull back on my word count goals, unfortunately. Because if I can't get books published, what's the point?

10:40 pm -

The Cardinals are in the World Series and we've been watching a ton of baseball as of late. But I've noticed, even outside of that, that on days when I walk 'n talk, I don't get much else done. As it was today.

I can't tell if it's because I'm at capacity in terms of energy or something else. What I do know is that at the end of my walk, I felt more energized than ever. I felt like I wanted to jump right in and get back to work. So what changed? How do I harness that momentum and push through to get a second block of work done on those days?

Tomorrow I need to stay home and get the aforementioned list of things done. I'm happy I wrote today, but I'm fresh out of outlines, beats, anything. I couldn't walk 'n talk tomorrow if I tried.

I keep reading content about directing passion into something positive. I want to, I really do. I want to get my work done, and I want it to be a happy place for me. I want to not be stressed out about money, but I also want to put my talents to their best uses.

Everything feels very mixed up right now, and I'm torn over how to get it all done and stay happy and healthy and sane. I'm starting to wonder if it's even possible. The numbers add up in terms of work hours per week—fewer than 50, even with all my projects. But the implementation has yet to gel for me. Is it just because the work is creative? Am I giving too much credence to the idea that people can work 40+ hours a week, productively?

It's so hard to tell. I might be back to the journal tomorrow... that's the only thing that seems to help me when I'm in these funks.

Challenge: Develop a Daily Fiction Editing Habit

Scenes beaten out this week: 0

Scenes revised this week: 0

Scenes edited on Kindle this week: 0

Scenes sent to Susan this week: 0

Books published this week: 0

Challenge: Pitch 15 Articles a Week

Pitched: 0

Assigned: 13

Completed: 0

Challenge: Write 100k Words of Fiction in a Month

Today: 7,394 words

This week: 16,628 words

October (so far): 51,977 words

August total (for the last week): 17,923 words
September total: 50,214 words

ABANDONING OCTOBER'S WORD COUNT GOAL... (LIFE OF A WRITER: DAY 61)

1:15 pm -

It just occurred to me that I have 1 week to write nearly 50k words. The goal sounds much more daunting than trying to walk 5 times in the next 8 days, which is what I've been telling myself.

Last night I came up with a potential answer for my editing woes...

Cycling.

I want to get editing done rapidly, and my greatest fear while editing is that at the end of each stage, the draft isn't good enough.

So, the best way to get the draft to where I want it is to get through tons of rounds of edits as quickly as possible. That means not worrying at all about making the book perfect on the first pass, just doing as many corrections as quickly as I can. When it feels right (which in my mind, is when I can send it to Susan and she'll love it), I can send it off and feel good with where it is.

This takes the pressure off of me and allows my creative side to work at its own pace, the same way it does with drafting.

Or at least that's the theory... I need to put it into practice to see if my hypothesis is true.

The biggest issue is, how to judge my progress? Susan's feedback is helpful, as are reviews after the fact (when it's too late to change things). I could track my time and see if books get published faster using this method. It's a bit more difficult to judge progress though, because there is an element of quality in the equation that is not as important during the drafting phase.

I always tell myself in the drafting phase that I'll fix things in the editing phase... and that's where I'm getting stuck. I need to treat my book like a dirty dish in a not-so-great dishwasher—it didn't come out squeaky clean the first time? Run it through another cycle!

Wait, does anyone else do this?

So, cycling. That's my newest scheme to getting this job done. I really want to see my books on the shelves, and soon.

7:15 pm -

I'm feeling... mooshy right now. Something in me is extremely misaligned and I just can't explain it right now.

I've decided that I'm going to abandon my 100k goal for this month. I really didn't want to do this, but I just realized that I want to focus on sorting out this whole editing process. That doesn't mean I'm not going to write at all (I fully intend to keep writing on a regular schedule), but it does mean that I'm not going to write 50,000 more words.

Like I said, I HATE doing this. It feels shitty to say I'm not going to meet a goal because I don't want to or don't feel like it. But right now I just have to follow my heart, which is telling me that I'm about to have a breakthrough on this editing stuff. I feel something shifting inside me, and I want to follow that urge.

There is more that I feel misaligned about, but this is enough for one day. I'll have to keep working on the rest. We can't always control things in life, but we can listen to ourselves as closely as we can and trust ourselves.

1 am (Oct. 25) -

I revised five scenes tonight as I watched some television. It's been not nearly the productive day I needed, but I have tomorrow too.

And I do feel better about the editing stuff. I think this could actually work, if I turned the TV off and got serious about getting these scenes done.

Still nothing on the freelancing stuff.

Challenge: Develop a Daily Fiction Editing Habit

Scenes beaten out this week: 0

Scenes revised this week: 5

Scenes edited on Kindle this week: 0

Scenes sent to Susan this week: 0

Books published this week: 0

Challenge: Pitch 15 Articles a Week

Pitched: 0

Assigned: 13

Completed: 0

Challenge: Write 100k Words of Fiction in a Month

Today: 7,394 words

This week: 16,628 words

October (so far): 51,977 words

August total (for the last week): 17,923 words

September total: 50,214 words

MOOSHY (LIFE OF A WRITER: DAY 62)

12:00 pm -

I have felt so off the last few weeks. Something isn't right. And I can't explain what it is.

I'm getting through revisions slowly, I think because I'm so bored by them. When I actually pause the television for a moment, I can get through them quickly. I'm sure if I timed myself, I'd go a lot faster too.

I'm eating like crazy, which is always a sure sign of stress, boredom, procrastination.

I want to walk again tomorrow.

I hate when things don't feel right.

I'm making a list of what I need to do today. I'll see if that helps.

I've noticed a pattern in my work. If I don't get the pre-work done, the work doesn't happen. For example, I have no beats right now. Which means I can't walk. I have no beats because I'm too far ahead in writing three different series, and haven't caught up on edits.

So I need to either start a new series (yay) or get the edits done, or both. Probably both.

The two books I have ready for Kindle edits need to be cycled—the Kindle edits need to be added to Scrivener, the Scrivener file needs to be recompiled, and then I'll be able to cycle back through the document on Kindle.

And if I can move my draft of the third series onto Kindle, I can do that while I'm cycling through my other edits.

I think my biggest problem right now is flow. Everything would be flowing if I planned correctly. But it's not because I don't have the pre-work done on a variety of things.

I think the first place to start is making a list of the pre-work. Get through those items, get through to the work, get everything humming along again at a rapid clip.

- Get unstuck.
- Get happy and productive again.
- Solve all my problems.
- Get a perfect life.

Okay, not the last one!

11:30 pm -

Cycling is going so slowly. It doesn't help that I'm bored out of my mind and have the television on in the background. It's just so hard to get through these edits! And boring. Did I mention boring?

I've put this and a few other things (like revisions) on my list of stuff to outsource, ASAP.

The good news is that I started outlines for 5 freelance articles. I'm hoping to press forward on those today, too. The psychological barriers to getting this started were ridiculous, but I'm glad it's finally moving forward.

As slow as the progress is, I feel like I'm FINALLY making it on editing and freelancing.

I think letting go of the word count goal was an important step.

But my concern is that I won't be able to do it all at once, which is what I need.

Challenge: Develop a Daily Fiction Editing Habit

Scenes beaten out this week: 0

Scenes revised this week: 5

Scenes edited on Kindle this week: 0

Scenes sent to Susan this week: 0

Books published this week: 0

Challenge: Pitch 15 Articles a Week

Pitched: 0

Assigned: 13

Completed: 0

Challenge: Write 100k Words of Fiction in a Month

Today: 7,394 words

This week: 16,628 words

October (so far): 51,977 words

August total (for the last week): 17,923 words

September total: 50,214 words

THE POWER OF PARTIALLY DONE (LIFE OF A WRITER: DAY 63)

9:50 am -

I feel much better today. Things are starting to gel, finally. I can see the ends of roads rather than just the beginnings, and that momentum will hopefully carry me through to getting something accomplished.

One thing I've noticed with editing is that I'm making progress, but it doesn't feel like I'm making progress. It's harder to judge the progress, especially with cycling, because I'm getting stuff partly done, over and over again.

I wish there was a better way to represent this so it would look like I'm making as much progress as I am. I think that would make me feel better. I like checking things off lists, and it's harder to start when there's nothing to check off after a big chunk of work time.

Freelancing feels a bit more linear, but for some reason it's harder to do. I'm misaligned with it right now. But financially, I need to get it done.

Challenge: Develop a Daily Fiction Editing Habit

Scenes beaten out this week: 0

Scenes revised this week: 5

Scenes edited on Kindle this week: 0

Scenes sent to Susan this week: 0

Books published this week: 0

Challenge: Complete 15 Articles a Week

Pitched: 0

Assigned: 13

Completed: 0

Challenge: Write 100k Words of Fiction in a Month

Today: 0 words

This week: 16,628 words

October (so far): 51,977 words

August total (for the last week): 17,923 words

September total: 50,214 words

CYCLING SEEMS TO BE WORKING... (LIFE OF A WRITER: DAY 64)

11:50 pm -

I'm finally starting to get through the editing, thanks to a shift in mindset. I realized today that if my goal is to get through each round of editing quickly, I can afford to make mistakes. This is similar to that mindset I had to develop with writing, to push through the first draft. I had to tell myself that nothing I wrote mattered, because I'd fix it in edits. So now, with editing, I'm telling myself that none of it matters because everything will be fixed in a later editing cycle.

Of course, that doesn't work forever. At some point, I want things to be good enough to send to Susan. Susan's feedback will tell me what's worth moving to the proofreading stage (it's good enough) vs. what needs to go back through the editing machine.

I feel great, though, having started to figure this out and just willy-nilly going through edits, correcting only what I see and not thinking too hard about it all. It's a lot simpler, honestly. And it's going much faster, thank God. Because I was really feeling like I was in editing hell for awhile there.

Unfortunately, in figuring out this process, I've let writing slack a bit. I can't write tomorrow, either, because I have no books outlined or beaten.

Tomorrow, I have a lot of work to do. I need to keep the editing machine going while also getting back to writing. As I keep saying, I'm determined to do both at once, making significant progress on both on a weekly basis.

Susan asked me why not alternate, a week of writing followed by a week of editing... and I don't think it will work for me. I don't want to write double the words in one week, and I don't want to edit double the words in one week either. Focus is probably awesome for some people, but I am all over the place. I get more energy from doing new things, and I love procrastinating on things by working on something else instead.

So, it seems like the next thing to do is outline something to write and keep the editing going on the three series I have. I'm about halfway through two manuscripts and ready to start on a third.

Where writing is concerned, I have 2 completed manuscripts of three different series that are still in edits, so I'm a bit remiss to start the next books in those series without getting the rest edited first. I just don't want to jump too far ahead. So I'm probably going to have to start something new, which isn't my preference, but in the long run it's not going to matter much.

Oddly enough, I'm considering jumping back to the Socialpunk series. I mentioned before that I'd hit a wall on this series, but the truth is, it makes sense to finish it before the Christmas season. If I can figure out the plot, it feels like a better alternative than starting a new series, from a business perspective.

And people really want this series out, which is another motivator. They've been waiting forever and I've kept mum on it because I don't have a projected publishing date.

The downsides to starting this series is that these books have difficult plotting and are forever long to write, which means I could easily write a few books in a new series much faster for the holiday rush. I'm also nervous about the editing, since it's a longer one and I'm starting the writing so close to Christmas. Who's to say I can get it finished in time? I would rather get as much finished as possible before the holidays, since I have no idea what will happen afterward.

I haven't decided yet. I tried to outline another book series yesterday, and didn't make it very far. I'm not particularly inspired to start something new, so maybe going with something I already have a setting and characters for is the way to go.

Or maybe the answer is to do both—Socialpunk plus one new series. I'll be rotating between the other three I'm working on as well, since all of them continue, but I don't mind having a lot of series going at once. All it means is that I have more fun switching between things.

A third option (I know I'm going on and on about this, just thinking out loud) is working on complimentary books for the WD&D series. I have a short series of novelettes for Milena, for example.

There's plenty to think about. If I could figure the editing thing out completely and know how long it took to do each book, I would probably stand a better chance at making a good business decision. As it is, I just have to move forward with something haphazardly and refine later. Doing something is still better than doing nothing... but I'd like to eventually have a schedule and release dates and all that good stuff.

But that's part of being an entrepreneur, right?

Challenge: Develop a Daily Fiction Editing Habit

Scenes beaten out this week: 0

Scenes revised this week: 3

Scenes edited on Kindle this week: 0

Scenes sent to Susan this week: 0

Books published this week: 0

Challenge: Pitch 15 Articles a Week

Pitched: 0

Assigned: 13

Completed: 0

Challenge: Write 100k Words of Fiction in a Month

Today: 0 words

This week: 0 words

October (so far): 51,977 words

August total (for the last week): 17,923 words

September total: 50,214 words

FEELING PEACEFUL (LIFE OF A WRITER: DAY 65)

12:30 pm -

I'm not sure I have a great reason to feel at peace, but I do today. I realized yesterday, as I was talking about understanding my editing process better so I can set launch dates, that I do at least understand my writing process well. That allows me to set a writing schedule for the rest of the year, which means I can plan out what I want to accomplish before the Christmas season.

My idea is to have 3 days of planned, this-has-to-get-done writing that can spill over into 4 days if necessary. I'll also have a few filler books that I can work on if I run out of stuff to do and still need to get my walks in.

That reminds me—my commitment to Lose Weight Slowly was at an all-time low last week. While I ate tons and tons of salad, I didn't do well on nearly any other metric, including the walks. Part of that was that I didn't want to focus too heavily on the fiction goal, but I'm definitely noticing the weight come back a bit, especially after not walking for nearly five days (the World Series partying doesn't help either).

OCTOBER 27TH LOSE WEIGHT SLOWLY UPDATE

I need to rededicate myself this week and really try to get those 4 big walks in. I feel like everything else could fall to the wayside and be okay, but the 4 big walks are a necessity, and getting only half of them in isn't going to cut it, especially on the losing weight goals.

5 pm -

I'm feeling good about today. My books are coming along nicely, and the only thing I have to get done is some beating and outlining.

10:30 pm -

I got all of my edits in, but I still have to do outlines and beats tomorrow. It's okay because it's probably unrealistic for me to go walking anyway (at least not on a long walk). But that also makes me nervous because I really need to get these walks in whenever I can. I think it will all be better when the beats are done and ready to go for a few more books.

Overall, an okay day. Not as productive as I wanted, but I think that's due to putting in a lot of edits. It feels unproductive, because I can't see my tangible progress and can't check something off my to-dos, but I have to remember that I'm getting books ready to publish so I can start earning from all the hard work I've been doing over the last few months. Without today, the books would not get out there.

Unfortunately, today and the last several days don't look as good on paper, even though I'm making progress. But it will be wonderful to have those books on sale.

Eye on the prize!

Challenge: Develop a Daily Fiction Editing Habit

Scenes beaten out this week: 0

Scenes revised this week: 3

Scenes edited on Kindle this week: 3

Scenes sent to Susan this week: 0

Books published this week: 0

Challenge: Write 15 Articles a Week

Pitched: 0

Assigned: 13

Completed: 0

Challenge: Write 100k Words of Fiction in a Month

Today: 0 words

This week: 0 words

October (so far): 51,977 words

August total (for the last week): 17,923 words

September total: 50,214 words

AN END TO THE STORY

My diary ended on Day 65, but I didn't want to leave this appendix in such a fuzzy place. It's true, I felt peaceful with my efforts toward the end of October and like I had finally gotten a grip on how to write fast when needed. As you may be able to surmise, though, my journey didn't end—and it still hasn't!

After a much needed break from recording my results, I was able to go back and process until about the end of 2013, when I still hadn't published any of the drafts I had written during my tracking months due to a non-existent editing process. In 2014, I published eight books and one short story by making several adjustments to my process since then. Here's a short summary of them:

I QUIT FREELANCING

It's obvious in hindsight that the reason I never hit any of my freelancing goals is because I didn't really want to hit my freelancing goals. I didn't want to freelance at all, in fact. Freelancing is difficult work, often undervalued, and almost always underpaid. On top of that, it's soooo not worth dealing with the clients, who often don't know what they want and can't spec out the content they need.

In one of my reflective moments last year, I was certain there was another way to pay my bills—and it turned out I was right. Since then, I've strung together a series of part-time jobs (20-30 hours per week) with various companies that needed copywriting services for the cool projects they were doing. I've been very, very selective and focused on companies with people that I admired at the helm and work that would challenge me. I also looked for companies that I would work for regardless of money, which made it easier to give them a deal when they guaranteed bulk hours.

I haven't made a full-time living from fiction writing yet, but I'm a lot closer than I was when I wrote those original entries. That has a lot to do with being able to find unique work arrangements that have been a win-win.

I'VE OUTSOURCED A LOT OF THE EDITING

I worked a lot with Susan during my challenge and afterward. We did all sorts of stuff with each other, including trading rough drafts for critique, meeting regularly to discuss our goals, and even collaborating on a bunch of content together (which worked out beautifully, until her life got a bit too hectic to keep up).

Working with someone else speeded up the editing process significantly. It's tough to work on your content by yourself because you simply can't see the problems in your manuscript. Furthermore, Susan and I also learned a lot from each other and we both drastically improved our writing in a short amount of time by working together.

Our collaboration on a billionaire romance series under my pen name was the pinnacle of my progress in 2014. The process was basically this: I handled the outline, beats, and drafts, then I handed it off to Susan who handled the revisions and editing as more of a ghostwriter than a critiquer. She returned the books to me in what she felt was "publish-ready" condition, and I proofed them (changing whatever I wanted) and loaded them to the digital vendors—Amazon, iTunes, Barnes and Noble, and so on.

Five out of the eight books I published last year were done this way, making it a game changer. I owe a significant amount of my progress to Susan—and while she doesn't work with me on every book, she and I created the foundation for what is now an important process in my business model.

I'm working with two other collaborators in addition to Susan, now. Susan still works with me under the pen name, though she's had to slow down due to her schedule and sometimes skips a book or two in a series. I'm sure we will continue to work together for a long time, though.

My second collaborator is someone I met at a writing conference I attended in late 2014. She has experience as an editor and is working on two series with me, both of which will be out under Monica Leonelle in the next year. We've only started to work together, but I basically gave her the same deal as Susan. The nice thing about it is that she works from home and sets her own schedule, same as me, so she has a lot more time to take on this kind of work, whereas Susan has a full-time job that requires her attention.

My third collaboration is with Sterling and Stone and it's also under my pen name, in collaboration with one of their pen names. That situation is a little different from the other two, because they are the ones producing the books. I'm doing drafts and a round of editing on the story we're working on together, but they'll be handling all of the production work, the launch, and half of the marketing, and I'll just get a percentage of the profits when they come in. With my collaborators, I pay them outright and I keep all the profits and copyright from a series, but I have to do the bulk of the work.

I feel great having so many collaborators because it puts me square in my areas of genius, which are creating a high level story that works, drafting quickly, and publishing and marketing. Since I struggled with editing so much, it's awesome to have others do it for me in the form of ghostwriting.

I'VE CREATED A SIMPLE SELF-EDITING PROCESS

I still do some books myself—for example, this one that you're reading right now! My old editing process was absolutely ridiculous and time-consuming, so I've since created a checklist of tasks to look at for each chapter or scene for fiction works. These include tasks like adding descriptions, improving characterizations, immersing the reader in the setting, and more. To compile my list, I read several self-editing books and looked through my reviews and editorial feedback from beta readers, critiquers, editors, and ghostwriters to see what my ticks are. I add to it regularly and also take away any task that I have repeated enough times to internalize (better to do it right the first time, if possible!).

I encourage everyone to optimize their own personal self-editing process with as much vigor as they optimize their writing speeds—for most authors, it's either the first or second most time-consuming process in a larger production process, and the place where these authors can save the most time (the other is during the draft process).

I've Stopped Using Word Count as a Metric

I love using word count as a metric. That said, if what gets measured gets managed, then you have to be very careful about choosing the right key performance indicators (KPIs). If all your tracking is word count, then you probably won't have many finished manuscripts. My process now is:

- Outline
- Beats
- Sketches
- Drafts
- Revisions (clean up a scene)
- Editing (whole book)
- Proofreading
- Publishing
- Marketing

That's a lot of steps, and each piece needs a dedicated amount of time. A lot of writers focus on writing more, and yes, that is the first step, but "writing" in and of itself is such a tiny part of making a business of writing.

A year after this challenge, I would say I spend roughly 15-20 hours on the Outline, Beats, Sketches, Drafts part and 15-20 hours a week on the Revisions, Editing, and Proofreading part of my work. During the challenge, however, I was only focused on the writing part, because that was the only metric I was tracking. Naturally, the other parts of this fell to the wayside in favor of more drafting.

I like what the guys at Sterling and Stone do, which is that they track every aspect of their process in terms of minutes and hours. They know (and say often, in fact) that it takes, say, 100 hours to produce a novel. And then, they only budget that out at about 3-4 hours a day, each. So they can get a full novel done in about 25 days, with both of them working on it at once. (They did this, in fact, with a project called Fiction Unboxed, in mid-2014.)

When I did my challenge, I identified fairly quickly that the first draft wasn't everything and that I needed to track metrics at every phase of the book, plus budget enough time for every phase. I don't think I ever did fully get around to doing that during the challenge (despite my good intentions), but it's certainly something I work toward now. Maybe I need a second round of the challenge?

I've Set Boundaries Around My Writing and Focused On Passion, Not Word Count

The greatest change I've made is to focus on enjoying my work and the freedom it provides for my life. The original reason I wanted to improve my writing speed was emotional—I felt like I was going to die with books still inside me, and those thoughts tortured me for years, making me paranoid, fearful, and frantic.

In 2014, however, I learned to lighten up and not stress so much.

I'm a healthy young person and (as far as I can tell) have all the time in the world to write the books I want and enjoy a safe, comfortable, and fulfilling life. If any of this is not true, then I want to die knowing that I spent most of my moments in a happy and optimistic state. There are a lot of things out of our control, but we can control our attitude and how we spend our 24 hours each day, so I've focused a lot on what keeps me motivated. Right now, those things are:

- Writing - not podcasting, not Youtubing, not marketing, not editing; rather, the purest form of my art. I like doing all the rest of it, but I love writing and telling my stories.

- Strengthening My Relationship - My fiancé is my number one priority and I'm very committed to our partnership and building a family together. That means that I support him and his career however I can, by cooking, cleaning, and laundering as needed. I also make effort to talk to him regularly about his life and support his goals as much as possible. I do the same for my dog to make sure she is happy, healthy, and comfortable.

- Friends and Family - I make time for them, period. Relationships need nurturing, and nurturing others supports my commitment to writing.

- My Health - Having just left my twenties, I'm much more aware of my health than ever before. I'm focusing much more on diet, specifically eating tons of fruits, veggies, wheatgrass, and more—and while I haven't fully nailed an exercise routine, it's also an area I'm attempting to improve.

- Space - I've tried to create a lot more space in my life whenever possible. This means saying no, quitting unprofitable projects, setting looser deadlines, and outsourcing as much as possible. I've noticed that creating space requires letting go, so I've tried to embrace it!

I hope this provides a satisfying end to this journey that I've shared with you. Thank you for sticking with me through it, and I hope you gleaned a lot of insight from it!

REMEMBER!

If you enjoyed this book, there are two things you can do that will really help spread the word about it:

#1: YOU CAN WRITE A REVIEW

As an independent author, reviews are one of the most important ways I have to get the word out. Your review will encourage others to grab the book. You can share anything, but here are a few ideas:

- What you liked about the book
- What you didn't like about the book
- Your favorite chapter/part in the book
- Three things you are going to implement from the book
- The results you hope to get or have already gotten from the book

Go to ProseOnFire.com/pof1 if you want to leave a review and help others discover a new way to write!

Also, make sure you send it to me at monicaleonelle@ gmail.com (my personal email address) so I can thank you properly for your support.

When you do, also tell me a little about yourself (optional, of course). Perhaps name ONE thing you want to change about your writing process. I'd love to hear from you—my email pals often inspire blog posts, which I love to dedicate to them!

#2: YOU CAN TELL THREE AUTHORS YOU KNOW ABOUT THIS BOOK

There are probably a few author friends who could benefit from this information, right? Why not send them an email or text with the title of the book right now? Takes just a few seconds, and you can do it from your phone!

Email or Text: Check out Write Better, Faster, by Monica Leonelle on Amazon! I enjoyed it and thought you would too.

I greatly appreciate all your support! Please let me know if I'm able to help you with anything in the future: monicaleonelle@gmail.com.

Sign Up For More

Be the first to know about upcoming books.

ProseOnFire.com/Storytellers/

ABOUT THE AUTHOR

Monica Leonelle was born in Germany and spent her childhood jet-setting around the world with her American parents. Her travels include most of the United States and Europe, as well as Guam, Japan, South Korea, Australia, and the Philippines.

She started publishing independently in 2009 and has since published over half a million words of fiction spread across five series, Socialpunk, Waters Dark and Deep, Emma + Elsie, and two under a pen name. In 2014, she published 8 books and one short story.

She writes about indie publishing at ProseOnFire. com. Her most recent non-fiction book, Write Better, Faster, has earned raving reviews from the independent publishing community for going deeper than anyone else into the topic of writing speed. She currently averages around 3,000 words per hour and writes 25,000+ words per week (most weeks).

Before becoming an independent author, Monica led digital marketing efforts at Inc. 100 companies like Hansen's Natural and Braintree.

Monica is a lifetime member of Sigma Pi Sigma honor fraternity and was a 2007 Chicago Business Fellow, graduating with an MBA from the Chicago Booth School of Business at 25 years old. She holds a Bachelor of Science in Computer Science with a minor in Physics from Truman State University.

She's been an avid blogger of marketing and business trends since 2007. Her ideas have been featured in AdAge, The Huffington Post, the AMEX OpenForum, GigaOm, Mashable, Social Media Today, and the Christian Science Monitor. In 2009, she was named one of the top 25 Tweeters in the city of Chicago by ChicagoNow, a subsidiary of the Chicago Tribune.

COPYRIGHT

Printed in Great Britain
by Amazon